BLACK LEGACY PRESS™
WWW.BLACKLEGACYPRESS.ORG

SLAVE NARRATIVES

VOLUME IV
GEORGIA NARRATIVES
PART 2

By
United States.
Work Projects Administration

Copyright © 2024 by BLACKLEGACYPRESS.ORG

All rights reserved. No part of this publication may be reproduced or transmitted in any form or by any means electronic or mechanical, including information storage and retrieval systems without permission in writing from the publisher, except for student research using the appropriate citations.

ISBN: 978-1-63652-202-9

SLAVE NARRATIVES

A Folk History of Slavery in the United States.
From Interviews with Former Slaves

**UNITED STATES.
WORK PROJECTS ADMINISTRATION**

TYPEWRITTEN RECORDS PREPARED BY
THE FEDERAL WRITERS' PROJECT
1936-1938
ASSEMBLED BY
THE LIBRARY OF CONGRESS PROJECT
WORK PROJECTS ADMINISTRATION
FOR THE DISTRICT OF COLUMBIA
SPONSORED BY THE LIBRARY OF
CONGRESS

WASHINGTON 1941

VOLUME IV

GEORGIA NARRATIVES
PART 2

Prepared by
the Federal Writers' Project of
the Works Progress Administration
for the State of Georgia

CONTENTS

Elisha Doc Garey 1
Leah Garrett 11
Mary Gladdy 17
Aunt Edie Dennis Has 21
Sarah Gray 31
Alice Green 35
Alice Green 41
Isaiah Green 51
Edwin Driskell 59
Margaret Green 63
Minnie Green 67
Wheeler Gresham 69
Heard Griffin 75
Reminiscences Of Slavery Days 81
Milton Hammond. 95
Jane Smith Hill Harmon Of Washington-Wilkes 103
Dosia Harris 109
Henderson Harris 121
Shang Harris 123
Tom Hawkins 131
Bill Heard 141

Emmaline Heard	151
Benjamin Henderson	179
Jefferson Franklin Henry	185
Robert Henry	198
John Hill	203
Laura Hood	211
Carrie Hudson	215
Charlie Hudson	223
Annie Huff	235
Bryant Huff	241
Easter Huff	249
Lina Hunter	257
Emma Hurley	275
Alice Hutcheson	281
Mrs. Amanda Jackson	289
Camilla Jackson	295
Easter Jackson	301
Snovey Jackson	305
Uncle Jake	313
Mahala Jewel	319
Benjamin Johnson	325
Georgia Johnson	331
Manuel Johnson	341

Susie Johnson 347

Estella Jones 351

Fannie Jones 357

Rastus Jones 361

PLANTATION LIFE
as viewed by ex-slave

ELISHA DOC GAREY
258 Lyndon Avenue
Athens, Georgia
Written by: Sadie B. Hornsby
Athens —

Edited by: Sarah H. Hall
Athens —

and

John N. Booth
District Supervisor
Federal Writers' Project
Res. 6 & 7
Augusta, Ga.

ELISHA DOC GAREY

Asked for the story of his early life and his recollections of slavery, Elisha replied: "Yes Ma'am, 'deed I'll tell you all I knows 'bout dem days." His next words startled the interviewer. "I knowed you was comin' to write dis jedgment," he said. "I seed your hand writin' and long 'fore you got here I seed you jus' as plain as you is now. I told dese folks what I lives wid, a white 'oman was comin' to do a heap of writin'.

"I was born on de upper edge of Hart County, near Shoal Crick. Sarah Anne Garey was my Ma and I was one of dem shady babies. Dere was plenty of dat kind in dem times. My own sister was Rachel, and I had a half sister named Sallie what was white as anybody. John, Lindsay, David, and Joseph was my four brothers.

"What did us chillun do? Us wukked lak hosses. Didn't nobody eat dar 'less dey wukked. I'se been wukkin' ever since I come in dis world.

"Us lived in log huts. Evvy hut had a entry in de middle, and a mud chimbly at each end. Us slep' in beds what was 'tached to de side of de hut, and dey was boxed up lak wagon bodies to hold de corn shucks and de babies in. Home-made rugs was put on top of de shucks for sheets, and de kivver was de same thing.

"I still 'members my grandma Rachel. De traders fotched her here f'um Virginny, and she never did learn to talk plain. Grandma Sallie Gaines was too old for field wuk, so she looked atter de slave babies whilst deir Ma's was wukkin' in de field. Grandpa Jack Gaines was de shoemaker.

"Most of de time I was up at de big house waitin' on our white folks, huntin' eggs, pickin' up chips, makin' fires, and little jobs lak dat. De onliest way I could find to make any money in dem days was to sell part'idges what I cotched in traps to dem Yankees what was allus passin' 'round. Dey paid me ten cents apiece for part'idges and I might have saved more of my money if I hadn't loved dat store boughten pep'mint candy so good.

"What I et? Anything I could git. Peas, green corn, 'tatoes, cornbread, meat and lye hominy was what dey give us more dan anything else. Bakin' was done in big old ovens what helt three pones of bread and in skillets what helt two. Big pots for bilin' was swung over de coals in de fireplace. Dey was hung on hooks fastened to de chimbly or on cranes what could be swung off de fire when dey wanted to dish up de victuals. Hit warn't nothin' for us to ketch five or six 'possums in one night's huntin'. De best way to tote 'possums is to split a stick and run deir tails thoo' de crack—den fling de stick crost your shoulders and tote de 'possums 'long safe and sound. Dat way dey can't bite you. Dey's bad 'bout gnawin' out of sacks. When us went giggin' at night, us most allus fotched back a heap of fishes and frogs. Dere was allus plenty of fishes and rabbits. Our good old hound dog was jus' 'bout as good at trailin' rabbits in de daytime as he was at treein' 'possums at night. I was young and spry, and it didn't seem to make no diff'unce what I et dem days. Big gyardens was scattered over de place whar-some-ever Marster happened to pick out a good gyarden spot. Dem gyardens all b'longed to our Marster, but he fed us all us wanted out of 'em.

"All dat us chillun wore in summer was jus' one little shirt. It was a long time 'fore us knowed dere was folks anywhar dat put more dan one piece of clothes on chillun in summer. Grandpa Jack made de red shoes us wore widout no socks in winter. Our other winter clothes was cotton shirts and pants, and coats what had a little wool in 'em. Summer times us went bar headed, but Unker Ned made bullrush hats for us to wear in winter. Dere warn't no diff'unt clothes for Sunday. Us toted our shoes 'long in our hands goin' to church. Us put 'em on jus' 'fore us got dar and tuk 'em off again soon as us got out of sight of de meetin' house on de way back home.

"Marse Joe Glover was a good man and he never whupped his Niggers much. His wife, our Miss Julia, was all right too—dat she was. Deir three chilluns was Miss Sue, Miss Puss, and Marster Will. Marse Joe done all his own overseein'. He used to tuck his long white beard inside his shirt and button it up.

"Dat was a fine lookin' turn-out of Marse Joe's—dat rock-a-way car'iage wid bead fringe all 'round de canopy, a pair of spankin' black hosses hitched to it, and my brother, David, settin' so proud lak up on de high seat dey put on de top for de driver.

"Dere warn't no slave, man or 'oman, livin' on dat plantation what knowed how many acres was in it. I 'spects dere was many as 500 slaves in all. Marster 'pinted a cullud boy to git de slaves up 'fore day, and dey wukked f'um sunup to sundown.

"Jails? Yes Ma'am, dere was sev'ral little houses dat helt 'bout two or three folks what dey called jails. White folks used to git locked up in 'em but I never did see no Niggers in one of dem little jailhouses. I never seed no Niggers sold, but I did see 'em in wagons gwine to Mississippi to be sold. I never seed no slave in chains.

"Some few slaves could read and write, and dem what could read was most allus called on by de others for preachin'. Charlie McCollie was de fust cullud preacher I ever seed. White folks 'lowed slaves to make brush arbors for churches on de plantations, and Nigger boys and gals done some tall courtin' at dem brush arbors. Dat was de onliest place whar you could git to see de gals you lakked de best. Dey used to start off services singin', 'Come Ye Dat Loves De Lawd.' Warn't no pools in de churches to baptize folks in den, so dey tuk 'em down to de crick. Fust a deacon went in and measured de water wid a stick to find a safe and suitable place—den dey was ready for de preacher and de canidates. Evvybody else stood on de banks of de crick and jined in de singin'. Some of dem songs was: 'Lead Me to de Water for to be Baptized,' 'Oh, How I love Jesus,' and 'Oh, Happy Day dat Fixed my Choice.'

"I hates to even think 'bout funerals now, old as I is. 'Course I'se ready to go, but I'se a thinkin' 'bout dem what ain't. Funerals dem days was pretty much lak dey is now. Evvybody in de country would be dar. All de coffins for slaves was home-made. Dey was painted black wid smut off of de wash pot mixed wid grease and water. De onliest funeral song I 'members f'um dem days is:

> 'Oh, livin' man
> Come view de ground
> Whar you must shortly lay.'

"How in de name of de Lawd could slaves run away to de North wid dem Nigger dogs on deir heels? I never knowed nary one to run away. Patterollers never runned me none, but dey did git atter some of de other slaves a whole lot. Marse Joe Allus had one pet slave what he sont news by.

"When slaves come in f'um de fields at night, dey was glad to jus' go to bed and rest deir bones. Dey stopped off f'um field wuk at dinner time Saddays. Sadday nights us had stomp down good times pickin' de banjo, blowin' on quills, drinkin' liquor, and dancin'. I was sho' one fast Nigger den. Sunday was meetin' day for grown folks and gals. Boys th'owed rocks and hunted birds' nests dat day.

"Chris'mas mornin's us chillun was up 'fore squirrels, lookin' up de chimbly for Santa Claus. Dere was plenty to eat den—syrup, cake, and evvything.

"New Year's Day de slaves all went back to wuk wid most of 'em clearin' new ground dat day. Dere was allus plenty to do. De only other holidays us had was when us was rained out or if sleet and snow drove us out of de fields. Evvybody had a good time den a frolickin'. When us was trackin' rabbits in de snow, it was heaps of fun.

"Marse Joe had piles and piles of corn lined up in a ring for de corn shuckin's. De gen'ral pitched de songs and de Niggers would follow, keepin' time a-singin' and shuckin' corn. Atter all de corn was shucked, dey was give a big feast wid lots of whiskey to drink and de slaves was 'lowed to dance and frolic 'til mornin'.

"If a neighbor got behind in geth'rin' his cotton, Marse Joe sont his slaves to help pick it out by moonlight. Times lak dem days, us ain't never gwine see no more.

"I ain't never seed no sich time in my life as dey had when Marse Will Glover married Miss Moorehead. She had on a white satin dress wid a veil over her face, and I 'clare to goodness I never seed sich a pretty white lady. Next day atter de weddin' day, Marse Will had de infare at his house and I knows I ain't never been whar so much good to eat was sot out in one place as dey had dat day. Dey even had dried cow, lak what dey calls chipped beef now. Dat was somepin' brand new in de way of eatin's den. I et so much I was skeered I warn't gwine to be able to go 'long back to Marse Joe's plantation wid de rest of 'em.

"Old Marster put evvy foot forward to take care of his

slaves when dey tuk sick, 'cause dey was his own property. Dey poured asafiddy (asafetida) and pinetop tea down us, and made us take tea of some sort or another for 'most all of de ailments dere was dem days. Slaves wore a nickel or a copper on strings 'round deir necks to keep off sickness. Some few of 'em wore a dime; but dimes was hard to git.

"One game us chillun played was 'doodle.' Us would find us a doodle hole and start callin' de doodle bug to come out. You might talk and talk but if you didn't promise him a jug of 'lasses he wouldn't come up to save your life. One of de songs us sung playin' chilluns games was sorter lak dis:

> "Whose been here
> Since I been gone?
> A pretty little gal
> Wid a blue dress on."

"Joy was on de way when us heared 'bout freedom, if us did have to whisper. Marse Joe had done been kilt in de war by a bomb. Mist'ess, she jus' cried and cried. She didn't want us to leave her, so us stayed on wid her a long time, den us went off to Mississippi to wuk on de railroad.

"Dem Yankees stole evvything in sight when dey come along atter de surrender. Dey was bad 'bout takin' our good hosses and corn, what was $16 a bushel den. Dey even stole our beehives and tuk 'em off wropt up in quilts.

"My freedom was brought 'bout by a fight dat was fit 'twixt two men, and I didn't fight nary a lick myself.

Mr. Jefferson Davis thought he was gwine beat, but Mr. Lincoln he done de winnin'. When Mr. Abraham Lincoln come to dis passage in de Bible: 'My son, therefore shall ye be free indeed,' he went to wuk to sot us free. He was a great man—Mr. Lincoln was. Booker Washin'ton come 'long later. He was a great man too.

"De fust school I went to was de Miller O. Field place. Cam King, de teacher, was a Injun and evvywhar he went he tuk his flute 'long wid him.

"Me and my fust wife, Essie Lou Sutton, had a grand weddin', but de white folks tuk her off wid 'em, and I got me a second wife. She was Julia Goulder of Putman County. Us didn't have no big doin's at my second marriage. Our onliest two chillun died whilst dey was still babies."

Asked about charms, ghosts and other superstitions, he patted himself on the chest, and boasted: "De charm is in here. I just dare any witches and ghosties to git atter me. I can see ghosties any time I want to.

"Want me to tell you what happened to me in Gainesville, Georgia? I was out in de woods choppin' cordwood and I felt somepin' flap at me 'bout my foots. Atter while I looked down, and dere was one of dem deadly snakes, a highland moccasin. I was so weak I prayed to de Lawd to gimme power to kill dat snake, but he didn't. De snake jus' disappeared. I thought it was de Lawd's doin', but I warn't sho'. Den I tuk up my axe and moved over to a sandy place whar I jus' knowed dere warn't no snakes. I started to raise my axe to cut de wood and somepin' told me to look down. I did, and dere was de same snake right twixt my foots again. Den and dere I kilt him, and de Sperrit passed th'oo me sayin': 'You is meaner dan dat snake; you kilt him and he hadn't even bit you.' I knowed for sho' den dat de Lawd was speakin'.

"I was preachin' in Gainesville, whar I lived den, on de Sunday 'fore de tornado in April 1936. Whilst I was in dat pulpit de Sperrit spoke to me and said: 'Dis town is gwine to be 'stroyed tomorrow; 'pare your folks.' I told my congregation what de Sperrit done told me, and dem Niggers thought I was crazy. Bright and early next mornin' I went down to de depot to see de most of my folks go off on de train to Atlanta on a picnic. Dey begged me to go along wid 'em, but I said: 'No, I'se gwine to stay right here. And 'fore I got back home dat tornado broke loose. I was knocked down flat and broke to pieces. Dat storm was de cause of me bein' hitched up in dis here harness what makes me look lak de devil's hoss.

"Tuther night I was a-singin' dis tune: 'Mother how Long 'fore I'se Gwine?' A 'oman riz up and said: 'You done raised de daid.' Den I laughed and 'lowed: 'I knows you is a Sperrit. I'se one too.' At dat she faded out of sight.

"I think folks had ought to be 'ligious 'cause dat is God's plan, and so I jined de church atter Christ done presented Hisself to me. I'se fixin' now to demand my Sperrit in de Lawd.

"Yes Ma'am, Miss, I knowed you was a-comin'. I had done seed you, writin' wid dat pencil on dat paper, in de Sperrit."

United States. Work Projects Administration

Slave Narratives

RICHMOND COUNTY EX-SLAVE INTERVIEW

LEAH GARRETT

Written by: Louise Oliphant
Federal Writers' Project
Augusta, Georgia

Edited By: John N. Booth
District Supervisor
Federal Writers' Project
Residencies 6 & 7
Augusta, Georgia

LEAH GARRETT

Leah Garrett, an old Negress with snow-white hair leaned back in her rocker and recalled customs and manners of slavery days. Mistreatment at the hands of her master is outstanding in her memory.

"I know so many things 'bout slavery time 'til I never will be able to tell 'em all," she declared. "In dem days, preachers wuz just as bad and mean as anybody else. Dere wuz a man who folks called a good preacher, but he wuz one of de meanest mens I ever seed. When I wuz in slavery under him he done so many bad things 'til God soon kilt him. His wife or chillun could git mad wid you, and if dey told him anything he always beat you. Most times he beat his slaves when dey hadn't done nothin' a t'all. One Sunday mornin' his wife told him deir cook wouldn't never fix nothin' she told her to fix. Time she said it he jumped up from de table, went in de kitchen, and made de cook go under de porch whar he always whupped his slaves. She begged and prayed but he didn't pay no 'tention to dat. He put her up in what us called de swing, and beat her 'til she couldn't holler. De pore thing already had heart trouble; dat's why he put her in de kitchen, but he left her swingin' dar and went to church, preached, and called hisself servin' God. When he got back home she wuz dead. Whenever your marster had you swingin' up, nobody wouldn't take you down. Sometimes a man would help his wife, but most times he wuz beat afterwards.

"Another marster I had kept a hogshead to whup you on. Dis hogshead had two or three hoops 'round it. He buckled you face down on de hogshead and whupped you 'til you bled. Everybody always stripped you in dem days to whup you, 'cause dey didn't keer who seed you naked. Some folks' chillun took sticks and jobbed (jabbed) you all while you wuz bein' beat. Sometimes dese chillun would beat you all 'cross your head, and dey Mas and Pas didn't know what stop wuz.

"Another way marster had to whup us wuz in a stock dat he had in de stables. Dis wuz whar he whupped you when he wuz real mad. He had logs fixed together wid holes for your feet, hands, and head. He had a way to open dese logs and fasten you in. Den he had his coachman give you so many lashes, and he would let you stay in de stock for so many days and nights. Dat's why he had it in de stable so it wouldn't rain on you. Everyday you got dat same number of lashes. You never come out able to sit down.

"I had a cousin wid two chillun. De oldest one had to nuss one of marster's grandchildren. De front steps wuz real high, and one day dis pore chile fell down dese steps wid de baby. His wife and daughter hollered and went on turrible, and when our marster come home dey wuz still hollerin' just lak de baby wuz dead or dyin'. When dey told him 'bout it, he picked up a board and hit dis pore little chile 'cross de head and kilt her right dar. Den he told his slaves to take her and throw her in de river. Her ma begged and prayed, but he didn't pay her no 'tention; he made 'em throw de chile in.

"One of de slaves married a young gal, and dey put her in de "Big House" to wuk. One day Mistess jumped on her 'bout something and de gal hit her back. Mistess said she wuz goin' to have Marster put her in de stock and beat her when he come home. When de gal went to de field and told her husband 'bout it, he told her whar to go and stay 'til he got dar. Dat night he took his supper to her. He carried her to a cave and hauled pine straw and put in dar for her to sleep on. He fixed dat cave up just lak a house for her, put a stove in dar and run de pipe out through de ground into a swamp. Everybody always wondered how he fixed dat pipe, course dey didn't cook on it 'til night when nobody could see de smoke. He ceiled de house wid pine logs, made beds and tables out of pine poles, and dey lived in dis cave seven years. Durin' dis time, dey had three chillun. Nobody wuz wid her when dese chillun wuz born but her husband. He waited on her wid each chile. De chillun didn't wear no clothes 'cept a piece tied 'round deir waists. Dey wuz just as hairy as wild people, and dey wuz wild. When dey come out of dat cave dey would run everytime dey seed a pusson.

"De seven years she lived in de cave, diffunt folks helped keep 'em in food. Her husband would take it to a certain place and she would go and git it. People had passed over dis cave ever so many times, but nobody knowed dese folks wuz livin' dar. Our Marster didn't know whar she wuz, and it wuz freedom 'fore she come out of dat cave for good.

"Us lived in a long house dat had a flat top and little rooms made like mule stalls, just big enough for you to git in and sleep. Dey warn't no floors in dese rooms and neither no beds. Us made beds out of dry grass, but us had cover 'cause de real old people, who couldn't do nothin' else, made plenty of it. Nobody warn't 'lowed to have fires, and if dey wuz caught wid any dat meant a beatin'. Some would burn charcoal and take de coals to deir rooms to help warm 'em. Every pusson had a tin pan, tin cup, and a spoon. Everybody couldn't eat at one time, us had 'bout four different sets. Nobody had a stove to cook on, everybody cooked on fire places and used skillets and pots. To boil us hung pots on racks over de fire and baked bread and meats in de skillets.

"Marster had a big room right side his house whar his vittals wuz cooked. Den de cook had to carry 'em upstairs in a tray to be served. When de somethin' t'eat wuz carried to de dinin' room it wuz put on a table and served from dis table. De food warn't put on de eatin' table.

"De slaves went to church wid dey marsters. De preachers always preached to de white folks first, den dey would preach to de slaves. Dey never said nothin' but you must be good, don't steal, don't talk back at your marsters, don't run away, don't do dis, and don't do dat. Dey let de colored preachers preach but dey give 'em almanacs to preach out of. Dey didn't 'low us to sing such songs as 'We Shall Be Free' and 'O For a Thousand Tongues to Sing'. Dey always had somebody to follow de slaves to church when de colored preacher was preachin' to hear what wuz said and done. Dey wuz 'fraid us would try to say something 'gainst 'em."

United States. Work Projects Administration

MARY GLADDY,

EX-SLAVE

Place of birth: On the Holt plantation, in Muscogee County, near Columbus, Georgia.

Date of birth: About 1853.

Present residence: In rear of 806½ 6th Avenue, Columbus, Georgia.
Interviewed: July 30, 1936.

MARY GLADDY

Her story: "I was a small girl when the Civil War broke out, but I remember it distinctly. I also remember the whisperings among the slaves—their talking of the possibility of freedom.

"My father was a very large, powerful man. During his master's absence, in '63 or '64, a colored foreman on the Hines Holt place once undertook to whip him; but my father wouldn't allow him to do it. This foreman then went off and got five big buck Negroes to help him whip father, but all six of them couldn't 'out-man' my daddy! Then this foreman shot my daddy with a shot-gun, inflicting wounds from which he never fully recovered.

"In '65, another Negro foreman whipped one of my little brothers. This foreman was named Warren. His whipping my brother made me mad and when, a few days later, I saw some men on horseback whom I took to be Yankees, I ran to them and told them about Warren—a common Negro slave—whipping my brother. And they said, 'well, we will see Warren about that.' But Warren heard them and took to his heels! Yes, sir, he flew from home, and he didn't come back for a week! Yes, sir, I sholy scared that Negro nearly to death!

"My father's father was a very black, little, full-blooded, African Negro who could speak only broken English. He had a son named Adam, a brother of my father, living at Lochapoka, Ala. In 1867, after freedom, this granpa of mine, who was then living in Macon, Georgia, got mad with his wife, picked up his feather bed and toted it all the way from Macon to Lochapoka! Said he was done with grandma and was going to live with Adam. A few weeks later, however, he came back through Columbus, still toting his feather bed, returning to grandma in Macon. I reckon he changed his mind. I don't believe he was over five feet high and we could hardly understand his talk.

"Since freedom, I have lived in Mississippi and other places, but most of my life has been spent right in and around Columbus. I have had one husband and no children. I became a widow about 35 years ago, and I have since remained one because I find that I can serve God better when I am not bothered with a Negro man."

Mary Gladdy claims to have never attended school or been privately taught in her life. And she can't write or even form the letters of the alphabet, but she gave her interviewer a very convincing demonstration of her ability to read. When asked how she mastered the art of reading, she replied: "The Lord revealed it to me."

For more than thirty years, the Lord has been revealing his work, and many other things, to Mary Gladdy. For more than twenty years, she has been experiencing "visitations of the spirit". These do not occur with any degree of regularity, but they do always occur in "the dead hours of the night" after she has retired, and impel her to rise and write in an unknown hand. These strange writings of her's now cover eight pages of letter paper and bear a marked resemblance to crude shorthand notes. Off-hand, she can "cipher" (interpret or translate) about half of these strange writings; the other half, however, she can make neither heads nor tails of except when the spirit is upon her. When the spirit eases off, she again becomes totally ignorant of the significance of that mysterious half of her spirit-directed writings.

"Aunt" Mary appears to be very well posted on a number of subjects. She is unusually familiar with the Bible, and quotes scripture freely and correctly. She also uses beautiful language, totally void of slang and Negro jargon, "big" words and labored expressions.

She is a seventh Day Adventist; is not a psychic, but is a rather mysterious personage. She lives alone, and ekes out a living by taking in washing. She is of the opinion that "we are now living in the last days"; that, as she interprets the "signs", the "end of time" is drawing close. Her conversion to Christianity was the result of a hair-raising experience with a ghost—about forty years ago, and she has never—from that day to this—fallen from grace for as "long as a minute".

To know "Aunt" Mary is to be impressed with her utter sincerity and, to like her. She is very proud of one of her grandmothers, Edie Dennis, who lived to be 110 years old, and concerning whom a reprint from the Atlanta Constitution of November 10, 1900, is appended.

Her story of Chuck, and the words of two spirituals and one slave canticle which "Aunt" Mary sang for her interviewer, are also appended.

AUNT EDIE DENNIS HAS
REACHED GOOD OLD AGE

—SPECIAL—

(FROM ATLANTA CONSTITUTION,
NOVEMBER 10, 1900.)

AUNT EDIE DENNIS HAS REACHED GOOD OLD AGE

Quite a remarkable case of longevity is had in the person of Edie Dennis, a colored woman of Columbus, who has reached the unusual age of 109 years of age and is still in a state of fair health.

Aunt Edie lives with two of her daughters at No. 1612 Third Avenue, in this city. She has lived in three centuries, is a great-great grandmother and has children, grandchildren, great-grandchildren and great-great-grandchildren, aggregating in all over a hundred persons. She lives with one of her "young" daughters, sixty-six.

Edie Dennis is no doubt one of the oldest persons living in the United States. Cases are occasionally reported where 105 years is reached, but 109 years is an age very seldom attained. A wonderful feature of this case is that this old woman is the younger sister of another person now living. Aunt Edie has a brother living at Americus, Georgia, who is 111 years old.

United States. Work Projects Administration

Notwithstanding her great age, Aunt Edie is in fairly good health. She is naturally feeble and her movements are limited. Even in her little home, from which she never stirs. Although she is feeble, her faculties seem clear and undimmed and she talked interestingly and intelligently to a Constitution reporter who called upon her recently.

Aunt Edie was born in 1791, just eight years before the death of George Washington occurred. She was a mother when the war of 1812 took place. The establishment of Columbus as a city was an event of her mature womanhood. The Indian War of the thirties she recalls very distinctly. She was getting old when the Mexican War took place. She was an old woman when the great conflict between the states raged. She was seventy-five years of age when she became free.

It is quite needless to say that Aunt Edie was a slave all her life up to the year 1866. She was born in Hancock County, Georgia, between Milledgeville and Sparta. She was the property of Thomas Schlatter. She came to Columbus just after the town had been laid off, when she was a comparatively young woman. She became the property of the family of Judge Hines Holt, the distinguished Columbus lawyer. She says that when she first came here there was only a small collection of houses. Where her present home was located was then nothing but swamp land. The present location of the court house was covered with a dense woods. No event in those early years impressed itself more vividly upon Aunt Edie's mind than the Indian War, in the thirties. She was at the home of one of the Indians when she first heard of the uprising against the whites, and she frankly says that she was frightened almost to death when she listened to the cold-blooded plots to exterminate the white people. Not much attention was paid to her on account of her being a Negro. Those were very thrilling times and Aunt Edie confesses that she was exceedingly glad when the troubles with the red men were over. Another happening of the thirties which Aunt Edie recalls quite distinctly is the falling of the stars. She says quaintly that there was more religion that year in Georgia than there ever was before or has been since. The wonderful manner in which the stars shot across the heavens by the thousands, when every sign seemed to point to the destruction of the earth, left a lasting impression upon her brain.

Aunt Edie says that she was kindly treated by her masters. She says that they took interest in the spiritual welfare of their slaves and that they were called in for prayer meeting regularly. Aunt Edie was such an old woman when she was freed that the new condition meant very little change in life for her, as she had about stopped work, with the exception of light tasks about the house.

There seems to be no doubt that Aunt Edie is 109 years old. She talks intelligently about things that occurred 100 years ago. All her children, grandchildren, etc., asserts that her age is exactly as stated. Indeed, they have been the custodians of her age, so to speak, for nearly half a century. It was a matter of great interest to her family when she passed the 100 mark.

Aunt Edie is religious and she delights in discussing scriptural matters. She has practical notions, however, and while she is morally sure she will go to a better world when she dies, she remarks, "That we know something about this world, but nothing about the next."

Perhaps this is one reason why Aunt Edie has stayed here 109 years.

> NOTE: Mary Gladdy (806½ - Sixth Avenue, Columbus, Georgia). A grand-daughter of Edie Dennis, states that her grandmother died in 1901, aged 110.

• The Story Of Chuck, As Told By Mary Gladdy.

Chuck was a very intelligent and industrious slave, but so religious that he annoyed his master by doing so much praying, chanting, and singing.

So, while in a spiteful mood one day, this master sold the Negro to an infidel. And this infidel, having no respect for religion whatsoever, beat Chuck unmercifully in an effort to stop him from indulging in his devotions. But, the more and the harder the infidel owner whipped Chuck, the more devout and demonstrative the slave became.

Finally, one day, the infidel was stricken ill unto death; the wicked man felt that his end was near and he was afraid to die. Moreover, his conscience rebuked him for his cruel treatment of this slave. The family doctor had given the infidel up: the man apparently had but a few hours to live. Then, about 8 o'clock at night, the dying man asked his wife to go down in the slave quarter and ask Chuck if he would come to his bedside and pray for him.

The white lady went, as requested, and found Chuck on his knees, engaged in prayer.

"Chuck", she called, "your master is dying and has sent me to beg you to come and pray for him."

"Why, Maddom", replied Chuck, "I has been praying fer Marster tonight—already, and I'll gladly go with you."

Chuck then went to his Master's bed side and prayed for him all night, and the Lord heard Chuck's prayers, and the white man recovered, was converted, joined the church, and became an evangelist. He also freed Chuck and made an evangelist of him. Then the two got in a buggy and, for years, traveled together all over the country, preaching the gospel and saving souls.

NOTE: Mary Gladdy believes this to be a true story, though she knew neither the principals involved, nor where nor when they lived and labored. She says that the story has been "handed down", and she once saw it printed in, and thus confirmed by, a Negro publication—long after she had originally heard it.

United States. Work Projects Administration

• Keep The Fire Burning While Your Soul's Fired Up.

Fire, fire, O, keep the fire burning while your soul's fired up.
O, keep the fire burning while your soul's fired up;
Never mind what satan says while your soul's fired up.
You ain't going to learn how to watch and pray,
Less you keep the fire burning while your soul's fired up.

Old Satan is a liar and a cunjorer, too;
If you don't mind, he'll cunjor you;
Keep the fire burning while your soul's fired up.
Never mind what satan says while, your soul's fired up.

Sung for interviewer by:
Mary Gladdy, Ex-slave,
806½ - Sixth Avenue,
Columbus, Georgia.
December 17, 1936.

• The Gospel Train

Never seen the like since I've been born,
The people keep a-coming, and the train's done gone;
Too late, too late, the train's done gone,
Too late, sinner, too late, the train's done gone;
Never seen the like since I've been born,
The people keep a-coming, and the train's done gone;
Too late, too late, the train's done gone.

Went down into the valley to watch and pray,
My soul got happy and I stayed all day;
Too late, too late, the train's done gone;
Too late, sinner, too late, the train's done gone;
Never seen the like since I've been born,
The people keep a-coming and the train's done gone.
Too late, too late, the train's done gone.

Sung for interviewer by:
Mary Gladdy, ex-slave,
806½ - 6th Avenue,
Columbus, Georgia,
December 17, 1936

• Old Slave Canticle.

> My sister, I feels 'im, my sister I feels 'im;
> All night long I've been feelin 'im;
> Jest befoe day, I feels 'im, jest befoe day I feels 'im;
> The sperit, I feels 'im, the sperit I feels 'im!
>
> My brother, I feels 'im, my brother, I feels 'im;
> All night long I've been feelin 'im,
> Jest befoe day, I feels 'im, jest befoe day, I feel 'im;
> The sperit, I feels 'im!

According to Mary Gladdy, ex-slave, 806½ - 6th Avenue, Columbus, Georgia, it was customary among slaves during the Civil War period to secretly gather in their cabins two or three nights each week and hold prayer and experience meetings. A large, iron pot was always placed against the cabin door—sideways, to keep the sound of their voices from "escaping" or being heard from the outside. Then, the slaves would sing, pray, and relate experiences all night long. Their great, soul-hungering desire was freedom—not that they loved the Yankees or hated their masters, but merely longed to be free and hated the institution of slavery.

Practically always, every Negro attendant of these meetings felt the spirit of the Lord "touch him (or her) just before day". Then, all would arise, shake hands around, and begin to chant the canticle above quoted. This was also a signal for adjournment, and, after chanting 15 or 20 minutes, all would shake hands again and go home—confident in their hearts that freedom was in the offing for them.

United States. Work Projects Administration

A SHORT TALK
WITH SARAH GRAY—

EX-SLAVE

A paper submitted
by Minnie B. Ross

Revision of original copy
and typing by
J. C. Russell

Talk with ex-slave
SARAH GRAY
M. B. Ross

1/25/37

SARAH GRAY

Sarah Gray is an aged ex-slave, whose years have not only bent her body but seem to have clouded her memory. Only a few facts relating to slavery could, therefore, be learned from her. The events she related, however, seemed to give her as much pleasure as a child playing with a favorite toy.

The only recollection Sarah has of her mother is seeing her as she lay in her coffin, as she was very young when her mother died. She remembers asking her sisters why they didn't give her mother any breakfast.

Sarah's master was Mr. Jim Nesbit, who was the owner of a small plantation in Gwinnett County. The exact number of slaves on the plantation were not known, but there were enough to carry on the work of plowing, hoeing and chopping the cotton and other crops. Women as well as men were expected to turn out the required amount of work, whether it was picking cotton, cutting logs, splitting rails for fences or working in the house.

Sarah was a house slave, performing the duties of a maid. She was often taken on trips with the mistress, and treated more as one of the Nesbit family than as a slave. She remarked, "I even ate the same kind of food as the master's family."

The Nesbits, according to Sarah, followed the customary practice of the other slave owners in the matter of the punishment of slaves. She says, however, that while there were stories of some very cruel masters, in her opinion the slave owners of those days were not as cruel as some people today. She said occasionally slave owners appointed some of the slaves as overseers, and very often these slave-overseers were very cruel.

When the war began, the Nesbits and other plantation owners grouped together, packed their wagons full of supplies, took all of their slaves, and started on a journey as refugees. They had not gone very far when a band of Yankee soldiers overtook them, destroyed the wagons, took seventy of the men prisoners and marched off taking all of the horses, saying they were on their way to Richmond and when they returned there would be no more masters and slaves, as the slaves would be freed. Some of the slaves followed the Yankees, but most of them remained with their masters' families.

They were not told of their freedom immediately on the termination of the war, but learned it a little later.

As compensation, Mr. Nesbit promised them money for education. She declares, however, that this promise was never fulfilled.

Sarah Gray's recollections of slavery, for the most part, seem to be pleasant. She sums it up in the statement, "In spite of the hardships we had to go through at times, we had a lot to be thankful for. There were frolics, and we were given plenty of good food to eat, especially after a wedding."

The aged ex-slave now lives with a few distant relatives. She is well cared for by a family for whom she worked as a nurse for 35 years, and she declares that she is happy in her old age, feeling that her life has been usefully spent.

United States. Work Projects Administration

Slave Narratives

PLANTATION LIFE as viewed by Ex-Slave

ALICE GREEN
Athens
Georgia

Written by: Corry Fowler,
Athens —

Edited by: Sarah H. Hall
Athens
and
John N. Booth
District Supervisor
Federal Writers' Project
Residencies 6 & 7

ALICE GREEN

Alice Green's supposed address led the interviewer to a cabin with a padlocked front door. A small Negro girl who was playing in the adjoining yard admitted, after some coaxing, that she knew where Alice could be found. Pointing down the street, she said: "See dat house wid de sheet hangin' out in front. Dat's whar Aunt Alice lives now." A few moments later a rap on the door of the house designated was answered by a small, slender Negress.

"Yes Mam, I'm Alice Green," was her solemn response to the inquiry. She pondered the question of an interview for a moment and then, with unsmiling dignity, bade the visitor come in and be seated. Only one room of the dilapidated two-room shack was usable for shelter and this room was so dark that lamplight was necessary at 10:00 o'clock in the morning. Her smoking oil lamp was minus its chimney.

A Negro child about two or three years old was Alice's sole companion. "I takes keer of little Sallie Mae whilst her Mammy wuks at a boardin' house," she explained. "She's lots of company for me.

"Charles and Milly Green was my daddy and mammy. Daddy's overseer was a man named Green, and dey said he was a powerful mean sort of man. I never did know whar it was dey lived when Daddy was borned. Mammy's marster was a lawyer dat dey called Slickhead Mitchell, and he had a plantation at Helicon Springs. Mammy was a house gal and she said dey treated her right good. Now Daddy, he done field work. You know what field work is, hoein', plowin', and things lak dat. When you was a slave you had to do anything and evvything your marster told you to. You was jus' 'bliged to obey your marster no matter what he said for you to do. If you didn't, it was mighty bad for you. My two oldest sisters was Fannie and Rena. Den come my brothers, Isaac and Bob, and my two youngest sisters, Luna and Violet. Dere was seven of us in all.

"Slaves lived in rough little log huts daubed wid mud and de chimblys was made out of sticks and red mud. Mammy said dat atter de slaves had done got through wid deir day's work and finished eatin' supper, dey all had to git busy workin' wid cotton. Some carded bats, some spinned and some weaved cloth. I knows you is done seen dis here checkidy cotton homespun—dat's what dey weaved for our dresses. Dem dresses was made tight and long, and dey made 'em right on de body so as not to waste none of de cloth. All slaves had was home-spun clothes and old heavy brogan shoes.

"You'll be s'prised at what Mammy told me 'bout how she got her larnin'. She said she kept a school book hid in her bosom all de time and when de white chillun got home from school she would ax 'em lots of questions all 'bout what dey had done larned dat day and, 'cause she was so proud of evvy little scrap of book larnin' she could pick up, de white chillun larned her how to read and write too. All de larnin' she ever had she got from de white chillun at de big house, and she was so smart at gittin' 'em to larn her dat atter de war was over she got to be a school teacher. Long 'fore dat time, one of dem white chillun got married and tuk Mammy wid her to her new home at Butler, Georgia.

"Now my daddy, he was a plum sight sho' 'nough. He said dat when evvythin' got still and quiet at night he would slip off and hunt him up some 'omans. Patterollers used to git atter him wid nigger hounds and once when dey cotch him he said dey beat him so bad you couldn't lay your hand on him nowhar dat it warn't sore. Dey beat so many holes in him he couldn't even wear his shirt. Most of de time he was lucky enough to outrun 'em and if he could jus' git to his marster's place fust dey couldn't lay hands on him. Yes Mam, he was plenty bad 'bout runnin' away and gittin' into devilment.

"Daddy used to talk lots 'bout dem big cornshuckin's. He said dat when dey got started he would jump up on a big old pile of corn and holler loud as he could whilst he was a snatchin' dem shucks off as fast as greased lightin'.

"When Mammy was converted she jined the white

folks church and was baptized by a white preacher 'cause in dem days slaves all went to de same churches wid deir marster's famblies. Dere warn't no separate churches for Negroes and white people den.

"I warn't no bigger dan dis here little Sallie Mae what stays wid me when de War ended and dey freed de slaves. A long time atter it was all over, Mammy told me 'bout dat day. She said she was in de kitchen up at de big house a-cookin' and me and my sisters was out in de yard in de sandbed a-playin' wid de little white chillun when dem yankee sojers come. Old Miss, she said to Mammy: 'Milly, look yonder what's a-comin'. I ain't gwine to have nothin' left, not even a nickels worth, 'cause dere comes dem yankees.' Dey rid on in de yard, dem sojers what wore dem blue jackets, and dey jus' swarmed all over our place. Dey even went in our smokehouse and evvywhar and took whatever dey wanted. Dey said slaves was all freed from bondage and told us to jus' take anything and evvything us wanted from de big house and all 'round de plantation whar us lived. Dem thievin' sojers even picked up one of de babies and started off wid it, and den Old Miss did scream and cry for sho'. Atter dey had done left, Old Miss called all of us together and said she didn't want none of us to leave her and so us stayed wid her a whole year atter freedom had done come.

"Not many slaves had a chance to git property of deir own for a long time 'cause dey didn't have no money to buy it wid. Dem few what had land of deir own wouldn't have had it if deir white folks hadn't give it to 'em or holp 'em to git it. My uncle, Carter Brown, had a plenty 'cause his white folks holped him to git a home and 'bout evvything else he wanted. Dem Morton Negroes got ahead faster dan most any of de others 'round here but dey couldn't have done it if deir white folks hadn't helped 'em so much.

"Soon as I got big enough, I started cookin' for well-off white folks. Fact is, I ain't never cooked for no white folks dat didn't have jus' plenty of money. Some of de white folks what has done et my cookin' is de Mitchells, Upsons, Ruckers, Bridges, and Chief Seagraves' fambly. I was cookin' for Chief Buesse's mammy when he was jus' a little old shirttail boy. Honey, I allus did lak to be workin' and I have done my share of it, but since I got so old I ain't able to do much no more. My white folks is mighty good to me though.

"Now Honey, you may think it's kind of funny but I ain't never been much of a hand to run 'round wid colored folks. My mammy and my white folks dey raised me right and larned me good manners and I'm powerful proud of my raisin'. I feels lak now dat white folks understands me better and 'preciates me more."

Why, jus' listen to dis! When Mr. Weaver Bridges told me his mother had done died, he axed me did I want to go to the funeral and he said he was goin' to take me to de church and graveyard too, and sho' 'nough dey did come and git me and carry me 'long. I was glad dey had so many pretty flowers at Mrs. Bridges' funeral 'cause I loved her so much. She was a mighty sweet, good, kind 'oman.

"All my folks is dead now 'cept me and my chillun, Archie, Lila, and Lizzie. All three of 'em is done married now. Archie, he's got a house full of chillun. He works up yonder at de Georgian Hotel. I loves to stay in a little hut off to myself 'cause I can tell good as anybody when my chillun and in-laws begins to look cross-eyed at me so I jus' stays out of deir way.

"I'm still able to go to church and back by myself pretty reg'lar. 'Bout four years ago I jined Hill's Baptist Church. Lak to a got lost didn't I? If I had stayed out a little longer it would have been too late, and I sho' don't want to be lost."

PLANTATION LIFE

Interview with:

ALICE GREEN
156 Willow Street
Athens, Georgia

Written by: Sadie B. Hornsby
Athens —

Edited by: Sarah H. Hall
Athens —

Leila Harris
Augusta —

and

John N. Booth
District Supervisor
Federal Writers' Project

ALICE GREEN

Ex-Slave—Age 76

Residencies 6 & 7.

ALICE GREEN

Alice Green's address led to a tumble down shack set in a small yard which was enclosed by a sagging poultry wire fence. The gate, off its hinges, was propped across the entrance.

The call, "Alice!" brought the prompt response, "Here

I is. Jus' push de gate down and come on in." When a little rat terrier ran barking out of the house to challenge the visitor, Alice hobbled to the door. "Come back here and be-have yourself" she addressed the dog, and turning to the interviewer, she said: "Lady, dat dog won't bite nothin' but somepin' t'eat—when he kin git it." Don't pay him no 'tention. Won't you come in and have a seat?"

Alice has a light brown complexion and bright blue eyes. She wore a soiled print dress, and a dingy stocking cap partly concealed her white hair. Boards were laid across the seat of what had been a cane-bottomed chair, in which she sat and rocked.

Asked if she would talk of her early life the old Negress replied: "Good Lord! Honey, I done forgot all I ever knowed 'bout dem days. I was born in Clarke County. Milly and Charley Green was my mammy and pappy and dey b'longed to Marse Daniel Miller. Mammy, she was born and raised in Clarke County but my pappy, he come from southwest Georgia. I done forgot de town whar he was brung up. Dere was seven of us chillun: me and Viola, Lula, Fannie, Rene, Bob, and Isaac. Chillun what warn't big 'nough to wuk in de fields or in de house stayed 'round de yard and played in de sand piles wid de white chillun.

"Slaves lived in mud-daubed log huts what had chimblies made out of sticks and mud. Lordy Honey! Dem beds was made wid big high posties and strung wid cords for springs. Folks never had no wire bedsprings dem days. Our mattresses was wheat straw put in ticks made out of coarse cloth what was wove on de loom right dar on de plantation.

"I don't know nothin' 'bout what my grandmammies done in slav'ry time. I never seed but one of 'em, and don't 'member much 'bout her. I was jus' so knotty headed I never tuk in what went on 'cause I never 'spected to be axed to tell 'bout dem days.

"Money! Oh-h-h, no Ma'am! I never seed no money 'til I was a great big gal. My white folks was rich and fed us good. Dey raised lots of hogs and give us plenty of bread and meat wid milk and butter and all sorts of vegetables. Marster had one big garden and dere warn't nobody had more good vegetables den he fed to his slaves. De cookin' was done in open fireplaces and most all de victuals was biled or fried. Us had all de 'possums, squirrels, rabbits, and fish us wanted cause our marster let de mens go huntin' and fishin' lots.

"Us jus' wore common clothes. Winter time dey give us dresses made out of thick homespun cloth. De skirts was gathered on to tight fittin' waisties. Us wore brass toed brogan shoes in winter, but in summer Niggers went bar'foots. Us jus' wore what us could ketch in summer. By dat time our winter dresses had done wore thin and us used 'em right on through de hot weather.

"Marse Daniel Miller, he was some kinder good to Mammy, and Miss Susan was good to us too. Now Honey, somehow I jus' cain't 'member deir chilluns names no more. And I played in de sand piles all day long wid 'em too.

"Oh-h-h! Dat was a great big old plantation, and when all dem Niggers got out in de fields wid horses and wagons, it looked lak a picnic ground; only dem Niggers was in dat field to wuk and dey sho' did have to wuk.

"Marster had a carriage driver to drive him and Ole Miss 'round and to take de chillun to school. De overseer, he got de Niggers up 'fore day and dey had done et deir breakfast, 'tended to de stock, and was in de field by sun-up and he wuked 'em 'til sundown. De mens didn't do no wuk atter dey got through tendin' to de stock at night, but Mammy and lots of de other 'omans sot up and spun and wove 'til 'leven or twelve o'clock lots of nights.

"My pappy was a man what b'lieved in havin' his fun and he would run off to see de gals widout no pass. Once when he slipped off dat way de patterollers sicked dem nigger hounds on him and when dey cotched him dey most beat him to death; he couldn't lay on his back for a long time.

"If dey had jails, I didn't know nothin' 'bout 'em. De patterollers wid deir nigger hounds made slaves b'have deirselfs widout puttin' 'em in no jails. I never seed no Niggers sold, but Mammy said her and her whole fambly was sold on de block to de highes' bidder and dat was when Ole Marster got us.

"Mammy, she was de cook up at de big house, and when de white chillun come back from school in de atternoon she would ax 'em to show her how to read a little book what she carried 'round in her bosom all de time, and to tell her de other things dey had larn't in school dat day. Dey larned her how to read and write, and atter de War was over Mammy teached school and was a granny 'oman (midwife) too.

"Dey made us go to church on Sundays at de white folks church 'cause dere warn't no church for slaves on de plantation. Us went to Sunday School too. Mammy jined de white folks church and was baptized by de white preacher. He larnt us to read de Bible, but on some of de plantations slaves warn't 'lowed to larn how to read and write. I didn't have no favorite preacher nor song neither, but Mammy had one song what she sung lots. It was 'bout 'Hark from de Tombs a Doleful Sound.' I never seed nobody die and I never went to no buryin' durin' slav'ry time, so I cain't tell nothin' 'bout things lak dat.

"Lordy Honey! How could dem Niggers run off to de North when dem patterollers and deir hounds was waitin' to run 'em down and beat 'em up? Now some of de slaves on other places might have found some way to pass news 'round but not on Ole Marster's place. You sho' had to have a pass 'fore you could leave dat plantation and he warn't goin' to give you no pass jus' for foolishment. I never heared tell of no uprisin's twixt white folks and Niggers but dey fussed a-plenty. Now days when folks gits mad, dey jus' hauls off and kills one another.

"Atter slaves got through deir wuk at night, dey was so tired dey jus' went right off to bed and to sleep. Dey didn't have to wuk on Sadday atter dinner, and dat night dey would pull candy, dance, and frolic 'til late in de night. Dey had big times at cornshuckin's and log rollin's. My pappy, he was a go-gitter; he used to stand up on de corn and whoop and holler, and when he got a drink of whiskey in him he went hog wild. Dere was allus big eatin's when de corn was all shucked.

"Christmas warn't much diffunt from other times. Us chillun had a heap of fun a-lookin' for Santa Claus. De old folks danced, quilted, and pulled candy durin' de Christmastime. Come New Year's Day, dey all had to go back to wuk.

"What for you wants to know what I played when I was a little gal? Dat was a powerful long time ago. Us played in de sand piles, jumped rope, played hide and seek and Old Mother Hubbard."

At this time a little girl, who lives with Alice, asked for a piece of bread. She got up and fed the child, then said: "Come in dis here room. I wants to show you whar I burned my bed last night tryin' to kill de chinches: dey most eats me up evvy night." In the bedroom an oil lamp was burning. The bed and mattress showed signs of fire. The mattress tick was split from head to foot and cotton spilling out on the floor. "Dat's whar I sleep," declared Alice. The atmosphere of the bedroom was heavy with nauseous odors and the interviewer hastened to return to the front of the house desiring to get out of range of the chinch-ridden bed. Before there was time to resume conversation the terrier grabbed the bread from the child's hand and in retaliation the child bit the dog on the jaw and attempted to retrieve the bread. Alice snatched off her stocking cap and beat at the dog with it. "Git out of here, Biddy. I done told you and told you 'bout eatin' dat chile's somepin t'eat. I don't know why Miz. Woods gimme dis here dog no how, 'cause she knows I can't feed it and it's jus' plum starvin'. Go on out, I say.

"Lordy! Lady, dar's one of dem chinches from my bed a-crawlin' over your pretty white dress. Ketch him quick, 'fore he bites you." Soon the excitement was over and Alice resumed her story.

"Dey tuk mighty good care of slaves when dey got sick. Dey had to, 'cause slaves was propity and to let a slave die was to lose money. Ole Miss, she looked atter de 'omans and Ole Marster, he had de doctor for de mens.

I done forgot most of what dey made us take. I know dey made us wear assfiddy (asafetida) sacks 'round our necks, and eat gumgoo wax. Dey rubbed our heads wid camphor what was mixed wid whiskey. Old folks used to conjure folks when dey got mad at 'em. Dey went in de woods and got certain kinds of roots and biled 'em wid spider webs, and give 'em de tea to drink.

"One day us chillun was playin' in de sand pile and us looked up and seed a passel of yankees comin'. Dere was so many of 'em it was lak a flock of bluebirds. 'Fore dey left some folks thought dey was more lak blue devils. My mammy was in de kitchen and Ole Miss said: 'Look out of dat window, Milly; de yankees is comin' for sho' and dey's goin' to free you and take you and your chillun 'way from me. Don't leave me! Please don't leave me, Milly!' Dem yankees swarmed into de yard. Dey opened de smokehouse, chicken yard, corncrib, and evvything on de place. Dey tuk what dey wanted and told us de rest was ours to do what us pleased wid. Dey said us was free and dat what was on de plantation b'longed to us, den dey went on off and us never seed 'em no more.

"When de War was over Ole Miss cried and cried and begged us not to leave her, but us did. Us went to wuk for a man on halves. I had to wuk in de field 'til I was a big gal, den I went to wuk for rich white folks. I ain't never wuked for no pore white folks in my whole life.

"It was a long time 'fore Niggers could buy land for deirselfs 'cause dey had to make de money to buy it wid. I couldn't rightly say when schools was set up for de Niggers. It was all such a long time ago, and I never tuk it in nohow.

"I don't recollect when I married George Huff or what I wore dat day. Didn't live wid him long nohow. I warn't goin' to live wid no man what sot 'round and watched me wuk. Mammy had done larnt me how to wuk, and I didn't know nothin' else but to go ahead and wuk for a livin'. I don't know whar George is. He might be dead for all I know; if he ain't, he ought to be. I got three chillun. Two of 'em is gals, Lizzie and Lila, and one is a boy. My oldest gal, she lives in Atlanta." She ignored the question as to where her other daughter lives. "My son wuks at de Georgian Hotel. But understand now, dem ain't George Huff's chillun. Deir pappy was my sweetheart what got into trouble and runned away. I ain't gwine to tell his name.

"Honey, I jus' tell you de truth; de reason why I jined de church was 'cause I was a wild gal, and dere warn't nothin' too mean for me to do for a long time. Mammy and my sisters kept on beggin' me to change my way of livin', but I didn't 'til four years ago. I got sick and thought I was goin' to die, and den I begged de good Lord to forgive me and promised Him if He would let me git well 'nough to git out of dat bed, I would change and do good de rest of my life. When I was able to git up, I jined de church. I didn't mean to burn in hell lak de preachers said I would. I thinks evvybody ought to jine de church and live right.

"Oh-h-h! Lady, I sho' do thank you for dis here dime. I'm gwine to buy me some meat wid it. I ain't had none dis week. My white folks is mighty good to me, but Niggers don't pay me no mind.

"Has you axed me all you wants to? I sho' is glad 'cause I ain't had nothin' t'eat yit." She pulled down her stocking to tie the coin in its top and revealed an expanse of sores from ankle to knee. A string was tied above each knee. "A white lady told me dem strings soaked in kerosene would drive out de misery from my laigs," Alice explained. "Goodbye Honey, and God bless you."

United States. Work Projects Administration

AN OPINION OF SLAVERY

BY ISAIAH GREEN—EX SLAVE

Submitted by Minnie B. Ross

Typed by
J.C. Russell
1-25-37

An opinion of Slavery
By
Isaiah Green—Ex-Slave

AN EX-SLAVES OPINION OF SLAVERY

ISAIAH GREEN

Isaiah Green, an ex-slave, still has a clear, agile mind and an intelligent manner. With his reddish brown complexion, straight hair, and high cheek bones, he reminds you of an old Indian Chief, and he verifies the impression by telling you that his grandfather was a full blooded Indian.

Isaiah Green was born in 1856 at Greensboro, Ga. Cleary Mallory Willis and Bob Henderson were his parents, but he did not grow up knowing the love and care of a father, for his father was sold from his mother when he was only two years. Years later, his mother lost track of his father and married again. There were eleven children and Isaiah was next to the youngest.

His master was Colonel Dick Willis, who with his wife "Miss Sally" managed a plantation of 3,000 acres of land

and 150 slaves. Col. Willis had seven children, all by a previous marriage. Throughout the State he was known for his wealth and culture. His plantation extended up and down the Oconee River.

His slave quarters were made up of rows of 2-room log cabins with a different family occupying each room. The fireplaces were built three and four feet in length purposely for cooking. The furniture, consisting of a bed, table, and chair, was made from pine wood and kept clean by scouring with sand. New mattresses and pillows were made each spring from wheat straw.

Old Uncle Peter, one of the Willis slaves, was a skilled carpenter and would go about building homes for other plantation owners. Sometimes he was gone as long as four or five months.

Every two weeks, rations of meal, molasses and bacon were given each slave family in sufficient quantity. The slaves prepared their own meals, but were not allowed to leave the fields until noon. A nursing mother, however, could leave between times.

Large families were the aim and pride of a slave owner, and he quickly learned which of the slave women were breeders and which were not. A slave trader could always sell a breeding woman for twice the usual amount. A greedy owner got rid of those who didn't breed. First, however, he would wait until he had accumulated a number of undesirables, including the aged and unruly.

There was an old slave trader in Louisiana by the name of Riley who always bought this type of slave, and re-sold them. When ready to sell, a slave owner notified him by telegram. When Riley arrived, the slaves were lined up, undressed and closely inspected. Too many scars on the body meant a "bad slave" and no one would be anxious to purchase him.

Green related the story of his grand mother Betsy Willis. "My grandmother was half white, since the master of the plantation on which she lived was her father." He wished to sell her, and when she was placed on the block he made the following statement: "I wish to sell a slave who is also my daughter. Before anyone can purchase her, he must agree not to treat her as a slave but as a free person. She is a good midwife and can be of great service to you." Col. Dick Willis was there, and in front of everyone signed the papers.

The Willis plantation was very large and required many workers. There were 75 plow hands alone, excluding those who were required to do the hoeing. Women as well as men worked in the fields. Isaiah Green declares that his mother could plow as well as any man. He also says that his work was very easy in the spring. He dropped peas into the soft earth between the cornstalks, and planted them with his heel. Cotton, wheat, corn, and all kinds of vegetables made up the crops. A special group of women did the carding and spinning, and made the cloth on two looms. All garments were made from this homespun cloth. Dyes from roots and berries were used to produce the various colors. Red elm berries and a certain tree bark made one kind of dye.

Besides acting as midwife, Green's grandmother Betsy Willis, was also a skilled seamstress and able to show the other women different points in the art of sewing. Shoes were given to the slaves as often as they were needed. Green's step-father was afflicted and could not help with the work in the field. Since he was a skilled shoe maker his job was to make shoes in the winter. In summer, however, he was required to sit in the large garden ringing a bell to scare away the birds.

Col. Willis was a very kind man, who would not tolerate cruel treatment to any of his slaves by overseers. If a slave reported that he had been whipped for no reason and showed scars on his body as proof, the overseer was discharged. On the Willis Plantation were 2 colored men known as "Nigger Drivers." One particularly, known as "Uncle Jarrett," was very mean and enjoyed exceeding the authority given by the master. Green remarked, "I was the master's pet. He never allowed anyone to whip me and he didn't whip me himself. He was 7-ft. 9 in. tall and often as I walked with him, he would ask, "Isaiah, do you love your old master?' Of course I would answer, yes, for I did love him."

Col. Willis did not allow the "patterrollers" to interfere with any of his slaves. He never gave them passes, and if any were caught out without one the "patterrollers" were afraid to whip them.

Mr. John Branch was considered one of the meanest slave owners in Green County, and the Negroes on his plantation were always running away. Another slave owner known for his cruelty was Colonel Calloway, who had a slave named Jesse who ran away and stayed 7 years. He dug a cave in the ground and made fairly comfortable living quarters. Other slaves who no longer could stand Col. Calloway's cruelty, would join him. Jesse visited his wife, Lettie, two and three times a week at night. Col. Calloway could never verify this, but became suspicious when Jesse's wife gave birth to two children who were the exact duplicate of Jesse. When he openly accused her of knowing Jesse's whereabouts, she denied the charges, pretending she had not seen him since the day he left.

When the war ended, Jesse came to his old master and told him he had been living right on the plantation for the past 7 years. Col. Calloway was astonished; he showed no anger toward Jesse, however, but loaned him a horse and wagon to move his goods from the cave to his home.

There were some owners who made their slaves steal goods from other plantations and hide it on theirs. They were punished by their master, however, if they were caught.

Frolics were held on the Willis plantation as often as desired. It was customary to invite slaves from adjoining plantations, but if they attended without securing a pass from their master, the "patterrollers" could not bother them so long as they were on the Willis plantation. On the way home, however, they were often caught and beaten.

In those days there were many Negro musicians who were always ready to furnish music from their banjo and fiddle for the frolics. If a white family was entertaining, and needed a musician but didn't own one, they would hire a slave from another plantation to play for them.

Col. Willis always allowed his slaves to keep whatever money they earned. There were two stills on the Willis plantation, but the slaves were never allowed to drink whiskey at their frolics. Sometimes they managed to "take a little" without the master knowing it.

On Sunday afternoons, slaves were required to attend

white churches for religious services, and over and over again the one sermon drummed into their heads was, "Servants obey your mistress and master; you live for them. Now go home and obey, and your master will treat you right." If a slave wished to join the church, he was baptized by a white minister.

The consent of both slave owners was necessary to unite a couple in matrimony. No other ceremony was required. If either master wished to sell the slave who married, he would name the price and if it was agreeable to the other, the deal was settled so that one owner became master of both. The larger and stronger the man, the more valuable he was considered.

Slaves did not lack medical treatment and were given the best of attention by the owner's family doctor. Sometimes slaves would pretend illness to escape work in the field. A quick examination, however, revealed the truth. Home remedies such as turpentine, castor oil, etc., were always kept on hand for minor ailments.

Green remembers hearing talk of the war before he actually saw signs of it. It was not long before the Yankees visited Greensboro, Ga., and the Willis plantation. On one occasion, they took all the best horses and mules and left theirs which were broken down and worn from travel. They also searched for money and other valuables. During this period a mail wagon broke down in the creek and water soon covered it. When the water fell, Negroes from the Willis plantation found sacks of money and hid it. One unscrupulous Negro betrayed the others; rather than give back the money, many ran away from the vicinity. Isaiah's Uncle managed to keep his money but the Ku Klux Klan learned that he was one of the group. One night they kidnaped and carried him to the woods where they pinned him to the ground, set the dry leaves on fire, and left him. In the group he recognized his master's son Jimmie. As fate would have it the leaves burned in places and went out. By twisting a little he managed to get loose, but found that his feet were badly burned. Later, when he confronted the master with the facts, Col. Willis offered to pay him if he would not mention the fact that his son Jimmie was mixed up in it, and he sent the man to a hospital to have his burns treated. In the end, all of his toes had to be amputated.

Another time, the Yankees visited the Willis plantation and offered Green a stick of candy if he would tell them where the master hid his whiskey. Isaiah ignorantly gave the information. The leader of the troops then blew his trumpet and his men came from every direction. He gave orders that they search for an underground cellar. Very soon they found the well-stocked hiding place. The troops drank as much as they wanted and invited the slaves to help themselves. Later, when Col. Willis arrived and the mistress, who was furious, told him, she said, "If it hadn't been for that little villain, the Yankees would never have found your whiskey." The master understood, however, that Isaiah hadn't known what he was doing, and refused to punish him.

The Yankees came to the Willis plantation to notify the Negroes of their freedom. One thing they said stands out in Green's memory. "If your mistress calls you 'John,' call her 'Sally.' You are as free as she is and she can't whip you any more. If you remain, sign a paper so that you will receive pay for your work." Mrs. Willis looked on with tears in her eyes and shook her head sadly. The next day the master notified each slave family that they could remain on his plantation if they desired and he would give each $75.00 at Christmas. Looking at Isaiah's step-father, he told him that since he was afflicted he would pay him only $50.00, but this amount was refused. Wishing to keep the man, Col. Willis finally offered him as much as he promised the ablebodied men.

Some slave owners did not let their slaves know of their freedom, and kept them in ignorance as long as six months; some even longer.

Green's family remained on the Willis plantation until they were forced to move, due to their ex-master's extravagance. As Isaiah remarked, "He ran through with 3,000 acres of land and died on rented land in Morgan County."

Directly after the war, Col. Willis was nominated for the office of legislator of Georgia. Realizing that the vote of the ex-slaves would probably mean election for him, he rode through his plantation trying to get them to vote for him. He was not successful, however, and some families were asked to move off his plantation, especially those whom he didn't particularly like.

Years later, Green's family moved to Atlanta. Isaiah is now living in the shelter provided by the Dept. of Public Welfare. He appears to be fairly contented.

[HW: Isaac (Isaiah) Green]

Edwin Driskell

THE EXPERIENCES OF AN EX-SLAVE

EDWIN DRISKELL

Following is the account of slavery as told by Mr. Isaac Green, who spent a part of his childhood as a slave.

"I wus born in Greene County, Georgia, eighty-one years ago. My marster wus named Colonel Willis. He wus a rich man an' he had a whole lots o' slaves—'bout seventy-five or more. Besides my mother an' me I had nine sisters. I wus de younges' chile. I didn't know 'bout my father 'till after surrender, 'cause ol' marster sold him 'way fum my mother when I wus two years old.

"When I wus big enuff I had to go to de fiel' wid de res' o' de chillun an' drap corn an' peas. We'd take our heels an' dent a place in de groun' an' in every dent we had to drap two peas. Sometimes we'd make a mistake an' drap three seeds instead o' two an' if we did dis too often it meant de strap fum de overseer. On our plantation we had a colored an' a white overseer.

"My ol' marster never did whup me an' he didn't 'low none o' de overseers to whup me either. He always say: 'Dat's my nigger—I sol' his father when I coulda saved him—he wus de bes' man I had on de plantation.' De rest o' de slaves uster git whuppins sometimes fer not workin' like dey should. When dey didn't work or some other little thing like dat dey would git twenty-five or fifty lashes but de marster would tell de overseer: 'Don't you cut my nigger's hide or scar him.' You see if a slave wus scarred he wouldn't bring as much as one with a smooth hide in case de marster wanted to sell 'im, 'cause de buyers would see de scars an' say dat he wus a bad nigger.

"Sometimes de women uster git whuppins fer fightin'. Ol' marster uster tell my mother all de time dat he wus goin' to give her one-hundred lashes if she didn't stop fightin', but he never did do it though. My grandmother never did git whupped. Colonel Black, her first marster, wus her father an' when he went broke he had to sell her. When he went broke he put her on de block—in dem days dey put slaves on de block to sell 'em jes' like dey do horses an' mules now—he say to de gentlemen gathered 'roun: 'Dis is my nigger an' my chile; she is a midwife an' a extraordinary weaver an' whoever buys her has got to promise to treat her like a white chile.' My marster bought her an' he treated her like she wus white, too. He never did try to hit her an' he wouldn't let nobody else hit her.

"We always had a plenty to eat an' if we didn't we'd go out in somebody's pasture an' kill a hog or sheep an' clean him by a branch an' den hide de meat in de woods or in de loft of de house. Some of de white folks would learn you how to steal fum other folks. Sometimes ol' marster would say to one o' us: 'Blast you—you better go out an' hunt me a hog tonight an' put it in my smokehouse—-dey can search you niggers' houses but dey can't search mine.'

"Once a week de marster give us three pounds of pork,

a half gallon o' syrup, an' a peck o' meal. You had to have a garden connected wid yo' house fer yo' vegetables. De marster would let you go out in de woods an' cut you as large a space as you wanted. If you failed to plant, it wus jes' yo' bad luck. If you wanted to you could sell de corn or de tobacco or anything else dat you raised to de marster an' he would pay you. 'Course he wusn't goin' to pay you too much fer it.

"All de slaves had to work--my mother wus a plow han'. All de aged men an' women had to tend to de hogs an' de cows an' do de weavin' an' de sewin'. Sometimes ol' marster would let us have a frolic an' we could dance all night if we wanted to as long as we wus ready to go to de fiel' when de overseer blowed de bugle 'fo day nex' mornin'. De fiel' han's had to git up early enuff to fix dey breakfas' befo' dey went to de fiel'. We chillun took dinner to 'em at twelve o'clock. We used baskets to take de dinner in, an' large pails to take de milk in. Dey had to fix supper fer dey selves when dey lef' de fiel' at dark.

"All de clothes we wore wuz made on de plantation. De women had to card, spin an' weave de thread an' den when de cloth wuz made it wuz dyed wid berries. My step-father wuz de shoemaker on de plantation an' we always had good shoes. He beat ol' marster out o' 'bout fifteen years work. When he didn't feel like workin' he would play like he wuz sick an' ol' marster would git de doctor for him. When anybody got sick dey always had de doctor to tend to him."

Regarding houses, Mr. Green says: "We lived in log houses dat had wood floors. Dere wuz one window an' a large fireplace where de cookin' wuz done in de ashes. De chinks in de walls wuz daubed wid mud to keep de weather out. De beds wuz made by hand an' de mattresses wuz big tickin's stuffed wid straw."

Continuing he says: "Yo' actual treatment depended on de kind o' marster you had. A heap o' folks done a heap better in slavery dan dey do now. Everybody on our plantation wuz glad when de Yankee soldiers tol' us we wuz free."

EX-SLAVE INTERVIEW:

MARGARET GREEN
1430 Jones Street
Augusta, Georgia.

(Richmond County)

BY: Mrs. Margaret Johnson
Editor
Federal Writers' Project,
Augusta, Georgia.

EX-SLAVE INTERVIEW

Margaret Green,
1430 Jones Street,
Augusta, Georgia
(Richmond County)

MARGARET GREEN

Margaret Green, 1430 Jones Street was born in 1855 on the plantation of Mr. Cooke McKie in Edgefield County, South Carolina.

Margaret's house was spotlessly clean, her furniture of the golden oak type was polished, and the table cover and sideboard scarfs were beautifully laundered. Margaret is a small, trim little figure dressed in a grey print dress with a full gathered skirt and a clean, starched apron with strings tied in a big bow. She has twinkling eyes, a kindly smile and a pleasant manner.

"Yes, mam, I remembers slavery times very well. I wuz a little girl but I could go back home and show you right where I wuz when the sojers come through our place with their grey clothes and bright brass buttons. They looked mighty fine on their hosses ridin' round. I could show you right where those sojers had the camp".

Margaret described "the quarters" and told of the life. "Each fam'ly had a garden patch, and could raise cotton. Only Marse Cooke raised cotton; what we raised we et".

"Margaret were the slaves on your master's plantation mistreated?"

"What you say? Mistreat? Oh! you mean whipped! Yes, man, sometime Marse Cooke whip us when we need it, but he never hurt nobody. He just give 'em a lick or two make 'em mind they business. Marse Cooke was a good man, and he never let a overseer lay a finger on one of his niggers!"

"Margaret were you ever whipped?"

Margaret laughed; with her eyes twinkling merrily she replied, "Marse Cooke say he wuz gonna whip me 'cause I was so mischievious. He was on his horse. I broke and run, and Marse ain't give me that whippin' till yet!"

"Yes, mam, I hearn stories o' ghos'es and hants, but I never did b'lieve in none of 'em. I uster love to play and to get out of all the work I could. The old folk on the plantashun uster tell us younguns if we didn't hurry back from the spring with the water buckets, the hants and buggoos would catch us. I ain't never hurry till yet, and I never see a hant. I wished I could, 'caus' I don't b'lieve I would be scart."

"Margaret, did you learn to read?"

"Oh! no mam, that wus sumpin' we wuzn't 'lowed to do; nobody could have lessons. But we went to Church to the Publican Baptist Church. Yes, mam, I'se sho' dat wuz the name—the Publican Baptist Church—ain't I been there all my life 'till I been grown and married? We uster go mornin' and evenin', and the white people sat on one side and the slaves on the other."

Margaret said her mother was a seamstress and also a cook. Three other seamstresses worked on the plantation. There was a spinning wheel and a loom, and all the cotton cloth for clothing was woven and then made into clothes for all the slaves. There were three shoe makers on the place who made shoes for the slaves, and did all the saddle and harness repair.

Margaret was asked who attended the slaves when they were sick.

"Marse Cooke's son was a doctor", she replied, and he 'tended anybody who was bad sick. Granny Phoebe was the midwife at our plantashun and she birthed all the babies. She was old when I was a little gal, and she lived to be 105. Marse Cooke never let any of his slaves do heavy work 'till dey wuz 18 years old." Margaret's father went to the war with "Marse Cooke" as his body servant, and her mother went also, to cook for him!

"To tell you the truth, man," said the old woman, "I 'member more 'bout that war back yonder than I member 'bout the war we had a few years ago."

United States. Work Projects Administration

Minnie Green

Interviewed

Alberta Minor
Re-search Worker

MINNIE GREEN

Minnie is not an ex-slave, for she was "jes walkin'" when the war was over. Her parents were given their freedom in May but stayed on with Judge Green until fall, after the wheat cutting. The family moved to a two story house "out Meriwether Road" but didn't get along so well. Minnie was hungry lots and came to town to get scraps of food. When she was a "good big girl" she came to town one day with her hair full of cukle-burrs, dressed in her mother's basque looking for food, when she saw a man standing in front of a store eating an orange. She wanted that peeling. No one kept their cows and pigs up and when the man threw the peeling on the ground a sow grabbed it. Minnie chased the pig right down Hill Street, was hollering and making plenty of noise, when a lady, "Mis' Mary Beeks", came out and asked her "what's the matter?" "Right then and there I hired myself out to Miss Mary, and she raised me." Minnie played with white children, went to the "white folks" Church, and did not "associate with niggers" until she was grown. Every summer they went to the Camp Grounds for two weeks. They took the children, Minnie for nurse, a stove, a cow and everything they needed for that time.

She was nearly grown before she went to a colored church and "baptisin'" and it frightened her to see a person immersed, and come up "shoutin'". Minnie thought they was "fightin' the Preacher" so she didn't go back anymore.

Minnie firmly believes if a woman comes in your house first on New Years Day, it will bring you bad luck, and she has walked as far as 10 miles to get a man in her house first. If she meets a cross eyed person, she crosses her fingers and spits on them to break the bad spell. "Hooten' owls" are sure the sign of death and she always burns her hair combs because if you just throw them away and the birds get them to put in their nests, you'll have a "wanderin' mind."

Minnie is 72 years old, very active physically and mentally, lives among the Negroes now but greatly misses her "white folks."

  Minnie Green
  503 East Chappell Street
  Griffin, Georgia
  August 31, 1936.

WHEELER GRESHAM of WILKES COUNTY
GEORGIA

by

Minnie Branham Stonestreet
Washington-Wilkes
Georgia

Dec. 14, 1936.

WHEELER GRESHAM

Wheeler Gresham, 82 years old, tall, very erect, has white hair and beard, a quiet dignified manner, and faded old eyes that seem ever to be gazing back on those happy days he told about "when we war' in slavery." He is uneducated, having gone to school only one week in his life—gave up "tryin' to larn out er books."

Wheeler claims the distinction of having had three masters and loving them all equally well; he belonged to one and lived with the other two. It all happened in this wise:

His mother, Barbara Booker, belonged to "Marse Simmie and Marse Jabie Booker"—("Marse Simmie wuz the one what named me") his father, Franklin Gresham belonged to "Marse George Gresham." The Bookers and Greshams lived on adjoining plantations and were the best of friends and neighbors. They would not sell a slave no matter what happened, so when Barbara and Franklin wanted to marry they had the consent of their owners and settled down on the Booker plantation where Barbara continued her work and Franklin spending all his spare time with her, although he belonged to the Greshams and kept up his work for them. He had a pass to go and come as he pleased.

Wheeler tells of his life on the plantations for his time was spent between the two where he played with the other little slaves and with the white boys near his age. He enjoyed most playing marbles, hunting and fishing with the little Gresham boys. He never has had a punishment of any kind in all his whole long life, and said with much pride—"An' I ain't never been in no court scrape neither. No'm, my Marsters didn't 'low nobody ter 'buke dey han's. Ef a overseer got rough an' wanted to beat a nigger, he had to go right den and dar." He added: "Dem overseer fellows wuz rough anyhow, dey warn't our sort of folks. An' de owners what wuz mean to dey niggers wuz looked down on by 'spectable white folks lak dem what I belonged to."

"All us little niggers on the Booker plantation et in de white folks' kitchen, a big old kitchen out in de yard. De grown slaves cooked and et in dey cabins, but our Mistess wouldn't trust 'em to feed de little ones. My Gramma wuz de cook an' we had plenty of good victuals, we'd all set er round an' eat all we wanted three times er day."

Wheeler said that the Doctor who lived near by was always called in when the negroes were sick and they had the best of care; their owners saw to that. Of course there were simple home remedies like mullein tea for colds, Jerusalem Oak seed crushed up and mixed with syrup, given to them in the Springtime, and always that terrible "garlic warter" they so despised to take.

When death came the slave was buried on the plantation in the negro burial ground, a white preacher conducting the last rites. When a negro couple wanted to marry the consent of the owners was ceremony enough and they set up a home as man and wife and lived on "'thout all dis 'vocin' lak dey has terday."

Christmas was a big time with three or four days holiday on the plantations. Santa Claus found his way to the Quarters and left the little negroes stick candy and "reisens", and "dar wuz er plenty of pound cake fer everybody." Fourth of July was a big holiday and all the little boys white and black went a-fishing together that day.

Sundays were kept holy—no work was done on the Sabbath. On "meetin' days" everybody attended the neighborhood Church, white and black worshiped together, the darkies in the gallery built for them. On all other Sundays they went to Church, and everybody sat in one big Bible Class. Wheeler said his Mistess called up all the little negroes on the plantation on Sunday afternoons and taught them the catechism and told them Bible stories.

There was plenty of fun for the darkies in the Gresham and Booker community. They had dances, cornshuckings, picnics and all kinds of old time affairs. These were attended by slaves for some distance around, but they had to have passes or "de patter rollers would sho' git 'em. Us little niggers wuz feared to go 'bout much 'kase we heered so much erbout de patter rollers." Wheeler enjoyed the cornshuckings more than anything else, or rather he talked more freely about them. He said that the corn was piled high in the barn and the men and boys, after a big supper of "fresh meat and all kinds of good things, and plenty of sho' nough pound cake"—(that pound cake he can't seem to forget)—would gather around and to the tune of an old fiddle in the hands of a plantation musician, they would sing and shuck corn until the whole pile was finished. Many races were entered into and the winners proclaimed amid much shouting and laughter. This merriment and work lasted into the night.

Wheeler was quick to say that the happiest time of his life was those days of slavery and the first years immediately after. He was happy, had all that anyone needed, was well taken care of in every way. He spoke of their family as being a happy one, of how they worked hard all day, and at night were gathered around their cabin fire where the little folks played, and his mother spun away on her "task of yarn". His Mistress made all his clothes, "good warm ones, too." All the little negroes played together and there "wuz a old colored lady" that looked after them "an' kept 'em straight."

There was little talk of the war, in fact some of the slaves didn't know what "de white folks wuz er fightin' 'bout." Wheeler's two Booker masters, "Marse Simmie and Marse Jabie, went to de war, Marse Jabie wuz kilt dar." Very little difference was noticed in the plantation life—of course times were harder and there was a sadness around, but work went on as usual. When the war was over and the slaves called up and told they were free: "Sum wuz glad an' sum wuz sorry, dey all wuz at a wonder—at de row's en', didn't know whar ter go. De most of 'em stayed on lak we wuz, workin' fer our white folks. Dat's what my Pa an' Ma done, dey stayed on fer sometime after de war." Wheeler tells about a few Yankees coming through the country after the war: "Us niggers wuz all 'feared of 'em an' we run frum 'em, but dey didn't do nothin' to nobody. I dunno what dey cum er 'round down here fer."

Wheeler said he "nuver paid signs no mind—nuver paid no 'tention to all dem 'stitions an' sich lak." He didn't have any superstitions to tell only he did hear "ef a screech owl fly 'cross yo' do' hits er sign of a death in dat house, an' ef a whippowill calls at de' do' hit's er sign of death. Dat's what folks say, I don't know nothin' 'bout hit."

"I'm glad I knowed slavery, I had er better livin' in dem days dan I eber had since. No talk 'bout money in dem days—no mam, an' ef a doctor wuz needed he wuz right dar. I'se livin' ter day 'kase I got sich a good start, an' den too, I'se livin' on de days of my Pa and Ma. Dey wuz good folks an' lived ter be old. An' den too, I'se allus lived on a farm, ain't nuver knowed no t'other kind of life, an' dat's de healthiest and freest way ter live."

And, maybe, this gray old son of the soil is right—who knows?

74

FIRST COPY

OF

ARTICLE ENTITLED:

"AN INTERVIEW WITH HEARD GRIFFIN," EX-SLAVE.

by

Minnie B. Ross

Typed by
A. M. Whitley
1-29-37

HEARD GRIFFIN—EX-SLAVE

HEARD GRIFFIN

In order to catch Mr. Heard Griffin, the writer prepared herself for an early morning interview. His daughter previously informed her that it would be the only possible chance of seeing him. Why? because even at the age of 86 years he is still restless; and is forever in the streets. He can walk much faster than a young person; but memory and hearing are a little dimmed by age. By careful and tactful questioning, and by giving him ample time for thinking the writer was able to learn a few facts of slavery which are as follows:

Mr. Griffin was born May 19, 1850 in Waldon County, Monroe, Georgia. His mother Sarah Griffin birthed 11 children; but he did not clearly remember his father as their master sold him when he was a very small boy. Here he remarked. "They would take small babies from their mothers' arms and sell them."

Their master and mistress Mike and Lucinda Griffin owned about 200 acres of land and a large number of slaves. On this plantation was grown corn, cotton, wheat, etc. Long before day light, the master would come to the slave quarters and call each person one by one, "Get up. Get up." Very soon every one was up and fully dressed ready to begin the day's work. First, however, they drank one or two glasses of milk and a piece of corn bread, which was considered breakfast. Whether this amount of food was sufficient for a morning's meal didn't matter to their master. They simply had to make it last them until dinner. Smiling Mr. Griffin remarked, "It wouldn't be long before you would hear the "geeing and hawing" coming from the fields, the squealing of pigs and the barking of dogs—all sounds mingling together."

Every one had a certain amount of work to complete before the day ended; and each person worked in feverish haste to get it done and avoid the whipping which they knew was in store for them, should they fail. During the day Mr. Griffin's mother worked in the field, hoeing and plowing. At night she, as well as other women, had to spin thread into cloth until bed time. Each woman had to complete four cuts or be punished the next morning. "If it began raining while we worked in the fields, the overseer would tell everyone to put up their horses and to shelling corn in the cribs," remarked Mr. Griffin.

"Mike Griffin was the meanest man I've ever known," he continued. "He would sit down with nothing else to do, think of some man, send for him and for no reason at all, give him a good beating. He kept a long cowhide, which was almost an inch thick and with this he would almost beat folks to death. First you had to remove your clothing so that whipping would not wear them out. One day he beat a woman named Hannah so badly that she died the same night. Before daybreak he had carried the baby off and buried it. We never knew the burial place." Overseers too, were very mean, particularly those on the Griffin plantation. They followed the example of the man who hired them and as a result this plantation was known far and wide for its cruelty, fear and terror. [HW:] Many slaves would have attempted to run away but for fear of the pack of blood hounds kept for the purpose of tracking run away slaves.

"Patter-rollers" were busy, too, looking up slaves and whipping them for the flimsiest of excuses. Slaves often outran them to the woods and managed to return to their plantations unobserved. If a pass had a certain hour marked in it, for the slave's return, and he failed to return at the designated houses, this was an offense for which they were punished by the "patter-rollers." "Yes," remarked Mr. Griffin, "We were not even allowed to quarrel among ourselves. Our master would quickly tell us, 'I am the one to fight, not you.'" When a slave visited his relatives on another plantation the master would send along one or two of his children to make sure they did not attempt to run away.

Discarded bed clothing was given to slave families on the Griffin Plantation and often it was necessary to keep a big log fire in the winter, in order to sleep comfortably. Clothing for individual needs consisted of one pair of brogan shoes a year and homemade cotton garments, shirts, pants, dresses, etc. Every person went bare footed in the summer and saved their one pair of shoes for the winter.

Food consisting of meal, bacon meat, and syrup was given the slave families once a week. Occasionally "short" a second quality of flour was given them for their Sunday meals. The Griffins were not liberal in feeding their slaves, but would not object to their raising a little corn, and a few vegetables. They had to work their gardens at night, however, by the light of burning fat wood. Real coffee was on unheard-of luxury among slaves: so scorched or corn meal served the purpose just as well. On Christmas the master called each slave and gave him a dram of whiskey. No other food or fruit was given. [HW:]

Tin pans served as plates for the families. Spoons, knives, and forks were unheard of: "Many a day I have eaten mashed bread and milk from a trough and thought it was good," remarked Mr. Griffin.

Occasionally on other plantations slaves were allowed to earn money by selling vegetables, chickens, etc. On the Griffin Plantation they could only sell home made "gingercakes" for which a five-cent piece of paper money was received in return. There were three pieces of paper money used in those days: the five-cent, ten-cent, and fifteen-cent pieces.

Although the slaves did not have separate churches, they were expected to attend the white churches and occupy the benches placed in the back, purposely for them. After the coachman drove the white family to church he unhitched the horses from the carriage and carried them to the pasture where they remained until the services were over.

Marriages were very easily performed on the Griffin Plantation: After securing the consent of both owners the rest of the ceremony consisted only in having the couple jump the broom. In the event, the bride and groom lived on separate plantations the groom was given a pass to visit her on week ends, beginning Saturday afternoon and ending Sunday evening.

"Our master was too mean to let us have frolics," remarked Mr. Griffin; "we never knew anything, but work. Of course when we got sick we were given the best medical care possible. People didn't die, they always got well." Home remedies made from various roots were used for minor illnesses.

"When the Civil War broke out our master loaded his horses with his most valuable possessions and refugeed forty miles from his home," remarked Mr. Griffin. "On one occasion the Yanks came to our plantation and stole three of our best horses. I never saw a battle fought but often watched the Confederate soldiers drilling. We continued to work long after freedom was declared, not knowing that we were free. One day our master's son-in-law called us together and told us we were free. Most of us didn't know what to do but we were glad to get off of that plantation and away from old man Griffin." With a broad smile he continued: "Well that is all I can tell you Miss, but come back to see me again."

With the above remark Mr. Heard Griffin and I closed our interview. He reminded me, however, that he had been married five times and was the father of fifteen children, four of whom are still living. His daughter cares for him and tries to make his old age as happy and comfortable as she can without the aid of relief.

[HW: David Goodman Gullins]

SUBJECT	REMINISCENCES OF SLAVERY DAYS
DISTRICT	NO. 1 W.P.A.
EDITOR AND RESEARCH	RUTH A. CHITTY
SUPERVISOR	J. E. JAFFEE

October 16, 1936.

REMINISCENCES OF SLAVERY DAYS

It was a beautiful brisk morning in October when I turned into main street to call on one of the most unique and interesting characters that we have among our colored citizens.

Upon arriving at the house where Uncle Dave lives, I made my way through a side gate and the first thing that greeted me in his back yard was a sign, "No Truspassing." I called to a tenant who rents his home to inquire where I might find Uncle Dave. We looked about the premises, and called him, but no response. I was just about to leave in despair, when the colored girl said "maybe he can be found inside," whereupon we called him forth.

He greeted me with a deep peal of laughter, saying "now you done caught me sho, Mistiss!" I told him the story of my mission, and, after making various excuses he finally, with a studied reluctance, consented to talk to me a while. He called the colored girl and asked her to bring a chair into the yard, which he placed near his favorite out-door lounging place, and invited me to sit down. Then, with a hearty laugh he said, "now Miss, just what is it you want me to tell you?"

"I want you to tell me all about yourself back in slavery days and since, Uncle Dave."

"Miss, if I tell you all I know, then you will know as much about me as I know." Again he burst into laughter, and constrained by a high sense of propriety, but with perfect ease, he began to relate to me in a manner and style all his own, some of the facts connected with his life.

"Miss, my name is David Goodman Gullins. I was born in 1854 on the 27th day of December, in Putnam County, about 3½ miles from Eatonton, on the Greensboro Road. I was born in slavery, my father and mother being owned by Mr. J. W. Mappin. Marse Mappin was not a large slave holder, since he only had about thirty-five slaves, but he was what we call a 'coming man'. I do not remember how much land he owned, but nothing like some of the very wealthy land and slave owners. My owner was a comparatively young man, say middle aged, weighing about 190 pounds, with a fairly good education and withall a first rate man. My earliest recollection of him was his perfectly bald head. It looked like a peeled onion. He married a widow, Mrs. Elizabeth Lawson, who had two sons; one who was Judge Thomas G. Lawson of the Ocmulgee Circuit, and Zurst Lawson, who was killed in the war. My owners were very good to their slaves.

"My father's name was John Mappin. He of course went by the name of the owner. My mother's name was Catharine. She was bought from an owner by the name of

Milline by my master, and she became Catharine Mappin. I know nothing of their lives, their childhood, their struggles, hardships, etc., and where they came from. There were eleven boys and one girl in our family, I being the third oldest boy born. Three brothers born after me died in infancy. My mother raised only five of her sons to manhood, and my sister is still living in Eatonton, Ga. She is Gracie Roby. I have one brother still living, W. R. Gullins, a minister. He is somewhere in North Carolina. When this brother was born, Mistress had a lot of company, and all the ladies wanted to name the new baby for their best friends. So the baby was named Willie Richard Edgar Mappin for the best friends of the young ladies. He later dropped the name Edgar and goes by the name of Willie Richard Gullins.

"Uncle David you say your owners name was Mappin, why is your name Gullins?"

"Well, Miss, I'll have to digress a little to give you the history of the name. Every effect has a cause you know, and after I got old enough to reason things out, I wondered too why my name was Gullins, so I did some investigating and the story goes like this.

"When I was a very small boy back before the war, a circus came to town. I remember the clown, whose name was Gullins. My father, John Mappin, was so much like the clown in his ways and sayings, that afterwards everyone started calling him Gullins. This soon became a sort of nickname. Some years after when slaves were freed, they were all registered, most of them taking the family name of their owners. When time came for my father to register, the Registrar says, "John, what name are you going to register under, Mappin or Gullins? Everyone calls you Gullins, and they will always call you Gullins. My father, after thinking for a moment said, "just put down Gullins." By this time I was beginning to think that Uncle Dave was pretty much of a clown himself.

"Now Uncle Dave tell me your early impressions of your mother and father."

"Miss, my mother was one of the best women God ever made. Back in slavery time I recall the trundle bed that we children slept on. In the day it was pushed under the big bed, and at night it was pulled out for us to sleep on. All through cold, bitter winter nights, I remember my mother getting up often to see about us and to keep the cover tucked in. She thought us sound asleep, and I pretended I was asleep while listening to her prayers. She would bend down over the bed and stretching her arms so as to take us all in, she prayed with all her soul to God to help her bring up her children right. Don't think now that she let God do it all; she helped God, bless your life, by keeping a switch right at hand."

"Uncle Dave you didn't have to be chastised, did you?"

"I got two or three whippings every day. You see my mother didn't let God do it all. You know if you spare the rod you spoil the child, and that switch stimulated, regulated, persuaded and strengthened my memory, and went a long way toward making me do the things my mother told me to do. Hurrah for my mother! God bless her memory!"

"What about your father, Uncle Dave?"

"My father was a good man; he backed my mother in

her efforts to bring us up right. He told me many a time, 'Boy, you need two or three killings every day!'"

"Uncle Dave why were you so obstreperous?"

"Miss, you see I was the baby in the family a long time, as three brothers born after me died in infancy. I was petted and spoiled, and later on they had to whip it out of me.

"Of course the slavery question was fast drawing to its climax when I was born. Already war clouds seemed to cast a shadow. While freedom was not had in Georgia until 1865, I was hardly old enough to remember very much about the early customs of slavery in pre-war days. We had comfortable quarters in which to live. Our houses were built in long rows, house after house. My father was carriage driver and foreman of the other niggers. His title was B.N."

"Uncle Dave what does B.N. stand for?"

With this question to answer, Uncle Dave broke into a spasm of laughter, bending double first, then rocking from side to side, all the time laughing while I waited anxiously to know the secret. Then, throwing his head back, he came forth with great emphasis—"Why, he was what we called 'Big Nigger'." Then we both laughed.

"Uncle Dave what were the duties of your mother as a slave?"

"Every slave had his task, and my mother was cook for the family and the weaver. All of the clothing was made on the plantation from cotton and wool. The cotton was carded, spun and woven into cloth and died. Likewise, woolen garments was made from the wool clipped from the sheep raised for this purpose. All these garments were made right on the plantation."

"Uncle Dave what did you do when you were a little slave?"

"Well, there was a whole drove of us little niggers. We had lots of chickens, cattle, hogs, sheep, etc. I had to help get up the eggs, drive cattle, open gates, go on errands for Marster, and Marster most always took me on trips with him, letting me ride in the foot of his buggy. I was his favorite little pet nigger."

"You must have been the Little Big Nigger, Uncle Dave."

"I was always pushing an investigation, so when Marse Mappin take me on trips with him that was my favorite time to ask questions. I remember one hot August day we were driving along, and I had already asked numerous questions, and Marse had already told me to shut up. I remained quiet for a time, but the temptation was too great, and while Marse was wiping the perspiration off his bald head, I said, 'Marster, may I ask you one more question?' 'Yes, what is it David?' 'If a fly should light on your head wouldn't he slip up and break his neck?' When Marster shouted 'Shut up,' I did shut up. He used to tell his wife, Miss Elizabeth, 'You know Elizabeth, my little nigger, Dave, drives me nearly crazy asking questions about the stars, moon, sun, and everything.'

"My family lived continuously on the Mappin plantation until after the war. Perhaps the most grievous fault of slavery was its persistent assault upon the home life.

Fortunately, none of our family was ever sold, and we remained together until after the war. Marster Mappin was far above the average slave owner; he was good to his slaves, fed them well, and was a very humane gentleman. We had such quantities of food—good rations, raised on the plantation. We had cattle, goats, hogs, sheep, chickens, turkeys, geese, all kinds of grain, etc. Very often a beef was butchered, we had fresh meat, barbecued kids, plenty vegetables, in fact just plenty to eat, and the slaves fared well. On Sundays we had pies and cakes and one thing and another. A special cook did the cooking for the single slaves. I'll say our rations were 150% fit. Everyone had certain tasks to perform, and all that was done above certain requirements was paid for in some way. We always had meat left over from year to year, and this old meat was made into soap, by using grease and lye and boiling all in a big iron pot. After the mixture become cold, it was a solid mass, which was cut and used for soap. Those were good old days. Everybody had plenty of everything.

"There were strict rules governing slaves, but our master was never brutal. I being a child, never received any punishment from any one except my mother and my Mistress. Punishment was inflicted with a raw cow hide, which was cut in a strip about three inches wide, one end being twisted. This made a very powerful and painful weapon. There were unruly slaves, what we called desperadoes. There were 'speculators', too, who would get possession of these, and if a slave come into possession of one of these speculators, he either had to come under or else he was sure to die. The Lynch law was used extensively. Those slaves committing crimes against the state were more often considered unworthy of trial, though some were brought to trial, punishment being so many licks each day for so many days or weeks, or capital punishment. It is true that many crimes were put upon the slaves when the white man was guilty.

"We had plenty of amusements in those days, such as corn shuckings, dances, running, jumping and boxing contest. Saturday was the big frolicking time, and every body made the most of it. Slaves were allowed to tend little patches of their own, and were often given Saturday afternoons off to work their crops, then when laying-by time came, we had more time for our patches. We were allowed all we could make over and above our certain tasks. Marster used to buy me candy when he take me with him, but I can't remember him giving me spending money.

"We were not compelled to attend church on Sundays, but most of the slaves went from time to time. I was a Baptist, my family being Baptist, but I have long since put Christianity above creeds. I learned too, many years ago, that we can find in the contents of that old book we call the Bible, a solution to every problem we run up against."—Uncle Dave is a learned theologian, and has served many years as a minister, or Doctor of Divinity. He is very modest, and says that he wants no titles on his name. He believes that every man and every woman gets all the credit they deserve in this world. "Going back to the church services, we slaves attended the white folks churches. There were galleries built for the slaves in some of the churches, in others, there was space reserved in the back of the church for the colored worshippers. It was a custom to hold prayer meetings in the quarters for the colored sick. One of the slaves named

Charity had been sick a long time, just wasting away. One beautiful spring morning they came running for my mother saying that Charity was dying. I was a very small child, and ran after my mother to Charity's house. It was a very harrowing experience to me, as it required three women to hold Charity on the bed while she was dying. I became so frightened, I slipped into unconsciousness. They took me home, and after hours went by I still was unconscious, and Marster became so alarmed about me that they sent for Dr. Cogburn. He said that it was a thousand wonders that I ever came back, but he gave me some medicine and brought me around. About a year later, my hair turned white, and it has been white ever since. They used to gather herbs and one thing and another from the woods for simple maladies, but Marster always send for the doctor when things looked serious to him.

"In 1863, Miss Elizabeth was going to have big company at her house, and she was saving her strawberries for the occasion. I spied all these nice, ripe strawberries through the paling fence, and the whole crowd of us little niggers thought they needed picking. We found an opening on the lower side of the fence and made our way in, destroying all of those luscious ripe strawberries. When we had about finished the job, Mistress saw us, and hollered at us. Did we scatter! In the jam for the fence hole I was the last one to get through and Mistress had gotten there by that time and had me by the collar. She took me back to the house, got the cow hide down, and commenced rubbing it over me. Before she got through, she cut me all to pieces. I still have signs of those whelps on me today. In the fight I managed to bite her on the wrist, causing her to almost bleed to death. I finally got away and ran to a hiding place of safety. [HW:] They used soot and other things trying to stop the bleeding.

"When Marster come home he saw Miss Elizabeth with her hand all bandaged up, and wanted to know what the trouble was. He was told the story, so he came out to look for me. He called me out from my hiding place, and when he saw me with those awful whelps on me, and how pitiful looking I was, he said, "Elizabeth, you done ruint my little nigger, David." "I wouldn't have him in this fix for all the strawberries." I was very fond of strawberries in those days, but that experience put an end forever to my taste for them. So much for the strawberry business!

"Even a dog [HW: likes] kind treatment. Some days Mistress was good and kind to us little niggers, and she would save us the cold biscuits to give us when we brought in the eggs. Sometime, she would go two or three days without giving us any biscuits then she didn't get no eggs. We rascals would get up the eggs and go off and have a rock battle with them. Every effect has a cause— then Miss would wonder why she didn't get any eggs and call us all in for cold biscuits, then the eggs would come again. Of course we had our game of "tell". If one of the gang threatened to tell, then we all would threaten to tell all we knew on him, and somehow we managed to get by with it all.

"After the war, my father stayed on with Marster Mappin as a cropper running a two horse farm for himself. In the early 70's my father bought 12 acres of land from Judge Lawson near Eatonton, which was later sold in lots to different colored people, and became known as Gullinsville, and is still so called by some.

"In 1876, 26 day of November, I left my folks and came to Milledgeville to live. I worked for Mr. Miller S. Bell in the livery stable for $7.00 per month. Of this amount I sent $3.50 home to my parents. The next year I went on a farm with Mr. John Wall for $8.00 per month. The next year I had a better offer with Mr. R. N. Lamar to farm and act as general handy man for $9.00 per month. I saved my money and worked hard, and I would lend Mr. Lamar my yearly income at interest. In 1882, Mr. Lamar negotiated a trade with Mr. Samuel Evans for this piece of property right here. When they found out a Negro wanted to buy the property, there was more or less argument, but I sat right still and let Mr. Lamar handle the trade for me. I have owned other property, but I have sold everything else I had. My health failed, and I just settled down here to be quiet. I owned property on Chestnut Street in Atlanta and in Putnam County also. I have been saving all my life, everything."

On looking about me, I concluded he was indeed a thrifty person. An accumulation of every conceivable thing (junk) that had been discarded by others, Uncle Dave had brought home and carefully and neatly stored it away for subsequent use.

"Uncle Dave tell me something about your education."

"Well, when I was a boy back in Putnam County I went to night school. For a long time I was the only Negro in the class. My foundation work I got under a Mr. Whitfield, Mr. John Nix, and we had a Yankee teacher, Miss Claudia Young. In September 1885 I went to Atlanta and entered the academic department of what is now Morehouse College. I was graduated in academics in 1889 as valedictorian of the class—my subject being "We Are Coming", which was a theme on the progress of the Negro race. In 1891 I was graduated from the theological department as valedictorian, my subject then being "Why Do Nations Die".

"Now Miss, you ask me if I am superstitious. I show am. When I hear these owls at night I just get up and get me some salt and a newspaper and burn this, and I don't never hear that same owl again. Some folks say tie knots in the sheet, but I burn salt. I think the bellowing or lowing of cows and oxen or the bleating of sheep is a bad omen." Then Uncle David took me way back in the Bible and recited how the king was commanded to slay all the cattle and everything and they kept out some of the oxen and sheep. "I believe you should turn a clock face to the wall when a person dies. I believe in signs, yes mam!"

"Marster was good to his niggers, but they had to have a pass to leave the plantation. There were patrolers to look after the slaves and see that they did not run around without a pass. If they found one without a pass, he was strapped then and there by the patrolers. Of course I was too young in those days to run around at night, and my mother always had us in bed early. It was long after the war that I did my courting. I was to have married a girl before I went to Atlanta in the 80's, but she died. I later married a Yankee nigger in Atlanta. She belonged to the 400, and some how, she never could get used to me and my plain ways. We had four children, three boys and one girl. Two of the boys died, and I have living today, one daughter married and living in Washington, D.C. and my son and his family live in Alabama.

"My Marster did not go to the war, but we all worked

at home preparing food and clothes and other things for those who did go. Some of the slaves went as helpers, in digging ditches and doing manual labor. The Yankee soldiers visited our territory, killing everything in sight. They were actually most starved to death. Marster was all broken after the war. He had planned to buy another plantation, and increase his holdings, but the war sorter left us all like the yellow fever had struck.

"After a number of years in Mission work and in the ministry I was compelled to retire on account on my broken health. I owe my long life to my mother's training in childhood. There are four things that keep old man Gullins busy all the time—keeping out of jail, out of hell, out of debt, and keeping hell out of me. I learned to put my wants in the kindergarten, and if I couldn't get what I wanted, I learned to want what I could get. I believe it is just as essential to have jails as to have churches. I have learned too, that you can't substitute anything for the grace of God."

United States. Work Projects Administration

1-25-37

Minnie B. Ross.

EX SLAVE

MILTON HAMMOND.

After explaining the object of the visit to Mr. Hammond he smiled and remarked "I think that is a good piece of work you're doing; and I'll tell you all that I can remember about slavery, you see I was only a small boy then; yesterday though, I was 83 years old." Mr. Hammond led the way up a dark stairway down a dark hall to a door. After unlocking the door, he turned on a light which revealed a very dark room commonly furnished and fairly neat in appearance. The writer took a seat and listened to the old man relate the following incidents.

A slave boy by the name of Milton Hammond was born in Griffin, Georgia, October 20, 1853. His parents, Emily and James Hammond, had 10 children 8 boys and 2 girls of whom he was oldest. His mother, sisters and brothers used the name Hammond as this was their father's name. Although every number of his family with the exception of his father, belonged to Bill Freeman they always used his name. Mr. Hammonds family always lived in the town of Griffin and belonged to a class known as "Town Slaves".

When Mr. Hammond reached the age of 6 years their old master, Bill Freeman died and all the property money, slaves, etc., had to be re-sold at an administrations sale. Among his four children a plan was made to repurchase their favorite slaves; but many were sold to owners in different states particularly Mississippi and Louisiana. Mr. Hammonds father, desiring to keep his family near him, spoke to his master and asked that he appeal to the young mistress to purchase his family. "I remember the auction sale quite well, remarked Mr. Hammond. They stood us on the block side by side. The mistress held my baby brother in her arms; and they began to cry us off just as they do now. Of course my mistress came forward and bought us, and we returned home the same day we left". Slaves were always sorted and placed into separate groups or classes. For instance, the heavy robust ones were placed together and sold for large sums of money. The light weights were grouped and sold accordingly.

Although the Freemans owned a large plantation several miles from Griffin and had a large number of slaves, who lived on this plantation to do the work, they resided in town with only the Hammond family as their servants. Mr. Hammonds' grandmother acted as the cook for the household and his mother assisted her. His sister was the chamber-maid and kept the house spotlessly clean. Smiling, Mr. Hammond remarked, "Until I was older my job was that of playing, later I became my young mistress's carriage driver". Miss Adeline Freeman was the young mistress whom Mr. Hammond continued to speak of; and during the war period she did welfare work; that is, Mr. Hammond drove her and her mother around through different counties, soliciting medicines, rags for bandages, etc., which were sent, to the hospitals.

Mr. Hammond related the following experiences while driving through the country. "We always visited the richest slave owners, those who owned 2 and 3 hundred head of slaves, and often would remain in one community over night and probably the next day. After putting up the horses an and carriage I would follow my mistress into the dining room. She always saw to it that I sat at the same table with her. I never could drink milk or eat butter, so on more than one occasion other people would try to influence my mistress and tell her that if I belonged to them they would make me drink milk or beat me. She never noticed any of their remarks; but always gave me the same food that she ate.

"Often while driving, I would almost drop off to sleep and my old mistress would shout, "Milton aren't you sleepy?". "No ma'am", I would reply, "Why, yes you are; I'll slap your jaws". My young mistress would then take the reins and tell me to go to sleep."

Mr. Hammond continued—"Many a morning I have known the overseers on the plantation where we were stopping to blow the horn for every one to get up, long before sunrise prepare their breakfast and get to the fields. The old women were required to care for the young children while their mothers worked in the fields. Sometimes there would be a many as ten and fifteen for each to look after. Around noon they were fed from a trough which was about ten or fifteen feet in length. Pot liquor by the buckets was thrown in the trough until they were filled. The children with spoons in their hands would then line up on each side no sooner was the signal given than they began eating like a lot of pigs. The smaller ones would often jump in with their feet."

After the work in the fields was completed for the day,

women were then required to work at night spinning thread into cloth. Each woman had a task which consisted of making so many cuts a night. As Mr. Hammond remarked, "You couldn't hear your ears at night on some plantations, for the old spinning wheels". At 9 o'clock the overseer would blow the horn for every one to go to bed. The cloth woven by women was used to make men clothing also, and was dyed different colors from dye which was made by boiling walnut hulls and berries of various kinds. Color varied according to the kind of berry used. One pair of shoes, made to order, was given each person once a year.

One and two roomed log cabins were found on practically all the plantations. The number of rooms depended upon the number in the family. Sometimes one room would contain three and four bed scaffolds, so called by Mr. Hammond because of their peculiar construction. Some beds were nailed to the walls and all of them were built with roped bottoms. Home made tables and benches completed the furnishings of a slave home. There were no stoves, large fireplaces, five to six feet in length, served the purpose of stoves for cooking. Cooking utensils including an oven and very large pots were found in every home. Wooden plates and spoons were used on some plantations.

The rations for the next week were given each family on saturday nights, amounts varying according to the number in each family. Usually a small family received three lbs. of bacon, one peck of meal, and one quart of syrup.

Slaves on the Freeman plantation never knew anything but kind treatment. Their mistress was a religious woman and never punished unless it was absolutely necessary. On other plantations however, some slaves were treated cruelly. When a slave resented this treatment he was quickly gotten rid of. Many were sent to Mississippi and Texas. White offenders were sent to chain gangs, but there were no gangs for slaves. "Patter rollers" were known more for their cruelty than many of the slave owners and would often beat slaves unmercifully". "I remember one," remarked Mr. Hammond, "The Patter rollers fot after a man on our place." Booker went to see his wife and took along an old out of date pass. The Patter-rollers asked to see the pass which he quickly handed to them and kept walking. After inspecting the pass closely they called Booker and told him the pass was no good. "Well this is" he replied and started running just as fast as he could until he safely reached the plantation. "I never needed a pass."

Through the week the slaves were allowed to conduct prayer meeting in the quarters themselves; but on Sundays they attended the white churches for their weekly religious meetings. We were told to obey our masters and not to steal. "That is all the sermon we heard," remarked Mr. Hammond. Their services were conducted in the basement of the church in the afternoons.

Marriages on the Freeman Plantation, were conducted in much the same manner as they are today. Mr. Hammond only remembers attending just one marriage of a colored couple. A white minister performed the ceremony right in the mistress's yard as every one white and colored looked on. After the ceremony the usual frolic did not take place; however on other plantations frolics often took place immediately following a marriage. Whiskey served as refreshment for some while others had to content themselves with barbecue.

"When we got sick we were not allowed to suffer through negligence on the part of our owner", remarked Mr. Hammond. Family doctors of the white families attended the slaves and through them they were well cared for. Castor oil was the favorite home remedy used in those days and it could always be found on the family shelf.

"My first impression of the civil war was received when the methodist and Baptist Churches began to disagree", remarked Mr. Hammond. He continued,—"One day as my uncle and I worked on Miss Adeline's truck farm Wheeler's Calvary, a group of Confederate soldiers came to the field and forced us to give them our two best mules. In their place they left their old half starved horses. We immediately rode to town and informed the mistress of what had taken place. During this time Confederate soldiers were known to capture slaves and force them to dig ditches, known as breastworks. My mistress became frightened, and locked me in the closet until late in the evening. She then fixed a basket of food and instructed me as to the direction in which to travel back to the field. It was a common sight to see soldiers marching on to Macon, Ga., in the mornings and in the evenings see the same group on their way back running from the Yanks".

Mr. Hammond made the following statement concerning the end of the war. "Our mistress told us we were free; however, I was too young to realize just what freedom would mean to us, but somehow I knew that we would have to be responsible for our own upkeep. Doctors bills, medicines, clothing, (etc) would have to be paid by us from then on. After that we worked for anyone who would hire us and never earned over 25 or 30 cents a day. Sometimes our pay consisted of a peck of meal or a piece of meat."

As a close to the interview Mr. Hammond stated he married at the age of 23 and was the father of 7 children. He has lived in Atlanta for the past 65 years working at various jobs. At one time he owned a dray. "My old age is the result of taking care of myself and not being exposed." Besides this Mr. Hammond attends Bethel A.M.E. church regularly. As writer prepared to leave, Mr. Hammond remarked, "I never knew much about slavery, you see; I've always been treated as a free man".

United States. Work Projects Administration

JANE SMITH HILL HARMON
of
WASHINGTON-WILKES

by

Minnie Branham Stonestreet
Washington-Wilkes
Georgia

JANE SMITH HILL HARMON OF WASHINGTON-WILKES

A comical little old black woman with the happy art of saying and doing as she pleases and getting by with it, is Jane Smith Hill Harmon of Washington-Wilkes. She lives alone in her cabin off the Public Square and is taken care of by white friends. She is on the streets every day carrying her long walking stick which she uses to lean on and as a "hittin' stick". She doesn't fail to use it vigorously on any "nigger" who teases her. She hits hard and to hurt, but it seems they had rather hear what she has to say, and take the penalty, then to let her alone. Her wardrobe consists of out-of-style clothes and hats given her and it is her delight on Saturday afternoons to dress up in her finest and fanciest creations and come strutting along down town proud of the attention she is attracting.

Unlike most old people, Aunt Jane doesn't like to talk about the past. She enjoys life and lives in the present. It was hard to get her to tell anything much of her early life.

Finally, however, she grew a bit reminiscent and talked of the past for a little while.

"Yassum, I'se 88 years ole last gone May, an' I been in Washington, Georgy fuh 53 years an' I ain't been in no Council scrape an' no Cote nor nothin' bad lak dat, kase I 'haves myself an' don't lak niggers an' don't fool 'long wid 'em. No'm, I sho' ain't got no use fuh niggers 'tall. An' as fuh yaller niggers—huh! I jes' hates 'em—dey's de wust niggers de're is, dey's got dirty feets, an' dey's nasty an' mean, I hates 'em, I tells yuh!

"I wuz borned an' raised on de Smith plantation out here a piece frum town. I wuz one of fourteen chillun, I think I wuz de 10th 'un. We wuz well took keer of by our Marster an' his fust wife, she wuz jes' as good ter us as she could be, my fust Mistess wuz, but she died an' Marster married agin an' she wuz mean ter us little niggers. She'd whup us fuh nothin', an' us didn't known what ter do, kase our fust Mistess wuz so good ter us, but dat last 'oman, she sho' wuz mean ter us.

"My Marster had lots of slaves an' us all had work ter do. De fust work I done wuz churnin' an' I loved ter do 'hit kase I loved milk an' butter so good. I'd dance an' dance 'round dat ole churn, churnin' an' churnin' 'till de butter wuz come. I allus could dance, I cuts fancy steps now sometimes when I feels good. At one o' dem big ole country breakdowns (dances), one night when I wuz young, I danced down seben big strong mens, dey thought dey wuz sumpin'! Huh, I danced eb'ry one down!

"I uster play dolls wid de overseer's chillun, an' look fuh aigs, an' tote in wood an' pick up chips. Us had good times togeder, all us little niggers an' de little white chilluns. Us had two days at Chris'mus, an' no work wuz done on de place of a Sunday. Everybody white an' black had ter go ter Chu'ch. De overseer piled us all in de waggin an' took us whether us wanted ter go or no. Us niggers set up in de loft (gallery), an' de white folks wuz down in de Chu'ch too.

"Atter er while dey s'lected me out to be a housegirl an' den I slep' in de big house. All de little niggers et in de white folks' kitchen out'n er big tray whut wuz lak a trough. De cook put our victuals in de tray an' gib us a spoon an' pone er bread a piece an' made us set 'roun' dat tray an' eat all us wanted. 'Hit wuz good eatin', too.

"All durin' of de War my Marster wuz off fightin' an' de overseer wuz hard on us. We wuz glad when Marster cum home er gin. De Yankees wuz a-comin' an' Daddy Charles, he wuz a ole black man on de place, knowed 'bout Marster's money, an' he took hit all an' put it in er big box an' went out in de night time an' buried hit 'way down deep in some thick woods an' put leaves all over de place an' dem Yankees couldn't fin' hit nowhar, an' dey went on off an' let us 'lone.

"My Ma wuz a 'spert spinner an' weaver, an' she spun an' wove things ter be sont ter de Soldiers in de War. I 'members dat, her er spinnin' an' dey say hit wuz fer de soldiers.

"Atter we wuz free I went ter school er mont'. I fit so wid all de chillun I quit. Dey said I mustn't fight an' I knowed I couldn't git er long widout fightin' so I jes' quit an' ain't never been ter no mo' schools. My Marster said he wuz goin' ter have a school on de place fer all his niggers, but freedom cum an' he didn't do hit.

"I mari'ed in my white folks' kitchen, mari'ed de fust time when I wuz 19 years ole. I been mari'ed two times an' had good husban's. Dey wuz good ter me.

"Doctors? Doctors? I don't know nothin' 'bout no doctors! I ain't never been sickly. Dis year (1936) I done had to have mo' ter do wid doctors dan ever in my life. I'se gittin' now to whar I kain't walk lak I uster, all crippled up in my laigs wid sumpin'.

"Ain't nobody lef' now but me an' one o' my six chillun. He lives up in dat Phillerdelma (Philadelphia) an' I 'cided onst three er fo' year ergo, to go up da're an' live wid 'im. Lawdy, Lawdy, I ain't been so glad o' nothin' in my life as I wuz ter git back ter Washington, Georgy! I ain't goin' 'way frum here 'till I dies. Son is mari'ed, an' sich er 'oman as he's got! She's un o' dem smart No'th'n niggers. She 'bused de So'th an' de white folks down here all de time. I'd er beat her wid my stick ef'n I'd er had 'tection, but I wuz way off up da're in de No'th an' didn't know nobody. But I did found a gal what use ter live here an' went an' stayed wid her 'till I worked an' got 'nough money ter git home on. Jes' soon as I got here I went straight ter Mr. Sheriff Walton an' Mr. Sturdivant (Chief of Police) an' tole dem 'bout dat sassy hateful nigger up da're talkin' 'bout de So'th an' de white folks lak she done, an dat she say she wuz comin' down here ter see me. I axed dem when I got er letter sayin' she wuz a-comin' would dey take me ter Augusty ter meet her an' when she stept off'n de train ter let me take my stick an' beat her all I wanted ter fer talkin' 'bout my white folks lak she done. Dey said: "Aunt Jane, jes' you let us know an' we sho' will take you to Augusty ter meet her, an' let you beat her all you want ter." But she ain't never come—

she skeered, an she sho' better be, kase I'se home down here an got all de 'tection I needs. Ef'n she ever do come, I'm goin' ter beat her wid dis stick an sen' her back to her country up da're in dat Phillerdelma. She ain't got no sense an' no raisin, neider, talkin' 'bout de So'th an' my white folks what lives here."

And from the wicked flash from Aunt Jane's eyes, it will be well for her "sassy" daughter-in-law to stay "up No'th".

United States. Work Projects Administration

PLANTATION LIFE

As viewed by

Ex-Slave

DOSIA HARRIS
159 Valley Street
Athens, Georgia

Written by: Sadie B. Hornsby
Athens —

Edited by: Sarah H. Hall
Athens —
Leila Harris
Augusta —

and

John N. Booth
District Supervisor
Federal Writers' Project
Residencies 6 & 7.

DOSIA HARRIS
Ex-Slave—Age 78

DOSIA HARRIS

Dosia lives in a red painted frame house. Her very black skin, thick lips, and broad nose are typical of her African ancestry. She is tall, thin, and a little stooped, and her wooly hair is fast fading from gray to almost white. When she greeted the interviewer, she was wearing a blue striped dress which displayed a large patch of blue print on the front of the skirt over her knees. Over her dress a black silk blouse, lavishly trimmed with black beads, was worn for a wrap, and a pair of men's brown shoes, sans laces, completed her costume. Due to illiteracy Dosia has retained the dialect of the old southern darky.

Asked to relate her experiences as a slave, she replied: "Oo, Miss! What does you want to know 'bout dat for? Well, anyhow I was borned in Greene County. Mary and Auss Downs was my Ma and Pa. I cain't tell you whar dey come from.

"I played 'round de yard wid de rest of de chillun and picked a little cotton up and down de rows. I was de oniliest chile my Mammy had. My Pa was married two times, and I was his fust chile. I had four half sisters: Fannie, Clara, Daisy, and Martha Ann, but I never had no brothers.

"All de houses in de slave quarters was log cabins 'cept two. Dey was made of boards what was put on straight up and down. All de houses had chimblies made out of mud and sticks. De beds had high posties and some of 'em was nailed to de wall of de cabin. Dey didn't know nothin' 'bout no wire springs den, and dey strung de beds wid heavy cords for springs. Dey made mattress ticks out of coarse home-wove cloth; some was striped and some was plain unbleached white. Atter de wheat was thrashed evvy year de 'omans tuk deir ticks and emptied out de old straw and went and filled 'em wid new wheat straw. Wisht I had a nice fresh made wheat straw mattress now. Us had plenty of good quilts for kivver.

"Some of de slave chillun slept on de flo', but me, I

slept wid my grandma. She was Crecia Downs, and she done raised me, 'cause my Mammy died when I was three days old, or come to think of it, was I three weeks old when dat happened? I'se done got so old I forgits lots of things lak dat. Mammy died of some kind of fever dat was mighty catchin'. Twenty-five Niggers died on dat one plantation 'bout de same time, from dat fever. Atter grandma got too old to wuk in de field, she didn't do nothin' but piddle 'round de yard and bile slops for de hogs. Grandpa Joe Downs, he was de carpenter, but he done most any kind of wuk dat come up to be done; he wuked in de fields and driv cows, or jus' anything.

"Money! No Ma'am! All dey ever give slaves was a belly full of somepin t'eat, de clo'es dey wore, and de orders to keep on wukin'. Now come to think of it, I did see $8,000 of Jeff Davis fodder what de white folks th'owed 'way atter de War. Us chillun picked it up and played wid it.

"What did us have t'eat? Oo-o! Dey give us plenty good victuals. Dere was bread and meat; peas, greens, and other vegetables; all de milk us wanted, and sometimes dere was good old gingercakes made wid sorghum syrup. As for me, I laked fried fat meat and cornbread cooked in de ashes better dan greens and sweet things any old time. All de cookin' was done in great big open fireplaces dat was plum full of ovens, skillets and all sorts of long handled pans and things. Gentlemen! Dat pot would bile down wid dem peas in it 'fore you knowed it if you didn't watch it close. Dere never was no other bread good as what us baked in dem ovens and in de ashes.

"'Possums! You jus' makes my mouth water, talkin' 'bout 'possums. Folks thought so much of deir 'possum dogs dem days dey fed 'em 'til dey was jus' fat and lazy. Dey cotched de 'possums, singed and scraped de hair off of 'em, finished dressin' 'em and drapped 'em in de pot to bile 'til dey was tender. Den dey put 'em in bakin' pans and kivvered 'em over wid strips of fat meat and baked 'em jus' as nice and brown, and if dey had good sweet 'tatoes, dey roasted 'em in de ashes, peeled 'em, and put 'em on de big old platters wid de 'possums. Rabbits was plentiful too and I loves 'em 'til dis good day. Most of de young tender rabbits what dey cotched was fried, but if dey brung in some old tough ones dey was throwed in de pot wid a piece of fat meat and biled 'til dey was done. Squirrels was cooked jus' lak rabbits. Dere was plenty of fish down dar in Greene County whar us lived, but I never did eat 'em. Slaves would wuk all day and fish all night, but you never did ketch Dosia foolin' 'round no fish ponds. Slave famblies was 'lowed to have little gyarden patches if dey wanted 'em. I ricollect how I used to go to de gyarden in de winter and cut down collards atter frost had done hit 'em and fetched 'em to de house to be biled down for dinner.

"What us wore in summer? Well, it was lak dis—little Nigger chillun didn't stay out of de branch long 'nough to need much clothes in hot weather, but in de winter dey give us dresses made out of coarse cloth wove on de loom right dar on de plantation. Some of dem dresses was red and some was blue. De cloth was dyed wid red oak bark and copperas, and dey used indigo what dey raised on de place to dye de blue cloth. De waisties was close fittin' and sorter skimpy skirts was gathered on to 'em. De underskirts was unbleached white cloth made jus' lak de dresses only some skimpier. Old Marster raised plenty of cattle and saved de hides what he sont to de tannery to be got ready for my uncle, Moses Downs, to make our brogan shoes. Dem shoes had brass toes to keep 'em from wearing out too quick. Uncle Mose was sho' a smart shoemaker. He had to make shoes for all de slaves on de whole plantation.

"Marster Sam Downs owned us, and his wife, Miss Mary, was a mighty good somebody to belong to—"Old Mist'ess" us called her. I don't 'member nothin' 'tall 'bout Old Marster, 'cause he died 'fore I was knee high to a duck. Old Marster and Old Mist'ess had five chillun. Dey was: Miss Ellen, Marse Sam, Marse James Kelsey, Marse Tom, and Marse William. Old Miss sho' was good to us Niggers, 'cause she was raisin' us to wuk for her.

"When Marse William went to de War, he tuk my pappy wid him. Dey come back home on one of dem flyloughs, (furloughs) or somepin lak dat, end you jus' ought to have seed de way us chillun crowded 'round pappy when he got dar. One of his fingers had done got shot off in de fightin', and us chillun thought it was one of de funniest lookin' things us had ever seed, a man wid a short finger. He said dem yankees had done shot it off.

"Atter Old Marster died Old Mist'ess moved to a town called Woodstock, or was it Woodville? It was Wood-somepin' or nother. She hired old man John Akins to oversee de plantation, and she evermore did oversee him and de plantation too. She had a fine pacing mule what wouldn't throw her for nothin'. Evvy mornin' she got on dat mule and rid out to her plantation. She allus fetched us somepin' t'eat; most of de time it was a gingercake apiece.

"I couldn't rightly say how big dat plantation of hers

was. Oo-o! But it sho' was one more big place, and Niggers was scattered all 'round dar lak blackbirds. Dat old overseer, he sho' was mean to de slaves. He whupped 'em and he kept on whuppin' 'em, 'til sometimes it seemed lak he jus' beat on 'em to hear 'em holler. It warn't long atter midnight when he got 'em up to go to wuk and he kept 'em at hard labor 'til way atter sundown. De biggest things he whupped Niggers for was for runnin' 'way and for not doin' deir wuk right.

"Jails! Did you say jails? Yessum, dey had jails. You know slaves warn't civilized folks den—all dey knowed was to fuss end fight and kill one 'nother. Dey put de Niggers in dem jails 'til dey hung 'em.

"Grandma was sold on de block to Marse Sam's Pa, Marse Kelsey Downs, soon atter she was brung over to dis country from de homeland of de black folks. She never did larn to talk dis language right plain. Us used to git her to tell us 'bout when she was sold. De sale was in December but it was so far off dat corn was in tassel 'fore my pore grandmammy got to Greene County. She said dey camped at night and got up long 'fore day and was driv lak cows, a man in front and 'nother one back of 'em to keep 'em from branchin' out and runnin'.

"Niggers never had no chance to larn to read and write dem days. Dey went to meetin' at Shiloh—dat was de white folks church nigh Penfield—and Bethesda was 'nother of de white folks churches whar slaves was brought to listen to de preachin'. One thing sho', Niggers couldn't read de Bible, but dey jus' lumbered down 'bout de Lord from deir heads.

"Slaves didn't run off to no North dat I ever knowed

'bout. I heared tell 'bout one man named Si what run 'way wid dem yankees when dey come through and dey made a black yankee soldier out of him atter he jined up wid 'em. I heared tell of patterollers what cotched Niggers 'way from home 'thout no pass. Folks said dey brushed you off and sont you home if dey cotched you.

"All I knowed Niggers to do at night atter dey come in from de fields, was to eat supper and fling deirselfs on de beds and go right off to sleep, 'cept when dey wanted to hunt and fish, and most of dat sort of thing was done atter de crops was laid by or atter dey had done been gathered into de barns. On Saddy nights, de older womans ironed and fixed up for Sunday whilst de men was busy gittin' de harness and tools and things ready for de next week's wuk. Young folks never had nothin' but good times on deir minds. Dey danced, frolicked, and cut de buck in gen'ral. Dey didn't have no sho' 'nough music, but dey sho' could sing it down. One of de dance songs went somepin' lak dis:

> 'Oh! Miss Liza, Miss Liza Jane!
> Axed Miss Liza to marry me
> Guess what she said?
> She wouldn't marry me,
> If de last Nigger was dead.'

"Christmas was sho' one grand time. Der warn't no big heap of good things lak dey has now. Old Mist'ess give de Niggers a little flour and syrup for to make sweet cake. Dere was plenty of fresh hog meat and chickens and all sorts of dried fruits. I was allus plum crazy 'bout de rag doll grandma would make for my Christmas present. Come New Year's Day, it was time to go back to wuk and evvy slave was made to do a heap of wuk on dat day to start de year off right.

"Slaves had a big old time at cornshuckin's. Dey didn't care so much 'bout de somepin' t'eat jus' so dey got plenty of whiskey to drink, and when dey got all het up on dat you could hear 'em a mile away a'whoopin' and hollerin'. Sometimes dey kilt a cow and throwed it in a pot and biled it down wid dumplin's, seasoned hot wid red pepper."

Asked what games she played as a child, Dosia replied: "Gentlemen! What de giver'ment don't want to know, ain't wuth knowin' no how. What I played? Well, now, let me see: Mollie, Mollie Bright was one of our games; Hiding de Switch was de one whar you counted 'em out; dat countin' run lak dis: 'Ten, ten, double-ten, forty-five, fifteen.' Gentlemen! I could run lak a snake.

"Ha'nts? Why, I kin see dem things anytime. Dis hyar place whar I lives is full of ha'nts, but dese folks would git mad wid me if I told 'bout 'em. Now, back in Greene County, I kin talk 'bout dem ha'nts all right. Back dar Mrs. Babe Thaxton had a mighty pretty flower yard. She used to tell me dat if I let anybody git any flowers from her yard atter she was daid, she would sho' ha'nt me. She had done been daid a good while when I was gittin' some flowers from her yard and a gal come along and axed me to give her some. I started cuttin' flowers for her. At dat Miss Babe, she riz up over me lak she was gwine to burn me up. She looked at me hard and went off and sot in a tree whar she could look right down on me. I ain't never cut no flowers out of dat yard no more. Now 'bout Raw Head and Bloody Bones, Honey, don't you know dat ain't nothin' but a cows head what's done been skint? Old folks used to ax us: 'Has you seed Raw Head and Bloody Bones?' Us would run over one 'nother tryin' to git dar fust to see him, and it allus turned out to be jus' a old skint up cow head. Den in de nighttime us would have wild dreams 'bout dem old skint cow heads.

"De onliest song I ever heared de Niggers sing in de fields run somepin lak dis: 'Tarrypin, Tarrypin, (terrapin) when you comin' over, For to see your wife and fam-i-lee.' Dey must a been wantin' to eat turkle (turtle), when dey was a-singin' dat song.

"Old Mist'ess was mighty special good to her slaves when dey was sick. Fust thing she done was send for de doctor. I kin see him now. He rid horseback and carried his medicine in saddlebags. He used to put some kind of powders in a glass of water and give it to de sick ones. Dere was three old 'omans what Old Mist'ess kept to look atter sick slave 'omans. Dem old granny nurses knowed a heap about yarbs (herbs). May apple and blacksnake roots, king of de meadow, (meadow rue) wild asthma (aster) and red shank, dese was biled and deir tea give to de slaves for diffunt ailments." Asked to describe king of the meadow, she continued: "Honey, ain't you never seed none? Well, it's such a hard tough weed dat you have to use a axe to chop it up, and its so strong and pow'ful dat nothin' else kin grow nigh 'round it. Back in dem days folks wore tare (tar) sacks 'round deir necks and rubbed turpentine under deir noses. When deir ailments got too hot, lak when Mammy died, dey made 'em swallow two or three draps of turpentine.

"I ricollects dat when de news come dat dem yankees was on de way towards our plantation, Old Mist'ess tuk her old pacin' mule and all her money and made Uncle

Moses go down on de river wid her to help hide 'em. I told her I was gwine tell dem yankees she had done stole my uncle and hid him so he wouldn't hear 'bout freedom. And when dem yankees finally did git dar, dey was singin' some sort of a song 'bout freedom. I lit out to runnin', and it was way atter midnight 'fore Old Mist'ess found me. I was pretty nigh skeered to death. Dey called all de slaves together and told 'em dey was free as jack rabbits, and 'deed dat was de truth. Us stayed dar for years. It looked lak us warn't never gwine to leave.

"Grandma started out to wuk for herself as a granny 'oman, and Old Mist'ess give her a mule to ride on to make her trips from one farm to another. It was a long time 'fore Niggers could git 'nough money together for to buy land of deir own, and it seems lak it was a long time 'fore schools for Niggers was sot up.

"When me and Oscar Harris got married, us had a big weddin' wid evvything good to eat what us could git, and plenty of wine to drink. De dancin' and good time went on most all night. I had a reg'lar weddin' dress made out of pretty white swiss trimmed wid lots of lace and it had a long train. I wore long white gloves. Tucks went 'round my petticoat from de knees to de lace what aidged de bottom, and my draw's was white cambric, gathered at de knee wid a wide ruffle what was tucked and trimmed up pretty. I married on Saddy night and dat called for a second day dress, 'cause I jus' had to go to church next day and show dat man off. Anyhow, my second day dress was blue cotton wid white lace on it, and I wore a big white plumed hat draped down over one eye. Wid de second day dress I wore dem same draw's, petticoat, and gloves what I was married in. Me and Oscar's five chillun was Mary, Annie Belle, Daniel, Cleveland, and Austin.

"My old man and all my chillun is daid 'cept Daniel, and I don't know whar he is. I wants to git married again, but dese hyar jealious Niggers 'round hyar says if I does de giver'ment is gwine to cut off my old age pension, and I sho' don't want to loose dat money. No Sir!

"I didn't take in nothin' 'bout Lincoln, Davis or dat man Washington. Dem days chillun had to take a back seat. When old folks wanted to talk, dey jus' sent chillun on 'bout dey business. One thing I does know: I'd sho' ruther have times lak dey is now. Yessum, I sho' had.

"I jined Randolph Baptist Church in Greene County 'cause I felt de urge and knowed it had done got to be my duty to jine up. I'se been a Baptist ever since, and will be one 'til I die; so was all my folks 'fore me. Folks when dey jine de church ought to live right so dey kin see de good Lord and have a restin' place atter dey is done wid dis sinful world. Yessum, I jined dat Randolph Baptist Church way down in Greene County a long time ago."

Mary A. Crawford
Re-search Worker

Henderson Harris—Ex-Slave

HENDERSON HARRIS

Henderson Harris was born August 19, 1858, in Talbot County. His parents were Frederick and Adeline Harris of Jones County, but Henderson remembers nothing about them because they both were sold on the block and left him when he was just a few months old.

Mr. Bill Adams, Henderson's owner, lived on a large plantation on the old stage road between Macon and Columbus. There were about three hundred acres in this plantation and between thirty and fifty slaves.

Mr. Adams was just a "straight out farmer, and as good a marster as ever wore shoe leather. 'Marse Bill' was a putty hard man about business, and meant 'skat' when he said 'skat'".

He had a white preacher and a white doctor on his plantation, and expected all the Negroes to go to 'preachin'' on Sunday afternoon, and if any of them were sick enough to need a doctor, they had him. The doctor came around about once a month and every slave was looked after.

The slaves were allowed Saturday afternoons, provided there was no fodder or other stuff down in the field to be put into the barn loft in case of rain. From breakfast on they had all Sunday, even the cook and other house servants. "Ole Miss had the cook bake up light bread and make pies on Saturday to do at the big house through Sunday."

The first work that Henderson remembers doing was "totin peaches to the pigs" and "drapin' peas".

He recalls nothing about the Yankees coming through, but remembers the others telling how they burned the warehouse and drove off the cattle and hogs.

After freedom his mammy and daddy returned to 'ole Marster's' plantation and he and the other seven children lived with them and worked for 'Marse Bill'.

The old fellow is very superstitious and firmly believes that the "squinch" owl's note is a "sho sign o' death."

Henderson says that he is able to work and that he cleans yards, cuts wood, and does almost any kind of job [HW: that] he can find.

> Henderson Harris
> 808 E. Slaton Avenue
> Griffin, Georgia
> September 23, 1936.

Velma Bell
District #2
Augusta, Ga.

EX-SLAVE INTERVIEW
Uncle Shang Harris
Toccoa, Georgia (Stephens County)

SHANG HARRIS

"Uncle Shang" Harris, at the age of 97, is more vigorous than many men twenty years younger. Erect and stocky, holding his white woolly head high, he retains the full favor of living. When the interviewer entered his cabin he rose from the supper table wiping from his mouth the crumbs of a hearty meal, and peered uncertainly through the gathering dark.

"Does I 'member 'bout slav'ey times?" His face relaxed into a broad smile, "G-lory, hallelujah, I sho does! I was born den and freed den. What you wanter know? I kin tell you all about it." He led the way to two chairs near the stove.

"My marster was Mr. Bob Alexander. He lived in Franklin County jes' dis side o' Carnesville. He treated me good—yes mam, he sho did. My marster didn't have no beatin' o' his niggers. I didn't do no work back in dem times—nuttin' but play. Me and my sister belonged to de youngest boy (dey was seven boys in dat family) and we jes' climbed trees and frolicked all de time. We had plenty in de eatin' line too.

"But law chile, eve'ybody didn't have dat. Some de marsters tied dey niggers to posts and whupped 'em till dey nigh killed 'em. Lots of 'em run away and hid in de woods. De marsters would put de dogs after you jes' like a coon. Dey'd run you and tree you"—imitating the sound of baying dogs—"oh, glory, hallelujah—dat's de way dey done 'em! I'se seed bare feets all cracked up wid de cold. We don't have no cold weather now. Why, I'se seed big pine trees bust wide open—done froze, and de niggers would be out in dat kind o' weather. But dey'd ruther do dat dan stay and git beat to death. Many a night jes' 'bout dark, I'd be a-settin' in my cabin wid my ole lady (dat was after I got older) and see somebody prowlin' roun' in de bushes, and I'd know hit was some po' nigger was hidin' and didn't had nuttin' to eat. My marster nuse to say, 'Harris, when you see somebody hongry, gi' 'im sumpin' to eat'. We didn't never turn 'em down even when dey look so bad dey was right scarey.

"No'm, I never was sold. Mr. Bob nuse to say, 'I got hogs, horses, mules and cows to sell, but no niggers.' He had 'bout twenty slaves. De biggest portion of 'em stayed on de farm.

"Lots o' folks did sell dey niggers, and sometimes dey'd take yo' chile and go to Alabama or Virginia, and you wouldn't never see him no mo'. Dey kept de dark ones together and de bright ones together. Hit didn't make no diffunce 'bout families. Dey warn't no marryin' 'mongst de niggers way back in time. De marsters wanted you to increase to give 'em more niggers, but dey didn't had no marryin'. I had three wives and I got my fourth one now. Dey all treated me good.

"Dat mixed-up color in niggers come from slav'ey

times. Some de marsters beat de slave women to make 'em give up to 'em.

"Dey talks a heap 'bout de niggers stealin'. Well, you know what was de fust stealin' done? Hit was in Afriky, when de white folks stole de niggers jes' like you'd go get a drove o' horses and sell 'em. Dey'd bring a steamer down dere wid a red flag, 'cause dey knowed dem folks liked red, and when dey see it dey'd follow it till dey got on de steamer. Den when it was all full o' niggers dey'd bring 'em over here and sell 'em.

"No'm I never was hired out to nobody in slav'ey times. Didn't I tole you we didn't do no work? I never seed no money—not a nickel. De most money I ever seed was when my boss buried some when de Yankees was.

"We nuse to have frolics and break-downs all de time—quiltin's and finger-pickin's and dances and all sech as dat. Finger-pickin's was when we'd pick de cotton off de seeds by hand. We'd spread it down in front o' de fire place 'cause it was easier to pick when it was hot.

"Does I 'member de old songs? Hallelujah, I sho does!" The old darkey began to pat his foot and clap his hands while he sang, "Pickin' out de cotton an' de bolls all rotten", repeating the same line over and over to a sing-song melody as impossible of transcription as a bird-call. Suddenly his smiling face fell serious and the song stopped.

"But since de Lawd saved me from a life o' sin, I don't think about dem things. I don't 'member 'em much now. I been saved forty odd years."

"Was that a sinful song, Uncle Shang?"

"Dat's de devil's song, dat is. A-dancin' an' a stompin' dat-a-way!

"Folks nuse to have fights sometimes at de frolics but dey didn't do no killin'. Hit ain't like dat now. Dey stob you now, but dey didn't do dat den. Somebody'd always stop 'em 'fore it got dat fur."

"Yes'm, we sung spirituals. We sung 'De good oletime religion', an' sech as dat. I can't 'member all dem good songs now."

His middle-aged wife, washing dishes over the wood stove, struck up, "I am bound for de promise land," and he joined in with a firm voice. But neither remembered many songs distinctly.

"We didn't had no schools. Dey wouldn't let de white chillen tell us about books. One day I axed about sumpin' in a book, and one de chillen say, 'Mamma tole me not to learn you nuttin' or she'd whup me'."

Asked about holidays, Uncle Shang replied, "Thanksgiving we give thanks in de church on our knees. Warn't no slave gallery. White and colored all together and shouted together.

"Christmas we frolic and eat cake. We had serenades, too, on banjoes and old tin pans and whatever you wanted to make a noise. And a gallon o' liquor—anything you want!" with a loud laugh.

"Yes, mam, I 'members when de war broke out. Hit was on a Sunday morning, jes' as clear and bright as could be. And Gen'l Lee prayed till it thundered. Jes' 'fore de sun riz he was fixin' to go to a battle. He got down on his knees and he jarred de worl'. Yes, mam, hit thundered and when de folks heered it, dey all commenced runnin' todes him wid de butts o' dey guns, and stacked de guns 'round a sweet-apple tree." Uncle Shang was not quite clear as to who had stacked the guns, but he was sure it had been done.

"I 'members when de Yankees come too. De Yankees come in—well, hallelujah!—one Friday mornin' 'bout sun-up. Mamma took a notion to go out in de syrup-cane patch, and I was settin' on de fence. I could hear dem cannons a-boomin' and de sun was a-risin' so red jes' like blood. Den I seed de Yankees a-comin' wid dey blue coats on an' all dem brass buttons jes' a-shinin'. I holler, 'Mamma—look a-yo-o-onder!' One man had a flag wid red on it—dat's for blood. One man come in a hurry and say, 'All come to de house.'

"Den he look at me a-settin' on the fence, and he say, 'Hey, boy, you mighty fat'. He talk and he talk and by dat time de yard was full o' Yankees. 'Lemme ask you sump-in', he say, 'Where's de horses?' Wid dat, he shot off a pistol—BAM!

"My boss had done took 'em off. I say, 'I don' know nuttin' 'bout 'em.'

"All dey got from our house was a big sack o' flour. Dey didn't burn nuttin' o' ours. Dey say, 'You all feelin' so good, havin' a good time—we won't take nuttin.'

"De calvary was here 'fore de Yankees was. Dey had on blue coats, too. Dey make de boss haul corn all day a-Sunday to fed dey horses.

"Dey try to git de niggers to go back North wid 'em,

and dey had a big crowd o' colored goin', but I wouldn't go. A fust cousin to my Dad left 'cause dey beat him so. I think he done well in de North. But I didn't want to go.

"After freedom was, some de marsters wouldn't tell you. But our marster tole us. He said, 'You free as I is. If you want to stay wid me, all right. If not, you know where to go.'

"Mistis warn't like de boss," (mimicking a precise, slightly acid voice), "She say, 'I don't want to hear of no fightin' now. You'll git your arms cut off if you fight.'

"But de boss keep her cooled down. He say, 'Arms cut off—huh! You git yo's broke off if you don't hush.'

"After freedom, we didn't work for no regular wages—jes' knock about like chillen 'round de house. I don't know how old I was den, but I warn't no chicken. After while I worked on de railroad, de fust one here, what used wood burners. I helped build it. Dey's great tall pines growin' now where dat fill was made.

"White folks nuse to travel in wagons way back in time. When dey tuk de cotton to New York dey went to Athens in de wagons wid oxen or mules, and den to New York on de train. De ladies rid 'round town in carriages—Rockaways—dem low one-hoss things. De driver sat on top. He wore a big beaver hat and good clothes and heavy gloves.

"White folks had lots o' dances and eve'ything went well. People was mighty nice in dis country.

"One my young bosses was a doctor. Dey didn't give dem little pills you have now, what don't do no good.

Dey made tea out o' devil's shoestring, and yerbs out de woods, and blue mass pills. When babies come, dey had mid-wives. Dey didn't do nuttin' to cut de pains—you got to have dem.

"Yes, mam, I knows 'bout cunjurs—plenty o' cunjurs. Dem cunjur-folks takes weeds and yerbs, and fixes you so you can't sleep and can't eat and bark like a dog. One man told a girl he'd fix her so green flies 'ud follow her all de time—and dey did!

"One of 'em gin me some stuff once. Yes, mam, like to killed de old pap. I had done found some money in Alabama, and another man wanted me to gi' it to him so he put sumpin' in my coffee. When I tasted dat coffee I started cussin' (I was wicked den)—I couldn't sleep—couldn't rest. My nephew said, 'Somebody done hurt you!' My father-in-law tuk it off. He made some tea out o' rattle-snake master, and I drunk dat and swallowed a silver dime. Dat tuk de cunjur off. Some says it's good to take nine silver pieces and boil 'em and drink de water.

"I knows sumpin' 'bout ghoses, too, but my foots got temper in 'em and when I sees anything, I runs. People say dey ain't no sech thing, but dey is.

"Dey was a house—people couldn't live dere, but a fellow said he could go dere, so he went. Fust thing he seed a cat rarin' and pitchin' in de fireplace. Den dey was a kickin' up in de loft, and here come a big old dog a-spittin', and fire all spranglin' out. He rared and growled. Den in come a woman. He say, 'What'll you have, lady?' She say, 'Dey's ten thousand dollars buried right where I'm a-standin'.

"He stayed dere till he got it too. De devil was trying to scare him off, but she wanted him to have it.

"People nuse to bury lots o' money 'way back in time, and lots o' folks is found it.

"Good-luck and bad-luck signs, you say? Well, lemme see," The old man paused to reflect and scratch his head. "Well, de bes' luck sign is to git in wid de Lawd. Keep wid Him; He'll keep you sweet in yo' soul. God's goin' to come down de mid-air. I seen dat one time. Jesus come to me—you never seen de like of it—de chariots—oh, glory!—and de purtiest singin' you ever heered, O-oh—glory, hallelujah! Dat was jes' last year.

"I had a good life. I been enjoyin' myself. I enjoys myself now, but I so old now I jes' staggers over de place. Can't do no work but chop wood once in a while. I enjoys myself in prayer.

"When de relief folks fus' come here, dey wouldn't give me nuttin' but I been prayin' and glory to Jesus I been gittin' little sumpin' ever since dat time.

"De way things is goin' now, it's better dan in slav'ey times, 'cause dey ain't no knockin' and beatin'. Things is gone too fur for dat now. If eve'ybody would be o' one mind and serve de Lawd, dey wouldn't be no troubles.

"I don't know whether I'll get th'ough dis winter or not. Hit was mighty cold last year, and dey warn't much fuel. But I thanks de Lawd for all He's done for me, and I'se ready to meet Him when he comes."

PLANTATION LIFE as viewed by Ex-Slave

TOM HAWKINS
163 Bremen Street
Athens, Georgia.

Written by: Sadie B. Hornsby
Athens —

Edited by: Sarah H. Hall
Athens —

Leila Harris
Augusta, Ga.

TOM HAWKINS
Ex-Slave—Age 75.

TOM HAWKINS

Tom was nowhere to be seen when the interviewer mounted the steps of his cabin. Daisy, his wife, was ironing on the back porch and when she learned the object of the proposed interview, she readily agreed to induce Tom to talk. She approached a basement door and called: "Tom, here's one of dem giver'ment ladies what's come to hear you talk 'bout slavery days." Tom replied: "All right, Miss Daisy, I'se a-comin'." The old man soon appeared feeling his way with his cane carefully before each hesitant step. Tom is blind. Established comfortably in his favorite chair, he talked freely.

"I was borned on Marse Johnny Poore's plantation 'bout four miles f'um Belton, South Callina. Marse Johnny owned my Ma, Mornin' Poore, and all three of her chillun. Dey was me and Johnny, and Mollie. My Pa was Tom Hawkins and he was named for his owner. De Hawkins plantation was 'bout a mile f'um de Poore place. Atter Ma married Pap, dey each one had to stay on wid deir own Marster. Dey couldn't stay on de same plantation together. I don't 'member much 'bout Gran'ma Jennie Poore 'cept dat she was de cook at de big house. Gran'pa Wade Poore was de blacksmith and Marse Johnny got a big price when he sold him to Dr. Chandler. Some of de slaves made demselfs corded beds and others jus' had makeshifts. De beds and cabins was good 'nough for de Niggers den, 'cause dey never had knowed no better. Gangs of slaves slept together lak hogs in dem dirt-floored log cabins.

"Chilluns what was big 'nough to do anything had to wuk. I was a moughty little chap when dey started me in as houseboy. I slept on a trun'le (trundle) bed in Miss Annie's room. In de daytime my little trun'le bed was rolled back out of sight under Miss Annie's big old four poster teester bed. I kep' a fire burnin' in her room winter and summer. Night times she would call me. 'Tom! Tom!' Sometimes I was so soun' asleep I didn't answer. Den pop, she would hit me on de head wid her long stick. Den I knowed hit was time to fire up her pipe. She smoked dat pipe a pow'ful lot atter Marse Johnny died.

"Grown slaves made a little money, but I never got none 'til atter de war. I didn't have no cause to want no money. Miss Annie, she give me evvything I needed.

"Oh, but us had plenty of good things to eat on de Poore plantation—meat and bread wid lots of turnips and 'tatoes. 'Bout once a month dey give us lallyhoe. Dey calls dat 'lasses now. Us et our breakfast and dinner out of wooden bowls. Under a long shed built next to de kitchen was a long trough. At night dey crumbled cornbread in it, and poured it full of buttermilk. Grown folks and chilluns all gathered 'roun' dat old trough and et out of it wid deir wooden spoons. No Ma'am, dere warn't no fightin' 'roun' dat trough. Dey all knowed better'n dat.

"Us got 'possums and rabbits de best ways us could—cotch 'em in traps, hit 'em wid rocks, and trailed 'em wid dogs. Us lakked 'possums baked wid 'tatoes, but most of de rabbits was stewed wid dumplin's. All our cookin' was done on big open fireplaces. Dey didn't fry nothin' dem days; leastwise dey never give de slaves no fried victuals. Grown folks seined for fish in Big Crick and Saluda River at night, 'cause dey couldn't git away f'um field wuk in de day. Chillun cotch a heap of fish wid hook and line. De river and crick bofe run thoo' Miss Annie's plantation so us didn't have to ax for a pass evvy time us went a fishin'. Us allus had to have a pass if us left de plantation for anything or de patterollers was apt to git you and look out den, for you was sho' to git a larrupin' if dey cotch you off f'um home widout no pass.

"Dere warn't but one gyarden on de Poore plantation, and it was big enough to feed all de white folks and slaves too. Two whole acres of dat gyarden was sowed down in turnips.

"Chilluns didn't wear but one piece of clothes in summer; dat was a shirt. In winter dey doubled up on us wid two shirts. I 'members how dem shirt tails used to pop in de wind when us runned fast. Us chillun used to tie up de 'bacco, what us stole f'um Miss Annie, in de under-arm part of de long loose sleeves of our shirts. Us didn't git no shoes for our foots, winter or summer, 'til us was ten years old.

"Marse Johnny Poore, he was kilt in de war and den Old Mist'ess, she was our Miss Annie, looked atter de plantation 'til her only child, young Miss Ann, married Marse Tom Dean. Den he helped Miss Ann 'tend to her business. Dey was moughty good to us. Miss Annie done her own overseein'. She rid over dat plantation onct or twict a day on her hoss.

"Our white folks lived in a big old two-story house what sot off f'um de road up on a high hill in a big oak grove. Miss Annie's own room was a shed room on dat house. De upstairs room was kept for comp'ny. Unkle Wade Norris Poore was Miss Annie's car'iage driver. De car'iage was called a surrey den.

"Dar was 'bout four or five hunderd acres in our plantation. Miss Annie kept 'bout a hunderd slaves. She was all time sellin' 'em for big prices atter she done trained 'em for to be cooks, housegals, houseboys, carriage drivers, and good wash 'omans. She wukked 75 slaves in her fields. Her Niggers was waked by four o'clock and had to be in de field by sunup. Dey come in 'bout dark. Atter supper, de mens made up shoes, horse collars, and anything else lak dat what was needed; de 'omans spun thread and wove cloth.

"Miss Annie was her own whuppin' boss. She beat on 'em for most anything. She had a barrel wid a pole run thoo' it, and she would have a slave stretched out on dat barrel wid his clothes off and his hands and foots tied to de pole. Den Miss Annie would fire up her pipe and set down and whup a Nigger for a hour at a time. Miss Annie would pull my ears and hair when I didn't do to suit her, but she never whupped me. Miss Annie didn't need no jail for her slaves. She could manage 'em widout nothin' lak dat, and I never did hear of no jails in de country 'roun' whar us lived.

"Yes Ma'am, I seed Old Miss sell de slaves what she trained. She made 'em stand up on a block, she kept in de back yard, whilst she was a-auctionin' 'em off. I seed plenty of traders go by our place in wagons what dey had deir somepin' t'eat and beddin' in, and deir slaves was walkin' 'long behind de wagon, gwine on to be sold, but dere warn't none of 'em in chains.

"Dere warn't no schools whar slaves could git book larnin' in dem days. Dey warn't even 'lowed to larn to read and write. When Dr. Cannon found out dat his carriage driver had larned to read and write whilst he was takin' de doctor's chillun to and f'um school, he had dat Niggers thumbs cut off and put another boy to doin' de drivin' in his place.

"Washin'ton Church was de name of de meetin' house whar us Niggers on de Poore plantation went to church wid our white folks. Couldn't none of us read no Bible and dere warn't none of de Niggers on our plantation ever converted and so us never had no baptizin's. De preacher preached to de white folks fust and den when he preached to de Niggers all he ever said was: 'It's a sin to steal; don't steal Marster's and Mist'ess' chickens and hogs;' and sech lak. How could anybody be converted on dat kind of preachin'? And 'sides it never helped none to listen to dat sort of preachin' 'cause de stealin' kept goin' right on evvy night. I never did see no fun'rals in dem days.

"Niggers didn't run to no North. Dey run to de South, 'cause dem white folks up North was so mean to 'em. One Nigger, named Willis Earle, run off to de woods and made hisself a den in a cave. He lived hid out in dat cave 'bout 15 years.

"Old Miss give dem dat wanted one a cotton patch and she didn't make her slaves wuk in her fields atter de dinner bell rung on Saddays. De mens wukked in dem patches of deir own an Sadday evenin' whilst de 'omans washed de clothes and cleaned up de cabins for de next week. Sadday nights dey all got together and frolicked; picked de banjo, and drunk whiskey. Didn't none of 'em git drunk, 'cause dey was used to it. Dar was barrels of it whar dey stilled it on de place. On Sundays us went f'um cabin to cabin holdin' prayer meetin's. Miss Annie 'pointed diff'unt ones to look atter da stock evvy Sunday.

"Big times was had by all at Chris'mas time. De eats warn't no diff'unt 'cept dey give us sweet bread and plenty of lallyhoe (molasses) what was made on de plantation. Us had two weeks vacation from field wuk and dey let us go rabbit and 'possum huntin'. Us had a gran' time clear up to New Year's Day.

"Oh, us did have one more big time at dem cornshuckin's. De corn was hauled to de crib and de folks was 'vited in de atternoon 'fore de cornshukin' started dat night. When de mans got to shuckin' dat corn, de 'omans started cookin' and dey got thoo' 'bout de same time. Den us et, and dat was de best part of de cornshuckin' fun. Cotton pickin's was held on moonshiny nights. Dey picked cotton 'til midnight, and den dey had a little shakin' of de footses 'til day.

"Mens had good times at de quiltin's too. Deir white folkses allus give 'em a little somepin' extra t'eat at dem special times. But de 'omans what was cooks at de big house tied sacks 'roun' deir waisties under deir skirts, and all thoo' de day would drap a little of dis, and some of dat, in de sacks. When day poured it out at night, dare was plenty of good somepin' t'eat. De mens kept de fire goin' and if dey got hold of a tallow candle day lit dat to help de 'omans see how to quilt. Most of de quiltin's was at night and nearly all of 'em was in winter time.

"De best game us had was marbles, and us played wid homemade clay marbles most of de time. No witches or ghosties never bothered us, 'cause us kept a horseshoe over our cabin door.

"Miss Annie doctored us. In summer, she made us pull up certain roots and dry special leafs for to make her teas out of. Horehoun', boneset, and yellow root was de main things she used. She made a sort of sody out of de white ashes f'um de top of a hick'ry fire and mixed it wid vinegar for headaches. De black ashes, left on de bottom of de hick'ry fire, was leached for lye, what was biled wid grease to make our soap.

"I never will forgit de day dey told us de war was over and us was free. One of de 'omans what was down by de spring a washin' clothes started shoutin': 'Thank God-a-Moughty I'se free at last!' Marse Tom heared her and he come and knocked her down. It was 'bout October or November 'fore he ever told us dat us was free sho' 'nough. Dat same 'oman fainted dead away den 'cause she wanted to holler so bad and was skeered to make a soun'. De yankees come thoo' soon atter dat and said us was free and 'vited all de Niggers dat wanted to, to go 'long wid dem. I never will forgit how bad dem yankees treated Old Miss. Dey stole all her good hosses, and her chickens and dey broke in de smokehouse and tuk her meat. Dey went in de big house and tuk her nice quilts and blankets. She stood all of dat wid a straight face but when dey foun' her gold, she just broke down and cried and cried. I stayed on and was Miss Annie's houseboy long as she lasted. I was 21 when she died.

"Dem night riders done plenty of whuppin' on our plantation. Hit was a long time 'fore Niggers could git 'nough money to buy lan' wid and it was a good 20 years 'fore no school was sot up for Niggers in our settlement.

"I thinks Mr. Jefferson Davis and Mr. Lincoln was bofe of 'em doin' deir best to be all right. Booker Washin'ton, he was all right too, but he sho' was a 'maybe man.' He mought do right and den he moughtn't.

"Yes Ma'am, if Old Miss was livin' I'd ruther have slavery days back, 'cause den you knowed you was gwine to have plenty t'eat and wear, and a good place to sleep even if Mist'ess did make you wuk moughty hard. Now you can wuk your daylights plum out and never can be sho' 'bout gittin' nothin'.

"De fust time I married me and Ad'line Rogers stood up by da side of de big road whilst de preacher said his marryin' words over us, and den us went on down de road. Me and Ad'line had six chillun: Mary, Lucy, Annie, Bessie, John and Henry Thomas. Atter my Ad'line died, I married Daisy Carlton. I didn't have no weddin' needer time. Me and Daisy just got a hoss and buggy and driv' up to de house whar de Justice of de Peace lived, and he jined us in mattermony. Den us got back in de buggy and went back down de big road."

Tom began telling why he joined the church, when Daisy interrupted. "Now Tom," she said, "you just tell dis white lady what you told me 'bout how come you jined de church." "Now, Miss Daisy," pleaded Tom, "1 don't want to do dat." Daisy snapped: "I don't keer what you don't want to, you is gwine to tell de trufe, Tom Hawkins." At that, Tom giggled and began: "Well, Miss, hit was lak dis: I went to church one night a feelin' moughty good. I went up and kneeled at de altar whar dey was prayin' for converts, and a good lookin' yaller gal was kneelin' right in front of me. I accident'ly tetched her on de laig. I sho' didn't mean to do it. In dat 'cited crowd most anything was apt to happen. Dat gal, she kicked me in de eye, and bruised up my face. My nose and eyes started drippin' and I hollered out real loud: 'Oh, Lord have mussy.' Den I staged a faint. De brother's of de church tuk me outside. Dey was sho' I had got 'ligion. By dat time I was so 'shamed of myself, I went back inside de meetin' house and jined de church, 'cause I didn't want nobody to know what had done happened. I 'cided den and dar to change my way of livin'. Next time I seed dat yaller gal I axed her why she kicked me in de face and she said: 'Next time you do what you done den, I'se gwine to kill you, Nigger.'"

"Yes Ma'am, I thinks evvybody ought to be 'ligious."

United States. Work Projects Administration

EX-SLAVE INTERVIEW

BILL HEARD
475 Reese Street
Athens, Georgia

Written by: Miss Grace McCune
Athens —

Edited by: Mrs. Sarah H. Hall
Athens —

and

John N. Booth
District Supervisor
Federal Writers' Proj.
Residencies 6 & 7
Augusta, Georgia.

Sept. 12, 1938

BILL HEARD
Ex-Slave—Age 73.

BILL HEARD

Bill Heard's blacksmith shop, a sagging frame structure, in the forks of Oconee Street and Lexington Highway, is conveniently located for both local and traveling clientele.

An old voice singing Swing Low Sweet Chariot in a low tone but with a fervor known only to Negroes led the visitor through the shop, where there was no sight of the singer. Bill was eventually discovered seated on a cushion-covered nail keg beneath a large water-oak at the rear of the building. A large hymn book was placed across his knees, and the old Negro was happily singing away all by himself. His gray hair was partly covered by an old black cap, and his faded blue work skirt and pants showed evidence of long wear.

As the song ended Bill discovered that he was not alone. Off came his cap, and he scrambled to his feet with a smile. "Good evenin', Missy, how is you? Won't you have a seat and rest? Dese nail kegs makes a mighty good place to set when you is tired out, and it's powerful nice and cool under dis old tree." After his guest was comfortably seated on another cushioned keg, the aged smith resumed his perch. "I didn't hear you come into my shop, and I think dat's about de fust time anybody ever did come in dar widout me hearin' 'em. I used to be in dar so busy all de time, I never had no chance to rest up or practice my singin'. Times has changed in lots of ways since dem good old days. Some folks laughs when us calls 'em 'good old days,' and dey wants to know how come us thinks dey was good old days, when us had such hard wuk to do den. Course folks had to wuk hard and didn't have all dese new-fangled gadgets to wuk wid lak dey got now, but I still calls 'em de good old days 'cause folks was better off den; dey loved one another and was allus ready to lend a helpin' hand, 'specially in times of trouble.

"I don't know nothin' 'bout slavery times 'cept what my Mammy and Daddy told me. Daddy, he belonged to Marse Tom Heard down in Elbert County, 'bout 10 miles from Rucker place, nigh Ruckersville. Daddy said Marse Tom had about a hunnerd and twenty-five slaves on his place. Daddy was mighty little when Marse Tom got him, and he never bought none of Daddy's other kinfolks, so it was right hard for de little boy all by hisself, 'cause de other slaves on de plantation was awful mean to him. Dey wouldn't let him sleep in deir quarters, so he stayed up at de big house, and place to keep warm. Atter he got big enough to wuk, day treated him better.

"Evvybody cooked on fireplaces dem days, 'cause dere warn't no sto'-bought stoves. Marse Tom fed all his slaves at de big house; he kept 'em so regular at wuk dere warn't no time for 'em to do deir own cookin'.

"Slaves lived in one-room log cabins dat had rock chimblies, and each cabin had one little window wid a wooden shutter dey fastened at night and in bad weather. Deir beds was made out of pine poles fastened to de sides of dem old beds 'teesters,' 'cause de posties was so high. Ropes or cords was criss-crossed to hold 'em together and to take de place of springs. Nobody hadn't ever saw no iron springs on beds dem days. Dem big old ticks was generally filled wid wheat straw, but sometimes slaves was 'lowed to pick up waste cotton and wash, dry, and card it to stuff deir bed-ticks wid. But Missy, dat was jus' too much trouble when a good old straw tick slept so fine. Cheers was made out of oak splits, and cane and rye plaits was used for de cheer-bottoms. Dem old cheers sot mighty good and lasted a lifetime.

"Folks sho 'nough did live at home den; dey raised all sorts of vegetables sich as corn, 'taters, wheat, rye, and oats, and what's more, dey raised de cotton and wool to make de cloth for deir clothes. Cows, hogs, goats, sheep, chickens, geese, and turkeys was runnin' all over dem pastures, and dere warn't no lack of good victuals and home-made clothes. When hogs and cows was kilt to put meat in de smokehouse deir hides was tanned for leather to be used for harness and shoes, and a heap of times a piece of hide was used for a cheer-seat.

"Daddy said dey had a powerful hard time gittin' things lak soda, salt, sugar, and coffee durin' de war times. He said dat sometimes corn and okra seeds was parched right brown and ground up to be used for coffee, but it warn't nigh as good as sho 'nough coffee. When de salt had to be used if folks and critters was to keep well. Dey dug up de dirt under old smokehouses and biled it to git out de salt. Nobody didn't waste none of dat salt. No Surree! It was too hard to git. When it got so dey couldn't buy no soda, dey saved nice clean corncobs and burned dem into a fine powder what dey used for soda. Was it fit for bread-makin'? Why, Missy, dem biscuits made out of corncob soda and baked in dem old dutch ovens was fit for anybody to eat and enjoy. De onliest trouble 'bout it was gittin' 'em to bake enough of it.

"Slaves clothes was all made at home. Gals spun de thread and old 'omens wove de cloth on home-made looms; my Mammy was one of dem weavin' 'omans. Clothes for summer was jus' thin cotton, but cotton and wool was mixed for cold weather, and don't think dem wool and cotton clothes didn't keep out de cold; dey sho did. Deir clothes was dyed wid barks from trees, ink balls, walnut hulls, and red bud. Most evry plantation had its own shoemaker man dat tanned all de leather and made up all de shoes. Leather for slaves' shoes warn't allus tanned and shoes made out of untanned leather looked lak dey had done been dyed red.

"Dey had special mens on de plantation for all de special wuk. One carpenter man done all de fixin' of things lak wagons and plows, holped wid all de buildin' wuk, and made all de coffins.

"No, Missy, dere warn't no undertakers back in dem days, and folks had to pervide evvything at home. Corpses was measured and coffins made to fit de bodies. All de neighbors, fur and nigh, gathered 'round to set up wid de fambly.

"Funerals warn't so common den as now 'cause folks didn't die out so fast dem days. Dey tuk better keer of deyselfs, et right, wuked hard, and went to bed at night 'stid of folks runs 'round now; deir mammies and daddies never knows whar dey is. Folks don't teach chillun right, and dey don't make dem go to church lak dey should oughta.

"Folks didn't even git married back in dem days lak dey does now, leastwise slaves didn't. If a slave wanted to marry up wid a gal he knocked on his Marster's door and told him 'bout it. If his Marstar laked de idea he told him to go on and take de gal and to treat her right; dat was all dere was to slaves gittin' married.

"My Daddy said slaves went to de white folks' church 'til dey got some churches for colored folks. Church days was big days wid folks den 'cause dey didn't have meetin' evvy Sunday. Slave 'omans had percale or calico dresses, brogan shoes, and big home-made bonnets wid slats in de brims for Sunday-go-to-meetin' wear, and if it was cold dey wropt up in shawls. Menfolks wore cotton shirts and pants. Dey had grand preachin' dem days and folks got honest-to-goodness 'ligion.

"Folks wuked mighty hard dem days, 'specially durin'

plantin' and harvest time, 'til atter de corn was gathered and fetched out of de fields in dem old two-wheel carts dat was used to haul up all de craps. When de cornshuckin's started evvywhar dey tuk time about at de diffunt plantations. De fust thing dey done atter dey got together was to 'lect a general; he led de singin', and de faster he sung de faster de shucks flew. Plenty of corn liquor was passed 'round and you know dat stuff is sho to make a Nigger hustle. Evvy time a red ear of corn was found dat meant a extra drink of liquor for de Nigger dat found it. Atter de last ear of corn was shucked a big supper was served and dey danced and sung de rest of de night.

"When dey needed some new ground cleared up, dey had a logrollin'. Evvybody tried to out wuk de others, and if de job hadn't been finished 'fore night, dey kept right on at it by moonlight. One man wuked so hard tryin' to beat de others dat when he went to de spring for some water, he tuk one drink, raised his haid quick lak, and died right dar. He was plumb daid when dey picked him up!

"Dey give us our freedom in April and Daddy left Old Marster in May. He moved here nigh de old Pittner place whar I was borned. Daddy farmed for a-while and wuked at blacksmithin' for de white folks too, 'cause dat was de wuk he had been doin' for his Old Marster. De fust ricollections I've got is 'bout de days on dat old place. I ain't never gwine to forgit 'bout dem old cottonpickin's dey had when I was a youngster. Dey said dey was jus' lak dem cottonpickin's dey had 'fore de war. Dey would git up big crowds and pick cotton by de light of de harvest moon, and dat's 'most as bright as daylight. Evvybody holped and, fast as dey picked all de cotton on one farm and et a big supper, dey hustled on to de next place whar plenty of cotton, white in de fields and liquor, and good barbecue, and sich lak kept 'em happy and hustlin' 'most all night. When dey had done all de cottonpickin' dey could for one night dey stopped for dancin' and all sorts of frolickin'. Plenty of liquor in dem little brown jugs helped to make things 'most too lively sometimes. De few fights dey had when dey was drinkin' heavy didn't 'mount to much.

"Chillun loved hogkillin' times. Five or six mens would jine up and go from place to place in de community whar dere was lots of hogs to be kilt. When dem hogs was all butchered de folks would git together and sich a supper as dey would have! De mostest fresh meat sich as chit'lin's, haslets, pig foots, and sausage, wid good old collard greens, cracklin' bread, and hot coffee. I'm a-tellin' you, Lady, dat was good eatin', and atter you had done been wukin' in de hogkillin' dem cold days you was ready for victuals dat would stay by you.

"De fust place I ever went to school was in a little house on de old Bert Benyard place nigh Winterville, Georgy, and let me tell you, Missy, schoolin' warn't nothin' lak what it is now. Dem what lived nigh went home to dinner, but chillun dat lived a fur piece off fotch deir dinner to school in a tin bucket. Us was still livin' dar when Mr. John McCune moved from Whitfield County to dat old Pittner place. My Daddy wuked for him and I played 'round wid his boys.

"Daddy moved closer to town and opened up a blacksmith shop on Broad Street at what was called Wood's corner den. I helped him in de shop and went to school some. Folks had to wuk so hard to make enough to keep alive dat dey didn't git to go to school much. Athens was a heap diffunt den to what it is now; it was mostly woods, and de roads was awful. Dere warn't no paved streets, no street-lights, and no streetcars den. I 'members dem fust street-lights. Lawsey, Missy, folks was sho proud of dem lights and, when dey got dem little streetcars what was pulled by little mules, Athens folks felt lak dey lived in a real city. Dey had a big old town hall whar dey had all sorts of shows and big 'tainments.

"Times has changed, folks has changed, and nothin' ain't lak it used to be. When I was little it warn't no sight a t'all to see traders wid big droves of hogs, horses, cows, sheep, and goats, bringin' 'em to town to sell or trade for somepin dey needed. Daddy said dat durin' slavery time dey drove slaves 'long de road de same way and sold 'em jus' lak dey sold deir cattle.

"It was mostly woods and fields 'round here when I opened dis little shop 'bout 40 years ago. Johnson's store was sot up whar de Carither's Wagon Yard used to be, and soon paved streets was laid, and den fillin' stations, other stores, and de lak, sprung up in a hurry 'long here. Soon dere won't be no need of a blacksmith shop here, but I wants to stay on at wuk in my shop jus' as long as I kin, here in dis world of trouble whar I has had good times and hard times jus' lak de others. No other place wouldn't seem right.

"Me and my wife jus' runned away and got married widout havin' no big weddin' and atter us has done wuked together dese long years, us hopes to go to de heavenly home together. Our oldest gal is all us has left of our five chillun; she lives off somewhar in Washington, and us don't never hear from her no more. Us still has de boy us 'dopted long years ago; him and his wife lives wid us and dey keeps us from bein' too lonesome.

"I has made a good livin' right here in dis old shop, wuked hard, and saved my money, and now us is got a right nice little home out on Reese Street. De Good Lord has been wid us in all our troubles as well as in our good times, and I knows He is gwine to stay wid us de rest of de time and den He will take us home to Glory.

"I'se mighty glad you hunted me up, for I 'members dem old days, playin' wid your Daddy, down on de Pittner place. Atter us had all moved to Athens, he was still my friend. Come back to see me again, and just trust in de Good Lord; He will take keer of you."

As the visitor went down the street Bill's quavering voice was heard again. He was singin' Lord I'se Comin' Home.

United States. Work Projects Administration

A STORY OF SLAVERY

AS TOLD BY

EMMALINE HEARD—EX-SLAVE

A paper submitted by
Minnie B. Ross

Revision of original copy
and typing by J.C.Russell
1-26-37

Story of slavery by ex-slave

Emmaline Heard
Ex-Slave

M. B. Ross

EMMALINE HEARD

Emmaline Heard is a small, dark brown skinned woman who appears to be about 67 but is probably older. Her mind seems to be active, however, as she responds quickly to questions and expresses herself intelligently.

Henry County, near McDonough, Ga., is Emmaline's birthplace. Judging from her earliest childhood memories and what she learned from her mother, her birth must have occurred four or five years before freedom. Her parents, Lewis and Caroline Harper had eleven children, of whom she was the second youngest.

Mr. Roger and Mrs. Frances Harper were the owners

of the Heard family. The large Harper plantation was located near McDonough, bordering the McDonough highway. The Harper home, a large 2-story frame dwelling, faced the highway. The family consisted of twin boys and two girls, in addition to the father and mother. They also owned a large number of slaves, who occupied two rows of cabins, built close together, at some distance behind the "big house."

In those days before the War, slaves were moved from place to place and from State to State in droves, known as "speculators' droves," and sold at public auction. Emmaline Heard's father was born in Virginia, but was brought to Georgia and sold to the Harpers as a plow boy, at the age of eleven.

The slave's cabins were constructed of rough-hewn logs, with the cracks daubed with mud and, as Emmaline recalled it, were very warm; warmer, in fact, than many of their houses are today. The furniture consisted of a "corded" bed, wooden tables and benches. This "corded" bed was constructed by running rope or cord from the head to the foot and then from side to side. A wooden peg was driven into the holes to hold the cord in place. Pegs were a household necessity and had to be cared for just as a key is today. Most homes also included a quilt slab, a sort of table used to place quilts on, as a necessary part of the furniture.

Every woman had a certain amount of weaving and spinning to do at home after coming in from the fields. Emmaline says her mother had to card bats at night so that the two older sisters could begin spinning the next morning. A loom was almost as large as a small kitchen and was operated by hands and feet. Until midnight, the spinning wheels could be heard humming in the slave cabins. At the hour of twelve, however, a bell was rung, which was the signal for the slaves to cease their spinning and go to bed.

Dye for coloring the cloth was provided by collecting sweet gum, dogwood bark, and red clay. Mixing these together produced different colors of dye. Sweet gum and clay produced a purple; dogwood, a blue.

Two dresses a year were allowed the women, while two cotton shirts and two pair of cotton pants were given the men. Everyone received one pair of shoes. Emmaline's father was a shoemaker by trade and made shoes for both slaves and the Harper family. The slaves shoes were called "nigger shoes," and made from rough horse and mule hide. The white folks' shoes were made from soft calf leather. Mr. Harper had a tanning vat on his plantation especially for the purpose of tanning hides for their shoes. Emmaline said these tanning vats reminded her of baptismal holes. The water was very deep, and once her sister almost drowned in one. Barks of various kinds were placed in the water in these vats to produce an acid which would remove the hair from the hides. Layers of goat, calf, and horse hides were placed in the vats and, after a certain length of time removed and dried.

Meals on week days consisted principally of syrup and bread and they were glad, Emmaline stated, to see Saturday come, because they knew they would have biscuit made from "seconds" on Sunday. Butter seems to have been a delicacy but little known. "The only butter I remember eating before we were freed," Emmaline declared, "was that which my little mistress Fannie would slip to me." This led her mother to say, "Miss Fannie is so crazy about 'Em' I am going to give 'Em' to her for a cook."

Besides working as a plow hand, Emmaline's mother assisted Aunt Celia Travis in preparing the meals for the Harper family. Four or five pots each containing a different kind of food hung over the fire along the long fireplace. Just before dinner, the mistress would come in to inspect the cooking. If the food in any of the pots was not cooked to her satisfaction, she would sometimes lose her temper, remove her slipper and strike the cook.

Slaves on the Harper plantation arose when the horn was sounded at four o'clock and hurried to the fields, although they would sometimes have to wait for daylight to dawn to see how to work. The overseer rode over the plantation watching the slaves at work and keeping account of the amount of work performed by each. Any who failed to complete their quota at the close of the day were punished.

On the Harper plantation, a brush arbor was used for the slave's church. The trees and underbrush were cleared away to provide a sufficient space to accommodate the slaves and the trees evened off at a good height and the brush and limbs piled on top to form a roof. In rainy weather, of course, church services could not be held. Sometimes the slaves would slip behind the trees beside the white folks' church and listen to the singing and preaching. They would then go back to their brush arbor church, and preach the same gospel and sing the same songs they had heard in the white people's church.

Frolics were often given on the Harper plantation. They usually consisted of dancing and banjo playing.

Slaves from other plantations sometimes attended, but it was necessary to secure a pass from their master and mistress in order to do so. A prize was given to the person who could "buck dance" the steadiest with a tumbler of water balanced on the head. A cake or a quilt was often given as the prize.

A marriage ceremony was performed after both owners had given their consent, when bride and groom did not belong to the same master. Often neither owner would sell their slave to the other, in which case it was necessary for the husband to be given a pass in order to visit his wife.

Slaves were given treatment by the doctor when they became ill, but if the doctor stated that the slave was well enough to work, they had to go to the fields. Sick babies were left at home while the parents were at work in the field. No matter what sickness the child suffered, castor oil was the only remedy ever given.

Slaves who chanced to be visiting away from his plantation without a pass from his owner would be severely handled if caught by the Ku Klux Klan or "patterrollers" as they were more commonly called. Fear of the "patterrollers" was invoked to frighten children into good behaviour.

A few Civil War incidents impressed themselves upon Emmaline's memory although she was a very young child at the time. One day, she recalls, as she and her little mistress Fannie sat on the front fence facing the highway they saw a cloud of dust in the distance down the highway and soon a troop of soldiers in blue and silver uniforms marched by. The children, frightened by the sight of these strange soldiers, ran to the house to tell the mistress. Mrs. Harper instructed Emmaline's mother to run to the smokehouse, lock the door and bring her the key. In a few minutes the soldiers tramped into the kitchen and ate all of the food they could find. When they found the smokehouse locked they demanded the key from Mrs. Harper, and when she refused proceeded to break down the door and appropriated all the meat they could conveniently carry. They also robbed the cellar of its store of jellies and preserves, hitched the buggy mare to the wagon and drove off with the best of the mules tied behind, as Mrs. Harper and the family looked on in tears.

When the Harpers learned that the slaves were free, they offered Emmaline's father and mother a house, mule, hog, and cow if they would remain on their plantation, but they thought they might fare better elsewhere and hired out to a plantation owner in an adjoining county.

A few years later, when she became old enough to obtain on her own account, she came to Atlanta where she has lived ever since. She is now being cared for by a grand-daughter and a son. She is an ardent admirer of President Franklin D. Roosevelt and declared she would like to vote for him a hundred times.

• PART II

Mrs. Emmaline Heard, who resides at 239 Cain St., N.E. has proved to be a regular storehouse for conjure and ghost stories. Not only this but she is a firm believer in the practice of conjure. To back up her belief in conjure is her appearance. She is a dark browned skinned woman of medium height and always wears a dirty towel on her head. The towel which was at one time white gives her the weird look of an old time fortune teller. Tuesday December 8, 1936 a visit was made to her home and the following information was secured.

"There wuz onst a house in McDonough and it wuz owned by the Smiths that wuz slave owners way back yonder. Now this is the trufe 'cause it wuz told ter me by old Uncle Joe Turner and he 'spirense it. Nobody could live in this how I don't care how they tried. Dey say this house wuz hanted and any body that tried to stay there wuz pulled out of bed by a hant. Well sir they offered the house and $1000.00 to any one who could stay there over night. Uncle Joe sed he decided to try it so sho nuff he got ready one night and went ter this house to stay. After while says he something came in the room and started over ter the bed; but fore it got there he sed "What in the name of the Lord you wont with me." It sed "follow me there is a pot of gold buried near the chimney; go find it and you want be worried with me no more." Der nect morning Uncle Joe went out then and begin ter dig and sho nuff he found the gold; and sides that he got the house. Dis here is the trufe Uncle Joes' house is right there in McDonough now and any body round there will tell you the same thing cause he wuz well known. Uncle Joe is dead now."

Anudder story that happened during slavery time and wuz told ter me by father wuz this: The master had a old man on his plantation named Jimson. Well Jimson's wife wuz sick and had been fer nearly a year. One day there she wanted some peas—black eyed peas; but old man Harper didn't have none on his plantation so Jimson planned ter steal off that night and go ter old marse Daniels farm, which wuz 4 miles from Moore Harpers farm, and steal a few peas fer his wife. Well between mid-night and day he got a sack and started off down the road. Long after while a owl started hootin who o o o are e-e-e, who are o-o-o- and it sounded jest lak some one saying "who are you". Jimson got scared pulled off his cap and ran all the way to old man Daniels farm. As he run he wuz saying "Sir dis is me. Old Jimson" over and over again. Now when he got near the farm old Daniel heard him and got up in the loft ter watch him. Finally old Jimson got dar and started creeping up in the loft. When he got up there chile Marse Daniel grabbed his whip and almost beat Jimson ter death.

This here story happened in Mississippi years ago but der folks that tell it ter me sed it wuz the trufe. "There wuz a woman that wuz sick, her name wuz Mary Jones. Well she lingered and lingered till she finally died. In them days folks all around would come ter the settin up of somebody wuz dead. They done sent some men after the casket since they had ter go 30 miles they wuz a good while getting back so the folkses decided ter sing. After while they heared the men come up on the porch or somebody got up ter let em in. Chile jest as they opened the door that 'oman set straight up on that bed, and sich another runnin and gittin out of that house you never heard; but some folks realized she wuzn't dead so they got the casket out der way so the wouldn't see it cause they wuz fraid she would pass out sho nuff; just the same they wuz fraid of her too. The men went off and come back with pistols guns, sticks and every thing and when this 'oman saw em she sed don't run I wont bother you' but child they left there in a big hurry too. Well this here Mary went to her sister's house and knocked on the door and said "Let me in this is Mary I want to talk to you and tell you where I've been. The sisters' husband opened the door and let her in. This 'oman told 'em that God had brought her to and that she had been in a trance with the Lord. After that everyone wuz always afraid of that 'oman and they wouldn't even sit next 'ter her in church. They say she is still living.

This happened right yonder in McDonough years ago. A gal went to a party with her sweet'art and her ma told her not ter go well she went on any how in a buggy. When they got ter the railroad crossing a train hit the buggy, and killed the gal; but the boy didn't get hurted at all. Well while they wuz sittin up with this dead gal, the boy comes long there in his buggy with anudder gal in the buggy; and do you know that horse stopped right in front 'uv that house and wouldn't bulge one inch. No matter how hard he whipped that horse it wouldn't move instid he rared and kicked and jumped about and almost turned the buggy over. The gal in the buggy fainted. Finally a old slavery time man come along and told em to git a quart of whiskey and pour it around the buggy and the hant would go away so they did that and the spirit let 'em pass.

If a han't laked whiskey in they lifetime and you pour it round when theys at they will go away.

The following are true conjure stories supposedly witnessed by Mrs. Heard.

There wuz a Rev. Dennis that lived below the Federal Prison now he wuz the preacher of the hard shell baptist church in this community; This man stayed sick about a year and kept gittin different doctors and none 'uv them did him any good well his wife kept on at him till he decided ter go ter see Dr. Geech. His complaint wuz that he felt something run up his legs ter his thighs. Old Dr. Geech told him that he had snakes in his body and they wuz put there by the lady he had been going wid. Dr. Geech give him some medicine ter take and told him that on the 7th day from then that 'oman would come and take the medicine off the shelf and throw it away. Course Rev. Dennis didn't believe a thing he sed so sho nuff she come jest lak Dr. Geech sed and took the medicine away. Dr. Geech told him that he would die when the snakes got up in his arm. But if he would do lak he told him he would get alright. Dis 'oman had put this stuff in some whiskey and he drunk it so the snakes breed in his body. After he quit taking the medicine he got bad off and had ter stay in the bed; sho nuff the morning he died. You could see the snake in his arm, the print uv it wuz there. When he died the snake stretched out in his arm and died too.

I got a son named Jack Heard, well somebody fixed him. I wuz in Chicago when that happened and my daughter kept writing ter me ter come home cause Jack wuz acting funny and she thought maybe he wuz losing his mind. They wuz living in Thomasville then and every day he would go sit round the store and laugh and talk but jest as soon as night would come and he would eat his supper them fits would come on him. He would squeal jest lak a pig and he would get down on his knees and bark jest lak a dog. Well I come home and went ter see a old conjure doctors. He says ter me, "that boy is hurt and when you go home you look in the corner of the mattress and you will find it." Sho nuff I went home and looked in the corner uv the mattress and there the package. It wuz a mixture of hair his hair and blue stone wrapped up in red flannel with new needles running all through it. When I went back he says ter me, Emmaline have you got 8 dimes no I sed but I got a dollar. Well get that dollar changed inter 10 dimes and take 8 'uv em and give 'em ter me. Then he took Jack in a room took off his clothes and started ter rubbing him down with medicine all the same time, he wuz a saying a ceremony over him, then he took them 8 dimes put 'em in a bag and tied them around Jacks chest some where so that they would hang over his heart. Now wear them always says he ter Jack. Jack wore them dimes a long time but he finally drunk 'em up. Any way that doctor cured him 'cause he sho woulda died.

The following is a few facts, as related by Mrs. Heard, concerning an old conjure doctor known as Aunt Darkas.

"Aunt Darkas lived in McDonough, Georgia until a few years ago. She died when she wuz 128 years old; but chile lemme tell you that 'oman knowed jest what ter do fer you. She wuz blind but she could go ter the woods and pick out any kind of root or herb she wanted. She always sed the Lord told her what roots to get and always fore sun up you would see her in the woods with a short handled pick. She sed she had ter pick 'em fore sun up, I don't know why. If you wuz sick all you had ter do wuz go to see

Aunt Darkas and tell her. She had a well and after listening to your complaint she would go out there and draw a bucket of water and set it on the floor and then she would wave her hand over it and say something. She called this healing the water. After this she would give you a drink of water as she handed it ter you she would say, now drink, take this and drink. Honey, I had some uv that water myself and believe me it goes all over you and makes you feel so good. Old Aunt Darkas would give you a supply of water and tell you ter come back fer more when that wuz gone. Old Aunt Darkas sed the Lord gave her power and vision and she used ter fast fer a week at a time. When she died there wuz a piece in the paper 'bout her."

This here is sho the trufe and if you don't go out ter Southview Cemetary and see Sid Heard my oldest son he been out there over 20 years as sexton and book keeper. Yessir he tole it ter me and I believe it. This happen long ago 10 or 15 years. There wuz a couple that lived in Macon, Ga., but their home wuz in Atlanta and they had a lot out ter South View. Well they had a young baby that tuck sick and died so they had the babies funeral there in Macon then they put the coffin in the box placed the lable on the box then brought it ter Atlanta. Folkses are always buried so that they head faces the east. They say when judgement day come and Gabriel blow that trumpet every body will rise up facing the east. Well as I wuz saying they come here Sid Heard met im out yonder and instructed his men fer arrangements fer the grave and everything. A few weeks later the 'oman called Sid Heard up long distance. She said, "Mr. Heard." "Yesmam," he said. "I call you ter tell you me and my husband can't rest at all." "Why?" he asked. "Because we can hear our baby crying every night and it is worrying us ter death our neighbors next door says our baby must be buried wrong." Sid Heard sed, "Well I buried the baby according ter the way you got the box labled." "I'm not blaming you Mr. Heard but if I pay you will you take my baby up?" Sed she "Yes Mam I will if you want me to jest let me know the day you will be here and I'll have everything ready". "Alright," sed she. "Well," sed Sid Heard, "the day she wuz ter come she wuz sick and instead sent a carload of her friends. The men got busy and started digging till they got ter the box, when they took it up sho nuff after they opened it they found the baby had been buried wrong the head was facing the west instead of the east. They turned the box around and covered it up. The folks then went on back ter Macon. A week later the 'oman called up again. "Mr. Heard," she says. "Yes maam" says he. "Well I haven't heard my baby cry at all in the past week I wuzn't there but I know the exact date you took my baby up, cause I never heard it cry no more".

On December 3 and 4, 1936, Mrs. Emmaline Heard was interviewed at her home, 239 Cain Street. The writer had visited Mrs. Heard previously, and it was at her own request that another visit was made. This visit was supposed to be one to obtain information and stories on the practice of conjure. On two previous occasions Mrs. Heard's stories had proved very interesting, and I knew as I sat there waiting for her to begin that she had something very good to tell me. She began:

"Chile, this story wuz told ter me by my father and I know he sho wouldn't lie. Every word of it is the trufe; fact, everything I ebber told you wuz the trufe. Now, my pa had a brother, old Uncle Martin, and his wife wuz name Julianne. Aunt Julianne used ter have spells and fight and kick all the time. They had doctor after doctor but none did her any good. Somebody told Uncle Martin to go ter a old conjurer and let the doctors go cause they wan't doing nothing for her anyway. Sho nuff he got one ter come see her and give her some medicine. This old man said she had bugs in her head, and after giving her the medicine he started rubbing her head. While he rubbed her head he said: "Dar's a bug in her head; it looks jest like a big black roach. Now, he's coming out of her head through her ear; whatever you do, don't let him get away cause I want him. Whatever you do, catch him; he's going ter run, but when he hits the pillow, grab 'em. I'm go take him and turn it back on the one who is trying ter send you ter the grave." Sho nuff that bug drop out her ear and flew; she hollered, and old Uncle Martin ran in the room, snatched the bed clothes off but they never did find him. Aunt Julianne never did get better and soon she died. The conjurer said if they had a caught the bug she would a lived."

The next story is a true story. The facts as told by Mrs. Heard were also witnessed by her; as it deals with the conjuring of one of her sons. It is related in her exact words as nearly as possible.

"I got a son named Albert Heard. He is living and well; but chile, there wuz a time when he wuz almost ter his grave. I wuz living in town then, and Albert and his wife was living in the country with their two chillun. Well, Albert got down sick and he would go ter doctors, and go ter doctors, but they didn't do him any good. I wuz worried ter death cause I had ter run backards and for'ards and it wuz a strain on me. He was suffering with a knot on his right side and he couldn't even fasten his shoes cause it pained him so, and it was so bad he couldn't even button up his pants. A 'oman teached school out there by the name of Mrs. Yaney; she's dead now but she lived right here on Randolph Street years ago. Well, one day when I wuz leaving Albert's house I met her on the way to her school. 'Good evening, Mrs. Heard', she says. 'How is Mr. Albert?' I don't hardly know, I says, cause he don't get no better. She looked at me kinda funny and said, don't you believe he's hurt?' Yes mam, I said, I sho do. 'Well,' says she, 'I been waiting to say something to you concerning this but I didn't know how you would take it. If I tell you somewhere to go will you go, and tell them I sent you?' Yes mam, I will do anything if Albert can get better. 'All right then', she says, 'Catch the Federal prison car and get off at Butler St.' In them days that car came down Forrest Ave. 'When you get to Butler St.', she says, 'walk up to Clifton St. and go to such and such a number. Knock on the door and a 'oman by the name of Mrs. Hirshpath will come ter the door. Fore she let you in she go ask who sent you there; when you tell 'er she'll let you in. Now lemme tell you she keeps two quarts of whisky all the time and you have ter drink a little with her; sides that she cusses nearly every word she speaks; but don't let that scare you; she will sho get your son up if it kin be done.' Sho nuff that old 'oman did jest lak Mrs. Yaney said she would do. She had a harsh voice and she spoke right snappy. When she let me in she said, 'sit down. You lak whisky?' I said, well, I take a little dram sometimes. 'Well, here take some of this', she said. I poured a little bit and drank it kinda lak I wuz afraid. She cussed and said 'I ain't go conjure you. Drink it.' She got the cards and told me to cut 'em, so I did. Looking at the cards, she said: 'You like ter wait too long; they got him marching to the cemetery. The poor thing! I'll fix those devils. (A profane word was used instead of devils). He got a knot on his side, ain't he?' Yes, Mam, I said. That 'oman told me everything that was wrong with Albert and zackly how he acted. All at once she said: 'If them d——d things had hatched in him it would a been too late. If you do zackly lak I tell you I'll get him up from there.' I sho will, I told her. 'Well, there's a stable south east of his house. His house got three rooms and a path go straight to the stable. I see it there where he hangs his harness. Yes, I see it all, the devils! Have you got any money?' Yes, mam, a little, I said. 'All right then,' she said. 'Go to the drug store and get 5¢ worth of blue stone; 5¢ wheat bran; and go ter a fish market and ask 'em ter give you a little fish brine; then go in the woods and get some poke-root berries. Now, there's two kinds of poke-root berries, the red skin and the white skin berry. Put all this in a pot, mix with it the guts from a green gourd and 9 parts of red pepper. Make a poultice and put to his side on that knot. Now, listen, your son will be afraid and think you are trying ter do something ter him but be gentle and persuade him that its fer his good.' Child, he sho did act funny when I told him I wanted to treat his side. I had ter tell him I was carrying out doctors orders so he could get well. He reared and fussed and said he didn't want that mess on him. I told him the doctor says you do very well till you go ter the horse lot then you go blind and you can't see. He looked at me. 'Sho nuff, Ma,' he said, 'that sho is the trufe. I have ter always call one of the chillun when I go there cause I can't see how ter get back ter the house.' Well, that convinced him and he let me fix the medicine for him. I put him ter bed and made the poultice, then I put it ter his side. Now this 'oman said no one was ter take it off the next morning but me. I was suppose ter fix three, one each night, and after taking each one off ter bury it lak dead folks is buried, east and west, and ter make a real grave out of each one. Well, when I told him not ter move it the next morning, but let me move it, he got funny again and wanted to know why. Do you know I had ter play lak I could move it without messing up my bed clothes and if he moved it he might waste it all. Finally he said he could call me the next morning. Sho nuff, the next morning he called me, ma! ma! come take it off. I went in the room and he wuz smiling. I slept all night long he said, and I feel so much better. I'm so glad, I said, and do you know he could reach down and fasten up his shoe and it had been a long time since he could do that. Later that day I slipped out and made my first grave under the fig bush in the garden. I even put up head boards, too. That night Albert said, 'Mama, fix another one. I feel so much better.' I sho will, I said. Thank God you're better; so for three nights I fixed poultices and put ter his side and each morning he would tell me how much better he felt. Then the last morning I was fixing breakfast and he sat in the next room. After while Albert jumped up and hollered, 'Ma! Ma!' What is it, I said. 'Mama, that knot is gone. It dropped down in my pants.' What! I cried. Where is it? Chile, we looked but we didn't find anything, but the knot had sho gone. Der 'oman had told me ter come back when the knot moved and she would tell me what else ter do. That same day I went ter see her and when I told her she just shouted, 'I fixed 'em the devils!' Now, says she, do you where you can get a few leaves off a yellow peachtree. It must be a yellow peach tree, though. Yes, mam, I says to her. I have a yellow peachtree right there in my yard. Well, she says, get a handful of leaves, then take a knife and scrape the bark up, then make a tea and give him so it will heal up the poison from that knot in his side, also mix a few jimson weeds with it. I came home and told him I wanted ter give him a tea. He got scared and said, what fer, Ma? I had ter tell him I wuz still carrying out the doctor's orders. Well, he let me give him the tea and that boy got well. I went back to Mrs. Hirshpath and told her my son wuz well and I wanted to pay her. Go on, she said, keep the dollar and send your chillun ter school. This sho happened ter me and I know people kin fix you. Yes sir."

The next story was told to Mrs. Heard by Mrs. Hirshpath, the woman who cured her son.

I used to go see that 'oman quite a bit and even sent some of my friends ter her. One day while I wuz there she told me about this piece of work she did.

"There was a young man and his wife and they worked for some white folks. They had just married and wuz trying ter save some money ter buy a home with. All at onct the young man went blind and it almost run him and his wife crazy cause they didn't know what in the world ter do. Well somebody told him and her about Mrs. Hirshpath, so they went ter see her. One day, said Mrs. Hirshpath, a big fine carriage drew up in front of her door and the coachman helped him to her door. She asked him who sent him and he told her. She only charged 50¢ for giving advice and after you wuz cured it wuz up to you to give her what you wanted to. Well, this man gave her 50¢ and she talked ter him. She says, boy, you go home and don't you put that cap on no more. That cap? he says. That cap you wears ter clean up the stables with, cause somebody done dressed that cap for you, and every time you perspire and it runs down ter your eyes it makes you blind. You jest get that cap and bring it ter me. I'll fix 'em; they's trying ter make you blind, but I go let you see. The boy was overjoyed, and sho nuff he went back and brought her that cap, and it wasn't long fore he could see good as you and me. He brought that 'oman $50, but she wouldn't take but $25 and give the other $25 back ter him.

"What I done told you is the trufe, every word of it; I know some other things that happened but you come back anudder day fer that."

• EX-SLAVE MILDRED HEARD.

The following interviews were obtained from Mildred Heard, a young woman who has lived in the country most of her life and might easily be described as a child of nature. Although a full grown woman and the mother of two children she seems much older than her years, this is true I believe because she has always lived among much older people. She is fairly intelligent and expresses her thoughts clearly and without hesitation. Quite a few of the stories related here were handed down to her from the older residents of the settlement. These stories are related in her own words.

Animal Behavior—Cows "I have always lived around animals and used to spend whole days in the woods; but first I want to tell you about a story concerning cows; and this is the trufe too. Every New Years night when the whistles begin to blow, cows get down on their knees lift up their front legs and make a mumbling noise. This is true cause one night I made it my business to be around some cows when the whistles begin to blow and sho nuff they got down on their hind legs and started making that noise. I was so fraid I ran all the way home.

"I also remember we had a cow that would eat clothes. My grandmother took in a lot of washings and one day after she had hung out Mrs. Richardson's clothes she (the cow) ate up most all of the clothes. Grandma whipped her and had to pay the white lady for the clothes but that cow kept on eating clothes. A lady told us to sprinkle red pepper on the clothes and that would break her up. Sho nuff we did it and she kicked her heels over her head; but we never had any more trouble with that cow.

"Maybe, you don't know it but cows are funny about the water they drink especially cows raised at a dairy. If water is placed in a tub for a cow and you stick your hand in the water they will not drink it. I have done it and I know it to be true. The cow don't have to see you but the scent from your hand is in the water".

Birds

"If a bird leaves her nest and flies away and you take her eggs out of the nest and put them back the bird can tell it the minute she returns to her nest; and she will not have the nest on the eggs again. I tried this once to see if it was true. I moved the eggs from a birds' nest and placed them back and then I hid behind a tree to watch sho nuff the bird came back to her nest she looked at the nest and the eggs a long time and flew away. Every day I would watch; but she never returned to that nest."

"Once a little red bird got hurt and I caught it and

nursed it back to health and this bird began to act just like a pet. When I saw the bird was well enough to leave I tied a red string around it's leg so that I would know it if I saw it again. After that for three years my little bird used to fly back and sit on the steps until I would feed him and then he would fly away. My bird came back until it was caught by a cat. I was so sorry when my bird died I cried and buried it in the back yard."

Snakes

"I have walked through the woods and almost stepped on different kinds of snakes. I wouldn't be afraid cause I would know that unless the snake is in a quirl, that is, in a pose to bite you, he wouldn't bite you. If you smell a water mellon scent in the woods you know right then that a black snake is around. If the scent is like a honey suckle a highland moccasin is around somewhere. A rattlesnake smells like a billy goat. Always remember a snake can't bite until it gets posed neither can a snake bite you in the water. Some snakes lay eggs and hatch their young. A mother snake always protects her baby snakes by swallowing them if danger comes around." Grandma told me once that they were cleaning out a large hole for a baptizing pool; and saw a mother snake swallow about ten baby snakes. After they killed the mother snake they pulled out the 10 babies.

Fowls

We had a rooster that was raised from a biddie and for 5 years this rooster practically lived in the house and would not sleep any place but on the foot of the bed.

"Chickens get used to certain people feeding them

and you can't get them used to others, that is, it was true concerning my cousin. He had a lot of chickens and he used to feed them every day. My cousin took sick and died and after that his chickens would not eat anything given them by any one else. One by one the chickens died. My Aunt said his spirit came back for the chickens".

Bees.

"This is a true story concerning bees that belonged to my aunt Caroline Hooper. Aunt Caroline died and left 10 hives of bees. We noticed they kept going away and would not return. One day a lady named Mrs. Jordan asked if anyone had told the bees that Caroline was dead; and we told her no, "Well" she said, "go out to the hive and say to the bees Caroline is dead and that they will have a new owner." My uncle told the bees that they belonged to him now that Caroline was dead. After that none others left the hive."

Mildred Heard continued giving short facts concerning different animals.—"If you run a rabbit out of his bed and shoot at him I don't care if you run him five or more miles he will come right back to the same place." "Buzzards are born as white as snow but turn darker as they grow older. Another fact concerning buzzards is that they will eat any carcass except that of a mad dog, he will walk around the body of a dead mad dog and then fly away."

"I remember once we had a cat that was the pet of every one in our house so when she gave birth to kittens she went in the chifforobe and when we let her out we didn't know she had left kittens in there. Naturally they died and we buried them in the back yard. Everyday this mother cat would go to their grave and whine, finally she left home."

The following stories relate to

Birthmarks

As previously mentioned Mildred Heard has two small daughters and the story of birthmarks begins with her own experience concerning them. "My oldest Child Tina is marked by crying. I don't care how much you whip or beg her to stop crying she will not stop until she gets ready. During the time I was pregnant my aunt died and I went to the funeral and before I knew it I found myself crying and unable to stop.

"My youngest child Georgia is marked by a monkey. This mark is the result of a visit to Grants Park during the time I was pregnant. As I stood with the white baby I was nursing at the time a monkey fell and when he got up he started scratching his back. It all looked so funny I began to laugh. When Gloria was born her bead resembled a monkeys in shape and on the lower part of her back she had red marks and was very hairy. I was afraid she would never change but as she grew older the marks and the hair disappeared." note—I glanced at the child and it is quite true that the shape of her head slightly resembles that of a monkey.

The next stories were related by Mrs. Heard. Mildred's grandmother. "I know a white 'oman that lives in Thomasville now that marked her child by a horse. This 'oman got tickled at a horse with his tongue hanging out. When her baby was born he had feet and hands jest lak a horse and she nebber would let any one see this child's feet.

"Another 'oman, Alberta Turner, got scared of a turtle while she wuz fishing and right now her child got feet that spreads out just like a turtles and he walks with his feet straight out that way.

"Aunt Eattie Coffee who lives in Macedonia, Ga., had a baby born with 4 teeth that looked jest like pearls. The doctor told her that the baby would shed those teeth and if she lost 'em the baby would die.

"He told her to be sure and watch the baby and to give him the teeth when they came out. Sho nuff them teeth came out but they never knowed where they went and that baby she died".

• ROBERT HEARD—PORTRAIT OF AN EX-SLAVE
[HW: J. Jaffee]

As we approached the little dilapidated, one-room cabin on the Jackson County hilltop, the aroma of frying bacon smote our nostrils.

Uncle Robert Heard welcomed us and stopped tending his ash-cake, peas, and fat back long enough to squint over the top of the "specks dat Ole Mis had give him back in '70", then he took a long look at the mahogany clock that had "sot on her parlor fish boa'd". In spite of his ninety-six years his memory of the old days is still fresh and his body surprisingly active for a person of his age.

"Course I 'members all 'bout Marster and Mistis," he

asserted with an indignant air. "I wuz grown an' big nuff to pick out a 'oman fer myse'f in de fust year ov de war. Dey wuz 120 niggers on de place whar I wuz borned. Hit belonged to ole Gen'l Heard an' hit wuz clost to Washin'ton."

"My mammy died when I warn't nothin' but a little trot-about. She wuz name' Susan, an' my pa wuz name' John. De Gen'l went to Virginny an' bought 'em an' had 'em sont home in boxes wid cracks big nuff to feed 'em through. Mistis give us our fust names an' us tuck dey las' un."

"Us didn't have no overseer on our plantation. Gen'l Heard allus looked arter his niggers hisssef til he got too old an' den his son, Mars Tom, seed arter 'em. I ain't never see'd 'em beat but one slave an' dat wuz caze he got rowdy drunk. Dey allus gite us a note to de patty rollers (patrollers) when us wanted to go somewheres".

"Us went to work 'bout a half hour by sun an' quit at dusty dark. De mens done fiel' wuk an' de wimmins mostly hepped Mistis 'bout de house. Dey washed, milked, made candles, an' worked in de spinnin' room. Us didn't have to buy nothin' caze dey wuz evathing us needed on the plantation."

"On some places de bosses kep' nigger mens at stud but Gen'l Heard an' Mars Tom didn't low nobody to live in sin on dey plantation. Us wuz all married by a white preacher, just lak white folks. Us 'tended de white folk's church ever Sundey an' sot in de gal'ry. Dey warn't no dancin' or cyard playin' in Gen'l Heard's house. He said: 'If you serve the Lord you have no time to fiddle and dance.'"

"Old Marster wuz too old to go to de war but Mars Tom went an' I hyeard Mistis say he got kilt at de second Manassas. My Uncle Chris went to de war wid Mars Tom an' he come back wid only one arm. He say de blood on some uv dem battle fiel's come up to de top uv his boots.

"Gen'l Heard died whiles de war wuz ragin' an' Ole Mistis come out on de po'ch an' tolt us we wuz all free. Most all de niggers stayed on wid Mistis arter de war an' worked fer fo'ths. Us used her mules an' tools an' she give us rations just lak Marster had been a doin' afore dey wuz any war. She would uv been powerful rich ef Confederacy money hadn't uv been so wuthless. She had four loads uv it hauled outen de house an' dumped in a ditch.

"At Christmus time, us allus had a BIG frolic wid music an' dancin'. Us danced de cotillion an' beat on buckets wid gourds fer music. Marster give us a little toddy now an' den an' us had plenty uv it at Christmas. De frolic allus had to bust up at midnight caze Marster would git out his horse pistols an' start shootin' ef it didn't. Sometimes us ud have a Satidy off an' us ud all go fishin' or have a frolic. Candy pullin's wuz allus de bestes kind of fun.

"I ain't lak mos' ob dese yere flibberty-gibbet niggers. I don' believe in hants an' ghostes, but they's some things which I does think is signs of death. Ef somebody brings a axe in de house hits a sho sign. Yer better watch when a cow lows arter dark, or a dog barks at de moon in front uv yer do', or ef yer sneezes whiles eatin', caze hit mout mean dat de death angel is hangin' roun'. Ef somebody in de house dies yer better stop de tickin' uv de clock an' kiver all de lookin'-glasses wid white cloth or else dey's liable to be another death in de fam'ly.

"Yer can take dis or leave it, but whutever yer does, don' never take ashes out doors arter dark, caze hits sho to bring yer bad luck. Now I done tol' yer all I knows so let me finish cookin' dis yere mess of vittals so I kin git back to de cotton patch."

Thus dismissed, we took our departure, gingerly picking our way down the rickety steps. The last we heard of Uncle Robert was a snatch of Negro ballad sung in a high-pitched, nasal voice.

United States. Work Projects Administration

Whitley,
1-22-37

M. B. Ross.

Ex-Slave
Benjamin Henderson.

BENJAMIN HENDERSON

After acquainting Mr. Benjamin Henderson with the facts of the interview he informed the writer that he would be very glad to give as much information as he could concerning the period of "I was only seven years old when freedom was declared, but I can remember a few facts," he said. His speech is well chosen and after a short talk one is much impressed with his intelligence and youthful appearance.

Benjamin Henderson was born September 8, 1858 in Jasper County, Monticello, Ga., the youngest of three children. His father was Mr. Sam Henderson, master and owner of the Henderson plantation, and his mother was Mandy Henderson, a slave. Mr. Sam Henderson never married but operated his farm with the help of his mother, Mrs. Allie Henderson.

The Henderson plantation comprised 250 acres and Mr. Henderson owned only five slaves to carry the necessary work. Besides Benjamin's immediate family there was one other man slave, named Aaron. Cotton, cattle and vegetables were the chief products of the farm. The work was divided as follows: Benjamin's job was to keep the yards clean and bring up the calves at night; his older sister and brother, together with Aaron, did the field work; and his mother worked in the house as general servant.

The same routine continued from day to day, each person going about his or her particular job. Plenty of flour was raised on the plantation and the master had to buy very little.

The Henderson slave houses were of the one-room log type, with one window and one door; each cabin was furnished with a bed, chair, and table. Large fireplaces took the place of stoves for cooking. These were constructed four or five feet in width so that one or two pots or a side of meat could be suspended from a hook which was fastened on a rack in the stick and dirt chimney.

Each family was given a spinning wheel and loom. After the day's work each slave home was the scene of spinning and weaving cloth for the occupant's clothes and bedding.

The master gave each slave a pair of shoes; Benjamin received his first pair of shoes when he was five years old. All slaves went barefoot in summer months.

Summer rations on the Henderson plantations never varied from bacon and corn bread. In the fall each family was free to eat as many of the different vegetables as they wanted.

Wooden spoons, bowls, and trays, were kept clean by scouring regularly with sand. At Christmas those who asked for whiskey were given an ample amount; and occasionally each family was given a cake baked by Mr. Henderson's mother.

The master of the Henderson plantation, as well as other plantation owners', allowed their slaves to work individual cotton patches; when the cotton was picked he paid them their price for the amount they had raised. Slaves often earned money, too, by splitting rails at night and selling them to different plantation owners.

Although Mr. Sam Henderson was a kind master and hardly ever punished his slaves, there were some masters who were known for their cruelty. One in particular was an old man by the name of Shirley, who would pick up anything from a stick to a brush broom to punish his slaves.

Benjamin heard from his elders that some masters constructed stocks like those of old, and sometimes slaves were whipped while fastened in the stocks. One slave owner named Gay kept wristbands of iron, and also a gag made to fit into the mouth and fasten around the neck, which prevented rolling while being whipped. Besides being punished for disobedience, a slave was often punished because he failed to complete the required amount of work. There were certain amounts of work specified for each slave: 150 rails had to be split a day by the rail splitters; cotton pickers were supposed to pick 150 pounds of cotton a day. Should anyone fail to complete his daily task, a sound whipping was given. Slaves were punished by "patter rollers" or the government patrol, if caught off of their plantations without a pass. Often slaves outran the "patter rollers" and escaped the 75 lashes which were in store for them if they were caught. "Patter rollers" carried a crooked-handle stick which they would try to fasten around the slaves' necks or arms. However, the slaves soon learned that the "patter-rollers" stick would slide off their bare arms and backs, so they left their shirts if planning to make a visit without a pass.

The second Sunday of each month the slaves attended religious services. Since there were no separate churches provided, they were allowed to use the white churches with the white minister in charge. Benjamin Henderson remarked: "It was my job to ride behind the mistress to church and while the services were going on I took care of her riding skirt and tended the horse."

A slave desiring marriage with a slave on another plantation must get his master's consent after which he went to see the master of his prospective mate. If both agreed, the marriage was set for the following Saturday night. All marriages usually took place on Saturday nights. The master of the bridegroom would then pick a straw broom or a pole and give two slaves the job of holding the ends of it. To be devilish they often held the stick too high and would not lower it until the master asked them to. After the bridegroom made the jump over the stick, the knot of matrimony was considered tied. Without any more ceremony the bride became his legal wife. If it so happened that the bride and groom lived on different plantations the groom would be given two passes a week, one to visit her on Wednesday nights and another which permitted him to remain over the weekend, from Saturday until Monday morning. Following the marriage there would take place the usual "frolic" ending up with several members drunk. These were thrown into the seed house where they remained all night.

Slave owners guarded carefully against illness among their slaves. Home remedies such as certain oil, turpentine, teas of all sorts were used. If these did no good the doctor was called in; he usually brought along all varieties of medicine in his saddle bags and gave what was needed. Benjamin Henderson considers that people were much healthier in those days and did not need doctors often.

He tells this story: "My mistress had a daughter who was married and had three sons who were Confederate soldiers. I remember the day they rode up on their grey horses to take dinner and say goodbye to the family. When they were ready to leave their grandmother gave them an old testament and told them to take it and read it and make good soldiers of themselves. One son replied, 'Oh grandma it won't last long, we're going to bring old Lincoln's head back and set it on the gate post for a target.' But they didn't come back: all three were killed. The master of the plantation also enlisted in the army; he was able to come home every week or two".

After the war Benjamin's mother married and moved with her husband to another farm, where she spent the rest of her life. Some families moved to other plantations, and during the first year after the war they were forced to work for one-sixth of the crop raised. The next year plantation owners realized this amount was unfair and agreed to let the ex-slaves work for one-third of the crops raised. Finally they worked on halves. Even now, working on halves is common in rural villages.

Benjamin Henderson believes he has lived long because he has lived a clean, useful life filled with plenty of hard work. He married at the age of 28 years and was the father of five children, none of whom are living.

His physical condition prevents him from working at present, but he has not given up hope that he will soon be able to take care of himself again.

Slave Narratives

PLANTATION LIFE, AS VIEWED BY AN EX-SLAVE

Written By: Mrs. Sadie B. Hornsby
Athens —

Edited By: Mrs. Sarah. H. Hall
Athens —

and

John N. Booth
District Supervisor
Federal Writers' Project
Residencies 6 & 7
Augusta, Georgia

September 23, 1938.

JEFFERSON FRANKLIN HENRY
Ex-Slave—Age 78
Athens, Georgia

JEFFERSON FRANKLIN HENRY

The widespread branches of a white mulberry tree formed a canopy for the entire yard before Jefferson Henry's gray-painted cottage. Luxuriant hydrangeas in wooden tubs, August lilies in other containers on the old-fashioned flower steps, and a carefully pruned privet hedge gave the place an air of distinction in this shabby neighborhood, and it was not surprising to learn that a preacher, a man highly respected by his race, lived there.

A rap on the door brought quick response from a rumbling bass voice inside the house. "George, is you here already?" In another moment a short, stocky Negro man appeared in the doorway, a collar clutched in one hand, and a slightly embarrassed look on his face. "Good mornin'," he said. "Yes, mam, this is Jeff Henry. I thought you was George done come to take me to Atlanta. One of my good church members is to be buried thar today, and I'se got to preside over the funeral. I can talk to you a few minutes if you ain't got too much to ax me about."

Though Jeff used some dialect, it was not so noticeable as in the speech of most southern Negroes. A scant fringe of kinky gray hair framed his almost bald head, and he was dressed in his Sunday-best clothes; a gray suit, white shirt, and black shoes, worn but carefully polished.

"This old Negro has been here many a day," he began. "I 'members when all this side of town was in farms and woods with just a few houses scattered about." Just then George drove up and Jeff suggested that the interview be postponed.

At the appointed hour Jeff was waiting to resume his narrative. "I sho is done been wukin' this old brain of mine to bring back them old times 'fore freedom come," he announced. "Anyhow, I was born in Paulding County. Sam and Phyllis Henry was my pa and ma, and they was field hands. Me and James, William, John, Mittie, and Mary was all the chillun they had. Us just played 'round the yard mostly, 'cause thar warn't none of us big enough to do no field wuk wuth talkin' 'bout 'fore the end of the war.

"Slave quarters was off from the big house a piece, and they was built in rows lak streets. Most of the log cabins had one room; some had two, but all of them had plain old stack chimblies made of sticks and red mud. Our beds was just home-made makeshifts, but us didn't know no diffunce 'cause us never had seed no better ones. They sawed pine posts the right height and bored holes through them and through the slabs they had cut for the railin's, or side pieces. They jined the bed together with cords that they wove back and forth and twisted tight with a stout stick. Them cords served two purposes; they held the bed together and was our springs too, but if us warn't mighty keerful to keep 'em twisted tight our beds would fall down. Lak them old beds, the mattresses us had them days warn't much compared with what we sleeps on now. Them ticks was made of coarse home-wove cloth, called 'osnaburg,' and they was filled with straw. My! How that straw did squeak and cry out when us moved, but the Blessed Lord changed all that when he gave us freedom and let schools be sot up for us. With freedom Negroes soon got more knowledge of how a home ought to be.

"Grandma Ca'line is the onliest one of my grandparents I can 'member. When she got too old for field wuk, they tuk and used her as a cook up at the big house, and she done the weavin', spinnin', and milkin' too, and kept a eye on the slave chillun whilst the mammies was off in the field.

"No, mam, slaves warn't paid no money them days, and it's mightly little I'se got holt of since. Anyhow I warn't big enough then to do no wuk, even if folks had been payin' wages to slaves. The most I ever done 'fore the war ended was to fetch water to the kitchen and pick up chips to kindle up the fire when it got low. Matches was so scarce then that fires warn't 'lowed to go slap out, but they did burn mighty low sometimes in summer and us had to use fat lightwood splinters to git 'em started up again.

"Us et home produce them days. Folks didn't know nothin' 'bout livin' out of cans and paper sacks lak they does now. Thar was allus plenty of hog meat, syrup, milk and butter, cornbread, and sometimes us chillun got a biscuit. Thar was one big old garden on the place that had evvything in the way of vegetables growin' in it, besides the patches of beans, peas, 'taters, and the lak that was scattered 'round in the fields. The orchards was full of good fruit sich as apples, peaches, pears, and plums, and don't forgit them blackberries, currants, and figs what growed 'round the aidge of the back yard, in fence corners, and off places. Sho, us had 'possums, plenty of 'em, 'cause they let us use the dogs to trail 'em down with. 'Possums was biled 'til they was tender, then baked with sweet 'taters, and thar ain't no better way been found to fix 'em to this good day, not even if they's barbecued. Sho, sho, us had rabbits and squirrels by the wholesale, and fish too if us tuk time to do our fishin' at night. They never did lak to see slaves settin' 'round fishin' in the daytime.

"All the cookin' was done in a log cabin what sot a good little piece behind the big house. The big old fireplace in that kitchen held a four-foot log, and when you was little you could set on one end of that log whilst it was a-burnin' on t'other. They biled in pots hangin' from hooks on a iron bar that went all the way 'cross the fireplace, and the bakin' was done in skillets and ovens, but sometimes bread was wropt up in cabbage or collard leaves and baked in hot ashes; that was ashcake. Thick iron lids fitted tight on them old skillets, and most of 'em had three legs so hot coals could be raked under 'em. The ovens sot on trivets over the coals.

"Our clothes warn't nothin' to talk about. In summer boys wore just one piece and that looked lak a long nightshirt. Winter clothes was jean pants and homespun shirts; they was warm but not too warm. Thar warn't no sich things as Sunday clothes in them days, and I never had a pair of shoes on my foots in slavery time, 'cause I warn't big enough to wuk. Grown Negroes wore shoes in winter but they never had none in summer.

"Marse Robert Trammell and his wife, Miss Martha, was our marster and mistess. Miss Ada, Miss Emma, and Miss Mary 'Liza was the young misses, and the young marsters was named George Washin'ton and William Daniel. Marse Robert and his fambly lived in a log and plank house with a rock chimbly. He was buildin' a fine rock house when the war came on, but he never got it finished.

"Robert Scott, one of the slaves, was made foreman atter Marse Robert turned off his overseer. Gilbert was the carriage driver and 'sides drivin' the fambly 'round, he tuk Marse Robert's ma, Miss Betsey, to her church at Powder Springs. Miss Betsey was a Hardshell Baptist, and Marse Robert and his wife wouldn't go to church with her.

"That old plantation was a large place all right enough; I 'spects thar was 'bout four or five hunderd acres in it. Marse Robert warn't no big slave holder and he didn't have so awful many slaves. His foreman had 'em out in the fields by daylight and wuked 'em 'til dark. The women had a certain stint of thread to spin and cloth to weave 'fore they could go to bed at night. The menfolks had to shuck corn, mend horse-collars, make baskets, and all sich jobs as that at night, and they had to holp the women with the washin' sometimes. Most of that kind of thing was done on days when the weather was too hot for 'em to work in the fields.

"Marse Robert done his own whippin' of his slaves and, let me tell you, they didn't have to do much for him to whip 'em; he whipped 'em for most anything. They was tied, hand and foots, to a certain tree, and he beat 'em with a heavy leather strop. I'se seed him whip 'em heaps of times, and it was 'most allus in the mornin's 'fore they went to wuk. Thar warn't no jailhouse nigh whar us lived and Marse Robert never had no place to lock slaves up when they got too bad, so he just beat the meanness out of 'em. Thar was one slave he never tetched; that was his foreman and his name was Robert too, lak I done told you.

"I never seed no slaves sold on the block or auctioned off, and if any droves of slaves for sale passed our plantation I'se done forgot about it. No, mam, a slave warn't 'lowed to take no book in his hand to larn nothin'; it was agin' the law to permit slaves to do that sort of thing. If us went to any churches at all it had to be our white folks' churches, 'cause thar warn't no churches for Negroes 'til the war was over. Not a slave on our place could read a word from the Bible, but some few could repeat a verse or two they had cotch from the white folks and them that was smart enough made up a heap of verses that went 'long with the ones larned by heart. Us went to Poplar Springs Baptist church with Marse Robert's fambly; that church was 'bout 3 miles from whar us lived. Miss Betsey, she tuk Grandma Ca'line with her to the Hardshell Baptist church about 10 miles further down the road. Sometimes Grandma Ca'line would go by herself when Marse Robert's ma didn't go. Us just had church once a month.

"When a slave died evvybody on our plantation quit wuk 'til atter the buryin'. The home-made coffins was made of unpainted planks and they was lined with white cloth. White folks' coffins was made the same way, only theirs was stained, but they never tuk time to stain the ones they buried slaves in. Graves was dug wide at the top and at the bottom they was just wide enough to fit the coffin. They laid planks 'crost the coffins and they shovelled in the dirt. They never had larnt to read the songs they sung at funerals and at meetin'. Them songs was handed down from one generation to another and, far as they knowed, never was writ down. A song they sung at the house 'fore they left for the graveyard begun:

> 'Why do we mourn departed friends,
> Or shake at death's alarm.'"

At the grave they sung, Am I Born to Die, To Lay this Body Down?

"Slaves on our plantation never thought about runnin' off to no North. Marse Robert allus treated 'em fair and square, and thar warn't no need for 'em to run nowhar. That foreman of his, Robert Scott, did go off and stay a few days once. Marse Robert had started to whip his wife and he had jumped 'twixt 'em; that made Marse Robert so mad he run to the house to git his gun, so the foreman he got out of the way a day or two to keep from gittin' shot. When he come back, Marse Robert was so glad to git him back he never said a word to him 'bout leavin'.

"On Saddays the women wuked in the field 'til dinnertime, but the menfolks wuked on 'til a hour 'fore sundown. The women spent that time washin', cleanin' up the cabins, patchin', and gittin' ready for the next week. Oh! How they did frolic 'round Sadday night when they could git passes. Sundays they went to church but not without a pass for, if they ever was cotch out without one, them paterollers would beat 'em up something terrible.

"Sho, Christmastime was when slaves had their own fun. Thar warn't nothin' extra or diffunt give 'em, only plenty to eat and drink; Marse Robert allus made lots of whiskey and brandy. He give his slaves six days holiday and 'lowed 'em to have passes. They frolicked, danced, and visited 'round and called it havin' a good time. Wuk begun again on New Year's Day and thar warn't no more holidays 'til the next Christmas. No, mam, not many slave chillun knowed what Santa Claus was or what Christmas was meant to celebrate 'til they got some schoolin' atter the war was over.

"Sho, sho, us had cornshuckin's, all right enough. Sometimes Marse Robert raised so much corn us had to have more than one cornshuckin' to git it all shucked. The neighbors was 'vited and such a time as us did have atter the wuk was done. I was too little to do so much eatin', drinkin', and cuttin' the buck as the older ones done. 'Cuttin' the buck' is what I calls the kind of frolics they had atter they got full of liquor.

"Yes, mam, they had dances all right. That's how they got mixed up with the paterollers. Negroes would go off to dances and stay out all night; it would be wuk time when they got back, and they went to the field and tried to keep right on gwine, but the Good Lord soon cut 'em down. You couldn't talk to folks that tried to git by with things lak that; they warn't gwine to do no diffunt, nohow. When they ain't 'cepted at St. Peter's gate, I'se sho they's gwine to wish they had heeded folks that talked to 'em and tried to holp 'em.

"Weddin's? Didn't you know slaves didn't have sho'nough weddin's? If a slave man saw a girl to his lakin' and wanted her to make a home for him, he just axed her owner if it was all right to take her. If the owner said 'yes' then the man and girl settled down together and behaved theyselves. If the girl lived on one plantation and the man on another that was luck for the girl's marster, 'cause the chillun would belong to him.

"Right now I can't call to mind nothin' us played when I was a chap but marble games. Us made them marbles out of clay and baked 'em in the sun. Grown folks used to scare chillun 'bout Raw Head and Bloody Bones, but that was mostly to make chillun git still and quiet at night. I ain't never seed no ghost in my life, but I has heared a heap of sounds and warn't able to find out what made them noises.

"When slaves got sick Marse Robert was good enough to 'em; he treated 'em right, and allus sont for a doctor, 'specially when chillun was borned. Oil, turpentine, and salts was the medicines the doctors give the most of to slaves. 'Fore they was sick enough to send for the doctor the homefolks often give sick folks boneset and life-everlastin' teas, and 'most evvybody wore a little sack of asafetida 'round their necks to protect 'em from diseases.

"When freedom come I was down in the lower end of Clarke County on Marse George Veal's plantation whar Marse Robert had done sont Miss Martha and the chillun and part of the slaves too. My white folks was fleein' from the Yankees. Marse Robert couldn't come 'long 'cause he had done been wounded in battle and when they sont him home from the war he couldn't walk. I don't know what he said to the slaves that was left thar to 'tend him, but I heared tell that he didn't tell 'em nothin' 'bout freedom, leastwise not for sometime. Pretty soon the Yankees come through and had the slaves come together in town whar they had a speakin' and told them Negroes they was free, and that they didn't belong to nobody no more. Them Yankees said orders for that pernouncement had come from the President of the United States, Mr. Abraham Lincoln, and they said that Mr. Lincoln was to be a father to the slaves atter he had done freed 'em.

"It warn't long then 'fore Marse Robert sont my pa to fetch Miss Martha and her chillun, and the slaves too, back to the old plantation. Pa wuked for him 'til June of the next year and then rented a farm on shares.

"I heared 'bout night-riders, but I never seed none of 'em. It was said they tuk Negroes out of their cabins and beat 'em up jus' 'cause they belonged to the Negro race. Negroes was free but they warn't 'lowed to act lak free people. Three months atter the war, schools was opened up here for Negroes and they was in charge of Yankee teachers. I can't call back the name of the Yankee woman that taught me.

"It was several years before no Negroes was able to buy land, and thar was just a few of 'em done it to start with. Negroes had to go to school fust and git larnin' so they would know how to keep some of them white folks from gittin' land 'way from 'em if they did buy it.

"Slavery time customs had changed a good bit when I married Ella Strickland. Us had a common little home affair at her ma's house. I never will forgit how Ella looked that day in her dove-colored weddin' dress; it was made with a plain, close-fittin' waist that had pretty lace 'round the neck and sleeves. Her skirt was plaited, and over it was draped a overskirt that was edged with lace. The Good Lord gave us seven children, but three of 'em He has taken from the land of the livin'. Us still has two boys and two girls. Sam wuks at a big clubhouse in Washington, D.C., and his four chillun are the onliest grandchillun me and Ella's got, so far as us knows. Charlie's job is at the Pennsylvania Station. Both of our daughters is teachers; one of 'em teaches at the Union Baptist School, here in Athens, and the other's at a school in Statesboro, Georgia. Yes, mam, Ella's still livin', but she is bad off with her foots. If the Lord lets us both live 'til this comin' December, us will celebrate our 53rd. Weddin' anniversary.

"Now that its all been over more than 70 years and us is had time to study it over good, I thinks it was by God's own plan that President Abraham Lincoln sot us free, and I can't sing his praises enough. Miss Martha named me for Jeff Davis, so I can't down him when I'se got his name; I was named for him and Benjamin Franklin too. Oh! Sho, I'd ruther be free and I believes the Negroes is got as much right to freedom as any other race, 'deed I does believe that.

"Why did I jine the church? 'Cause I was converted by the power of the Holy Spirit. I thinks all people ought to be 'ligious, to be more lak Christ; He is our Saviour. I'se been in the church 53 years and 'bout 52 of them years I'se been a-preachin'. I went one year to the Atlanta Baptist College to git my trainin' for the ministry, and I would have gone back, but me and Ella got married. I'se been pastor of the Friendship Baptist Church 48 years. In all, I'se been pastor of eight churches; I'se got three regular churches now."

A Negro boy came to the door and asked Jeff to tell him about some work. As Jeff arose he said: "If you is through with me, I'll have to go now and help this boy. I'se 'titled to one of them books with my story in it free, 'cause I'se a preacher, and I knows I'se give you the best story you has wrote up yit."

Slave Narratives

SUBJECT: [HW: Robert Henry]—EX-SLAVE
DISTRICT: W.P.A. NO. 1
RESEARCH WORKER: JOSEPH E. JAFFEE
EDITOR: JOHN N. BOOTH
SUPERVISOR: JOSEPH E. JAFFFEE (ASST.)

PLANTATION LIFE, AS VIEWED BY AN EX-SLAVE

United States. Work Projects Administration

ROBERT HENRY

Uncle Robert Henry, an active 82, now lives with his daughter on Billups Street in Athens. At the time of our visit he was immaculate in dark trousers, a tweed sack coat, and a gayly striped tie. Naturally the question came to mind as to whether he found life more pleasant in his daughter's neat little cottage, with its well kept yards, or in the quarters on "Ole Marster's plantation." He seemed delighted to have an opportunity to talk about "slave'y days"; and although he could not have been more than 11 years old at the time, he has a very vivid recollection of the "year de war broke and freedom came."

His parents, Robert and Martha Henry, were born in Oglethorpe County and were later purchased by P.W. Sayles, who owned a 1,000-acre plantation about 18 miles from Washington, in Wilkes County. Ga. "Marster didn't have many niggers, not more'n 70," he stated.

Uncle Robert was the oldest of 8 children, 5 boys and 3 girls. "Pa wuz de butler at de big house," he declared with pride in his voice; and he went on to tell how his mother had been the head seamstress on the plantation and how, at the tender age of 8, his father had begun training him to "wait on Marster's table".

The picture of "Old Marster's" household, as the old man unfolds it to his listeners, is one of almost idyllic beauty. There was the white-pillared "big house" in a grove of white oaks on the brow of a hill with a commanding view of the whole countryside. A gravelled driveway led down to the dusty public road where an occasional stagecoach rattled by and which later echoed with the hoofbeats of Confederate Cavalry.

The master's house contained twelve rooms, each about 16 x 16 feet. The kitchen was in the back yard and food was carried to the dining room in the high basement to the big house by means of an underground passage. Two servants stood guard over the table with huge fans made of peacock feathers which they kept in continuous motion during meals to "shoo de flies away."

The slave quarters were on the banks of a creek down the hill behind the big house. Nearby were the overseer's cottage, the stables, and the carriage houses.

In the family were: "Marster, Mistis, Mis' Fannie, Mis' Sally, Mars' Thomas, Mars' Hickey, and Mars' Wyatt. Dey all 'tended a school on de plantation." Two of the boys went to the war but only one of them came back.

After the war the "Yanks" came by and took nearly all the stock that the servants hadn't hidden in the swamps and all the silver that "Ole Mistis" hadn't buried under the currant bushes.

Yes, in spite of the hard work required, life was very pleasant on the plantations. The field hands were at work at sun-up and were not allowed to quit until dark. Each slave had an acre or two of land which he was allowed to farm for himself. He used Saturday morning to cultivate his own crop and on Saturday afternoon he lolled around or went fishing or visiting. Saturday nights were always the time for dancing and frolicking. The master sometimes let them use a barn loft for a big square dance. The musical instruments consisted of fiddles; buckets, which were beaten with the hands; and reeds, called "blowing quills," which were used in the manner of a flute.

There were two churches on the plantation, "one for de white folks and one fer de niggers." The same preacher held forth in both congregations. When there were services in the white church there was no negro meetings; but negroes were allowed to sit in the gallery of the "white folk'" church.

The master regarded his slaves as valuable piece of [HW:] property and they received treatment as such. When they were ill the doctor would be sent for or "Old Mistis" would come to the cabins bringing her basket of oil, pills, and linament.

Food was always given out to the slaves from the commissary and the smokehouse. There was flour and corn meal, dried beans and other vegetables, and cured pork and beef in the winter. In season the servants had access to the master's vegetable garden and they were always given as much milk as they could use.

Life [HW:] was very pleasant in those times; but Uncle Robert, at ease in a comfortable rocker, would not agree that it was more to his liking than this present-day existence.

When the subject of signs and omens was broached he waxed voluble in denying that he believed in any such "foolishment." However, he agreed that many believed that a rooster crowing in front of the door meant that a stranger was coming and that an owl screeching was a sign of death. He suggested that a successful means of combatting the latter omen is to tie knots in the bed sheets or to heat a poker in the fire. In case of death, Uncle Robert says, to be on the safe side and prevent another death in the family, it is wise to stop the clock and turn its face to the wall and to cover all the mirrors in the house with white cloths. Uncle Robert's highly educated daughter smiled indulgently on him while he was giving voice to these opinions and we left him threatening her with dire punishment if she should ever fail to carry out his instructions in matters of this nature.

[HW: Robert Henry Ex-slave]
FEDERAL WRITERS' PROJECT
W.P.A. OFFICE
787 COBB STREET
ATHENS, GEORGIA
OCTOBER 16, 1936

Mr. John L. Peters, Director
W.P.A. District No. 2
708 Telfair Street
Augusta, Georgia

Attention:
Mrs. Carolyn P. Dillard
State Director
Federal Writers' Projects
Atlanta, Georgia

Dear Mr. Peters:

Attaching herewith story of an ex-slave prepared by Mr. John Booth from my notes and is in accordance with the instructions contained in your letter of October 13. The snap-shots are by Jaffee.

We have located a former slave of Dr. Crawford W. Long in Jackson county and we plan to interview the 'darky' in the very near future. We are anxious to get a very intimate picture of Dr. Crawford W. Long from the eyes of one of his personal servants.

Very truly yours,

[HW: Joseph E. Jaffee]
Joseph E. Jaffee
Asst. District Supervisor
Federal Writers' Project
W.P.A. District No. 1
JEJ:H

JOHN HILL
1525 Broad Street
Athens, Georgia

PLANTATION LIFE, AS VIEWED BY AN EX-SLAVE

Written By:
Grace McCune
Research Worker
Federal Writers' Project
Athens, Georgia

Edited By:
Leila Harris
Editor
Federal Writers' Project
Augusta, Georgia

JOHN HILL
Ex-Slave, Age 74
1525 W. Broad St.
Athens, Georgia

JOHN HILL

John Hill, an old Negro about 74 years old, was seated comfortably on the front porch of his little cabin enjoying the sunshine. He lives alone and his pleasure was evident at having company, and better still an appreciative audience to whom he could relate the story of his early days.

"My pa wuz George Washin'ton Hill. His old Marster wuz Mr. Aubie Hill, an' dey all lived on de Hill Plantation, in de Buncombe district, nigh whar Monroe, Georgia is now. My ma wuz Lucy Annie Carter, an' she b'longed to de Carter fambly down in Oglethorpe County, 'til she wuz sold on de block, on de ole Tuck plantation, whar dey had a regular place to sell 'em. Dey put 'em up on a big old block, an' de highest bidder got de Nigger. Marse George Hill bought my ma, an' she come to stay on de Hill plantation. Dar's whar my pa married her, an' dar's whar I wuz borned.

"When I wuz just a little tike, I toted nails for 'em to build de jailhouse. Dey got 'bout two by four planks, nailed 'em crossways, an' den dey drived nails in, 'bout evvy inch or two apart, just lak a checkerboard. When dey got it done, dat jail would evermo' keep you on de inside. Dere wuz a place wid a rope to let down, when de jailbirds would need somethin', or when somebody wanted to send somethin' up to 'em. No Ma'am, dat warn't de rope dey used to hang folkses wid.

"My pa stayed on wid old Marster 'bout ten years atter de War, den us moved to de farm wid de Walkers at Monroe, Georgia. Dat wuz Governor Walker's pa. Dere wuz a red clay bank on de side of de crick whar us chilluns had our swimmmin' hole, an' us didn't know when us wuz a frolickin' an' rollin' young Marse Clifford down dat bank, dat someday he would be gov'ner of Georgia. He evermo' wuz a sight, kivered wid all dat red mud, an' Mist'ess, she would fuss an' say she wuz goin' to whup evvyone of us, but us just stayed out of de way an' she never cotched us. Den she would forgit 'til de nex' time.

"When I wuz 'bout eight years old, dey 'lowed it wuz high time I wuz a larnin' somethin', an' I wuz sont to de little log schoolhouse down in de woods. De onliest book I had wuz just a old blue back speller. Us took corn an' 'tatoes 'long an' cooked 'em for dinner, for den us had to stay all day at school. Us biled de corn an' roasted 'tatoes in ashes, an' dey tasted mighty good.

"Us had corn pone to eat all de time, an' on de fust Sunday in de month us had cake bread, 'cause it wuz church day. Cake bread wuz made out of shorts, but dem biscuits wuz mighty good if dey wuz dark, 'stead of bein' white.

"Us had big gyardens, an' raised all sorts of vegetables: corn, peas, beans, 'tatoes, colla'ds, an' turnip greens. Us had plenty of milk an' butter all de time. An' Marster made us raise lots of cows, hogs, sheep, an' chickens, an' tukkeys.

"Dey warn't no ready made clo'es or no vittuls in cans at de sto'keepers' places, an' us didn't have no money to spend, if dey had a been dar. Us didn't have nothin' what us didn't raise an' make up. Cotton had to be picked offen de seed, an' washed an' cyarded, den ma spun de thread an' wove de cloth an' sometimes she dyed it wid ink balls, 'fore it wuz ready to make clo'es out of. De ink Marster used to write wid wuz made out of ink balls.

"I wuz still little when my ma died. De white folks' preacher preached her fun'ral from de tex' of Isaiah fifth chapter: fust verse, an' dey sung de old song, "Goin' Home to Die no Mo'." Den dey buried her on de place, an' built a rail fence 'roun' de grave, to keep de stock from trompin' on it. Sometimes several owners got together an' had one place to bury all de slaves, an' den dey built a rail fence all 'roun' de whole place.

"Hit wuz just lak bein' in jail, de way us had to stay on de place, 'cause if us went off an' didn't have no ticket de paddyrollers would always git us, an' dey evermore did beat up some of de Niggers.

"I 'members de Klu Klux Klan good. Dey kept Niggers skeered plum to death, an' when dey done sumpin' brash dey sho' got beat up if de Kluxers cotched 'em.

"One time de Kluxers come by our place on de way to beat a old Nigger man. I begged 'em to lemme go wid 'em, an' atter a while dey said I could go. Dere wuz horns on de mask dey kivvered up my head wid an' I wuz mighty skeered but I didn't say nothin'. Atter us got dar, dey tied de old man up by his hands to de rafters in his house. He wuz beggin' 'em to let him off an' yellin' 'O Lordy, have mussy!' Dere wuz a little gal dar an' I wanted to skeer her, so I started atter her, an' de old man tole her to hit me on de head. She picked up a shovel an' th'owed it an' cut my leg so wide open de blood just spilt down on de floor. I got so bad off dey had to take me back to old Marster, an' he fix me up. Hit wuz six months 'fore I could use dat leg good, an', I nebber did wanter go wid dem Kluxers no more.

"Us went to de white folkses church, but onct a year on de fust Sunday in Augus' de white folkses let de Niggers have dat day for camp meetin'. Dey fixed good dinners for us, an' let us go off in de woods an' stay all day. Dem chicken pies an' dem good old 'tato custards, 'bout one an' a half inches thick, made wid sea sugar, dey make your mouf water just to talk 'bout 'em. What wuz sea sugar? Why it wuz dat crawly, kind of grayish, lookin' sugar us used den. I wuz grown 'fore I ever seed no sho' 'nough white sugar.

"My pa hired me out to Mr. Ray Kempton to tote cotton to de gin on his plantation, when I wuz 'bout 16 years old. I wuz wukkin' dar when de fust railroad wuz laid, an' dey named de place Kempton station fer Marse Ray Kempton. I wuz paid five dollars a month an' board for my wuk, an' I stayed dar 'til I married.

"I wuz 'bout eighteen when I rode on de train for de fust time. Us rode from Social Circle to Washin'ton, Wilkes, to see my ma's folkses. Ma tuk a heap of ginger cakes an' fried chicken along for us to eat on de train, an' de swingin' an' swayin' of dat train made me so sick I didn't want to ride no more for a long time.

"Soon atter I wuz twenty years old, I married a gal from Washin'ton, Wilkes, an' us moved to Athens, an' I been livin' right here ever since. Us got here de last day de old whiskey house wuz open. Dey closed it down dat night. I wukked a long time wid de Allgood boys in de horse tradin' business an' den I wukked for Mr. an' Mrs. Will Peeples 'bout ten years. Dey runned a boardin' house, an' while I wuz dar, Dr. Walker come to board, an' I wuz mighty glad to wait on him, 'cause he wuz from Monroe an' had done been livin' on de old Walker place dat I stayed at when us wuz down dar.

"My uncle, Ambus Carter, wuz a preacher on Marse Jim Smith's place. He b'longed to Marse Jim durin' de War, an' he never did leave him. Atter freedom come, most of Marse Jim's Niggers lef' him, an' den he had what dey called chaingang slaves. He paid 'em out of jail for 'em to wuk for him. An' he let 'em have money all de time so dey didn't never git out of debt wid him. Dey had to stay dar an' wuk all de time, an' if dey didn't wuk he had 'em beat. He evermore did beat 'em if dey got lazy, but if dey wukked good, he wuz good to 'em. Sometimes dey tried to run away. Dey had dogs to trail 'em wid so dey always cotched 'em, an' den da whippin' boss beat 'em mos' to death. It wuz awful to hear 'em hollerin' an' beggin' for mussy. If dey hollered, 'Lord have mussy!' Marse Jim didn't hear 'em, but if dey cried, 'Marse Jim have mussy!' den he made 'em stop de beatin'. He say, 'De Lord rule Heb'en, but Jim Smith ruled de earth.'

"One time he cotched some Niggers down at de Seaboard Station, what had runned away from his place. He got de police, an' brung 'em back 'cause he 'lowed dey still owed him money. I wuz mighty sorry for 'em, for I knowed what dey wuz goin' to git when he done got 'em back on his place. Dat whippin' boss beat 'em 'til dey couldn't stan' up.

"But he wuz good to my uncle, an' treated him just lak one of de fambly. He helped him wid all his sermons, an' told him to always tell 'em to be observerant an' obejent to de boss man. He provided good fer his help an' dey always had plenty to eat. He used to try to git me to come an' stay wid him, but I didn't want to stay on dat place.

"Marse Jim used to have big 'possum hunts for his Niggers, an' he would sen' me word, an' I most always went, 'cause dem wuz good times den, when dey cooked de coons an' 'possums, an' eat an' drunk mos' of de night. Coon meat is most as good as lamb if you is careful to take out de musk sacs when you dress 'em to cook."

Smithsonia, the Jim Smith plantation, covered thousands of acres, but the words of the feeble old Negro showed that he could not imagine it possible for any farmer to own more than one hundred acres.

"Marse Jim had a hund'ud acre farm, an' he had to keep plenty of Niggers to look atter dat place, but I wuz 'fraid to go dar to stay, for it wuz sho' just lak de jailhouse.

"Dey ain't but four of our nine chilluns livin' now an' dey's all up Nawf. Dey done sont atter me when deir ma died, an' tried to git me to stay wid 'em, but its too cold up dar for dis old Nigger, so I just stays on here by myself. It don't take much for me to live on. In crop times I wuks in de fiel' a choppin' cotton, an' I picks cotton too. I'll just wait on here an' de waitin' won't be much longer, 'cause I'se a living right, an', 'Praise de Lawd,' I'se a gwine to Heb'en w'en I die."

United States. Work Projects Administration

Mary A. Crawford
Re-search Worker

Laura Hood
Ex-Slave

LAURA HOOD

Laura was born in Griffin December 23, 1850 on Mr. Henry Bank's place. Her mother, Sylvia Banks (called "Cely Ann" by the darkies) married her father, Joe Brawner, a carpenter, who was owned by Mr. Henry Brawner.

Joe and Sylvia were married in Mr. Henry Bank's parlor by this white preacher.

Mr. Banks, Laura's master, owned a tannery in Griffin and had "around fifty slaves" according to Laura's memory. Most of the slaves worked at the tannery, the others at Mr. Bank's home. Laura's mother was the cook in the Bank's home for over forty years. Joe, Laura's father, was a carpenter and the four little darkies of the family helped about the house and yard doing such work as feeding the chickens, sweeping the yards and waiting on the Mistress. Laura, herself was a "house girl", that is, she made the beds, swept the floors and sewed and helped the Mistress do the mending for the family.

When asked if the Master and Mistress were good to the slaves, Laura replied that they certainly were, adding, "Marse Henry was as good a man as ever put a pair of pants on his legs." As to the punishments used by the

Banks, Laura was almost indignant at such a question, saying that Marse Henry never whipped or punished his darkies in any way, that he did not believe in it. The only whipping that Laura herself ever had was one lick across the shoulders with a small switch used by her Mistress to keep her mother, Celie Ann, from whipping her.

Laura relates that the darkies worked all the time except Sunday. On Sunday they could do as they pleased so long as they went to church. All the Bank's darkies attended service in the "cellar" (basement) of the First Baptist Church and had a colored preacher.

When any of the darkies were sick if 'ole Marster' and 'ole Miss' could not "set them straight" they called in "ole Marse's" white doctor.

Mr. Banks, himself, was too old "to fight the Yankees" but young 'Marse Henry' fought but did not "get a scratch" and when he came home all of them were sure glad to see him.

"After freedom, when 'ole Mars' was gone, 'young Marster' was as good as gold to all the darkies." Laura can remember when he gave her $5.00 to $20.00 at a time."

She also recalls that when the slaves were freed that her ole Marse called all of the darkies around him out in the yard and told them that they were as free as he was and could leave if they wanted to, but if they would stay 'till Christmas and help him that he would pay them wages. All of them stayed except one Negro named "Big John" who left with a bunch of Yankees that came along soon after.

As to what happened at the Bank's home when the Yankees came through, Laura does not remember, but she does recall that the Banks family "refugeed to Florida to get out of the path of the Yankees."

"No, mam," said Laura in reply to the question "Did your master have his slaves taught to read and write?" "We never had any school of any kind on the Bank's place. 'Marse Henry did not believe we needed that."

Laura has lived in her present home since 1867 and recalls when Griffin was "mostly a big woods full of paths here and there." She recalls the "auction block" which was on or near the site of the present Court House.

The old woman is very feeble, in fact, unable to walk but is cared for by a niece.

    Laura Pood
    432 E. Solomon Street
    Griffin, Georgia
    September 23, 1936

United States. Work Projects Administration

PLANTATION LIFE as viewed by Ex-Slave

CARRIE HUDSON
258 Lyndon Avenue
Athens, Georgia.

Written by: Sadie B. Hornsby
Athens —

Edited by: Sarah H. Hall
Athens —

Leila Harris
Augusta —

and

John N. Booth
District Supervisor
Federal Writers' Project
Residencies 6 & 7.

CARRIE HUDSON
Ex-Slave—Age 75

CARRIE HUDSON

Carrie was asked to relate her memories of childhood days on the old plantation. "I'se done most forgot 'bout dem days," she replied, "but if you ax me some questions hit mought come back to me. Hit's such a fur way back dat I don't never think 'bout dem times no more." After a few reminders, the old Negress began eagerly volunteering her recollections.

"Slave traders fotched my Pa, he was Phil Rucker,

f'um Richmond, Virginny, and sold him to Marse Joe Squire Rucker. Ma, she was Frances Rucker, was borned on Marse Joe's place nigh Ruckersville, up in Elbert County, and all 10 of us chilluns was born on dat plantation too. Hester Ann, Loke Ann, Elizabeth, Mary, Minnie Bright, Dawson, Ant'ony, Squire and Philip was my sisters and brothers. Grandma Bessie done de cookin' at de big house. Grandpa Ant'ony had done died long 'fore I got big enough to know nothin' 'bout him.

"Miss, chilluns what was knee high to a duck had to wuk. 'Til dey was big and strong enough for field wuk, little Niggers done all sorts of piddlin' jobs. Dey toted water to de big house and to de hands in de fields, fotched in chips and wood, and watched de cows. Me? I nussed most of de time. If dere was any money give out for slaves' wuk de grown folkses got it all, for I never seed none and I never heared 'bout no Niggers gittin' none in slavery times.

"Us lived in log cabins scattered 'round de plantation. De biggest of 'em had two rooms and evvy cabin had a chimbly made out of sticks and red mud. Most of de chillun slept on pallets on de floor, but I slept wid my Pa and Ma 'cause I was so pettish. Most of de beds was made out of poles, dis a-way: Dey bored two holes in de wall, wide apart as dey wanted de bed, and in dese holes dey stuck one end of de poles what was de side pieces. Dey sharpened de ends of two more poles and driv' 'em in de floor for de foot pieces and fastened de side pieces to 'em. Planks was put acrost dis frame to hold a coarse cloth tick filled wid wheat straw. Ma had a ruffle, what was called a foot bouncer, 'round de foot of her bed. Beds up at de big house was a sight to see. Dey had high posties and curtains over de top and 'round de bottom of deir beds. Dem beds at de big house was so high dey had steps to walk up so dey could git in 'em. Oh, dey was pretty, all kivvered over wid bob' net to keep flies and skeeters off de white folkses whilst dey slept!

"Warn't nothin' short 'bout de eats. Our white folkses b'lieved in good eatin's. Dey give us bread and meat wid all de cabbage, colla'd and turnip greens us wanted, and us had 'matoes, 'tatoes, chickens and ducks. Yessum, and dere allus was plenty 'possums and rabbits cooked 'bout lak dey is now, only dere warn't no stoves in dem days. Pots for biling swung on racks dey called cranes, over de coals in big open fireplaces. Baking was done in ovens and skillets. Dere was allus lots of fishes in season, but I didn't do none of de fishin', 'cause I was too skeered of de water when I was a chap.

"All de cloth for our clothes was wove in de loom room up at de big house. Little gal's dresses was made just lak deir Ma's, wid full skirts gathered on to plain, close fittin' waisties. Little boys just wore shirts. Didn't no chillun wear but one piece of clothes in summer. Winter time us wore de same only dey give us a warm underskirt, and rough red brogan shoes. Didn't no Niggers wear shoes in warm weather durin' slavery times.

"Marse Joe Squire Rucker was de fust Marster of our plantation. Atter him and Miss Peggy done died, his son, Marse Elbert Rucker tuk up where his Pa left off. I can't call to mind nothin' 'bout Marse Joe and Miss Peggy 'cept what old folkses told me long atter dey done died, but I does 'member Marse Elbert and Miss Sallie and dey was just as good to us as dey could be. De onliest ones of dier chilluns I ricollects now is Miss Bessie, Miss Cora and Marsters Joe, Guy, Marion and Early. Dey all lived in a big fine house sot back f'um de road a piece.

"Marse Elbert's overseer was a Mr. Alderman. He got de slaves up early in de mornin' and it was black night 'fore he fotched 'em in. Marse Elbert didn't 'low nobody to lay hands on his Niggers but his own self. If any whuppin' had to be done, he done it.

"My brother, Squire, was de carriage driver and he was all time a-drivin' our white folkses to Ruckersville, and sometimes he driv' 'em far as Anderson, South Callina.

"To tell de truth, Missy, I don't know how many acres was in dat big old plantation. Dere just ain't no tellin'. Niggers was scattered over dat great big place lak flies. When dey come in f'um de fields at night, dem slaves was glad to just go to sleep and rest.

"Dey didn't do no field wuk atter dinner on Saddays. De 'omans washed, ironed and cleaned up deir cabins, while de mens piddled 'roun' and got de tools and harness and things lak dat ready for de next week's wuk.

"I heared 'em say dere was a jail at Ruckersville, but so far as I knows dere warn't no slaves ever put in jail. Niggers didn't have no chance to git in devilment, 'cause de overseers and patterollers kep' close atter 'em all de time, and slaves what stepped aside allus got a whuppin'. Dere warn't no time for to larn readin' and writin' on Marse Elbert's plantation. Dem slaves knowed what a Bible was but dey sho' couldn't read de fust line. Us went to white folkses church on Sundays, and while I never tuk in none of dem songs us sung, I sho'ly do ricollect moughty well how de Reverend Duncan would come down on dat preachin'.

"Lordy, Miss! Dere you is a-axing me 'bout folkses dyin', and I'se nigh dead myself! Brother 'lisha done prophesied you was a-comin' here for to write a jedgment, and hit makes me feel right creepy. Anyhow I seed a heaps of folkses died out and git put in dem homemade coffins what was black as sin. I sho' is glad dey done changed de color of coffins. I 'members how us used to holler and cry when dey come to de part of de fun'ral whar dey sung: 'Hark F'um De Tomb, A Doleful Sound.'

"Dere was a heap of baptizin's dem days and I went to most all of 'em, but I sho' warn't baptized 'til long atter I got grown, 'cause I was so skeered of de water. I kin see dem folkses now, a-marchin' down to de crick, back of de church, and all de can-i-dates dressed in de whites' white clothes, what was de style den. Evvybody jined in de singin', and de words was lak dis:

> 'Marchin' for de water
> For to be baptized.
> De Lord done lit de candle
> On de other side
> For to see his chilluns
> When dey gits baptized.'

"Niggers on Marse Elbert's place never knowed nothin' 'bout no North; if dey did dey wouldn't tell it to chilluns little as I was den. Dere was some sort of uprisin' a good piece f'um Ruckersville, but I can't tell you 'bout it 'cause I just heared de old folkses do a little talkin', what warn't enough to larn de whole tale. Chillun back dar didn't jine in de old folkses business lak dey does now.

"Sadday nights de young folkses picked de banjo, danced and cut de buck 'til long atter midnight, but Christmas times was when chilluns had deir bestes' good times. Marse Elbert 'ranged to have hog killin' close enough to Christmas so dere would be plenty of fresh meat, and dere was heaps of good chickens, tukkeys, cake, candies, and just evvything good. En durin' de Christmas, slaves visited 'roun' f'um house to house, but New Year's Day was wuk time again, and dere was allus plenty to do on dat plantation. Most all de Niggers loved to go to dem cornshuckin's, 'cause atter de corn was all shucked dey give 'em big suppers and let 'em dance. De cotton pickin's was on nights when de moon was extra bright 'cause dey couldn't do much lightin' up a big cotton field wid torches lak dey did de places where dey had de cornshuckin's. Atter cornshuckin's, dey mought be dancin' by de light of torches, but us danced in de moonlight when de cotton was picked and de prize done been give out to de slave what picked de most. Logrollin's was de most fun of all. De men and 'omans would roll dem logs and sing and dey give 'em plenty of good eats, and whiskey by de kegs, at logrollin's. De Marsters, dey planned de cornshuckin's, and cotton pickin's, and logrollin's and pervided de eats and liquor, but de quiltin' parties b'longed to de slaves. Dey 'ranged 'em deir own selfs and done deir own 'vitin' and fixed up deir own eats, but most of de Marsters would let 'em have a little somepin' extra lak brown sugar or 'lasses and some liquor. De quiltin's was in de cabins, and dey allus had 'em in winter when dare warn't no field wuk. Dey would quilt a while and stop to eat apple pies, peach pies, and other good things and drink a little liquor.

"Us had to tote water and nuss chillun 'stid of playin' no games. Us didn't know nothin' 'bout ghosties, hants, and sich lak. Our white folkses would whup a Nigger for skeerin' us chillun quick as anything. Dey didn't 'low none of dat. De onliest ghost I'se ever seed was just t'other day. I seed somebody pass my door. I hollered out: 'Who dat?' Dey didn't say nothin'. Brother 'Lisha here said it was a sperrit passin' by. He must be right, 'cause whoever it was, dey didn't say nothin' 'tall.

"Marse Elbert and Miss Sallie was sho' moughty good when deir Niggers tuk sick. Castor oil and turpentine was what dey give 'em most of de time. Horehound tea was for colds, and elderberry tea was to help babies teethe easier. Yessum, us wore beads, but dey was just to look pretty.

"All I knows 'bout how come us was sot free is dat folkses said Mr. Jefferson Davis and Mr. Abraham Lincoln got to fightin' 'bout us, and Mr. Lincoln's side got de best of Mr. Davis' side in de quarrel. De day dey told us dat us was free dere was a white man named Mr. Bruce, what axed: 'What you say?' Dey told him 'gain dat all de Niggers was free. He bent hisself over, and never did straighten his body no more. When he died, he was still all bent over. Mr. Bruce done dis to sho' de world how he hated to give his Niggers up atter dey done been sot free.

"When dem Yankees come thoo' dey stole evvything dey could take off wid 'em. Dey tuk Sue, my brother's nice hoss, and left him a old poor bag-of-bones hoss. Us stayed on wid our white folkses a long time atter de War.

"Edwin Jones was my fust husband and I wore a pretty dove colored dress at our weddin'. Jenny Ann was our onliest child. All but one of our eight grandchillun is all livin' now, and I'se got 24 great grandchillun. Atter Edwin died, I married dis here Charlie Hudson what I'se livin' wid now. Us didn't have no big weddin' and tain't long since us got married. Me and Charlie ain't got no chillun.

"I jined de church 'cause I got 'ligion and I knows de good Lord done forgive my sins. Evvybody ought to git 'ligion and hold it and jine de church.

"De way us is a havin' to live now is pretty bad 'cause us is both too old to wuk. Don't give me dem slavery days no more 'cause I would have to wuk anyhow if I was a slave again! Us couldn't set 'roun' and smoke our pipes and do as us please. I'd ruther have it lak it is now.

"I can't 'member no more to tell you, but I sho' has 'joyed dis talk. Yessum, dem days was a fur piece back."

[TR: date stamp: MAY 28 1938]

PLANTATION LIFE as viewed by Ex-Slave

CHARLIE HUDSON
258 Lyndon Avenue
Athens, Georgia

Written by: Sadie B. Hornsby
Athens —

Edited by: Sarah H. Hall
Athens —

Leila Harris
Augusta —

and

John N. Booth
District Supervisor
Federal Writers' Project
Res. 6 & 7.
Augusta, Ga.

CHARLIE HUDSON Ex-Slave—Age 80.

CHARLIE HUDSON

Charlie listened with eager interest to the story related by Carrie, his wife, and frequent smiles played over his wrinkled black face as her reminiscences awakened memories of younger days. His delight was evident when the interviewer suggested that he tell his own impressions of slavery and the period following the War between the States.

"Miss," he said, "I been takin' in what de old 'oman done told you. Dat was de beginnin' way back yonder and de end is nigh. Soon dere won't be nobody left livin' what was a sho' 'nough slave. It's somepin' to think about, ain't it?

"Anyhow, I was born March 27, 1858 in Elbert County. Ma lived on de Bell plantation and Marse Matt Hudson owned my Pa and kept him on de Hudson place. Dere was seben of us chillun. Will, Bynam, John and me was de boys, and de gals was Amanda, Liza Ann, and Gussie. 'Til us was big enough to wuk, us played 'round de house 'bout lak chillun does dese days.

"Slave quarters was laid out lak streets. Us lived in log cabins. Beds? Dey was jus' makeshift beds, what was made out of pine poles. De side of de house was de head of de beds. De side rails was sharpened at both ends and driv' in holes in de walls and foot posties. Den dey put boards 'cross de side rails for de mattresses to lay on. De coarse cloth bed ticks was filled wid 'Georgy feathers.' Don't you know what Georgy feathers was? Wheat straw was Georgy feathers. Our kivver was sheets and plenty of good warm quilts. Now dat was at our own quarters on Marse David Bell's plantation.

"Didn't evvybody have as good places to sleep as us. I 'members a white fambly named Sims what lived in Flatwoods. Dey was de porest white folks I ever seed. Dey had a big drove of chillun and deir Pa never wukked a lick in his life—He jus' lived on other folkses' labors. Deir little log cabin had a partition in it, and 'hind dat partition dere warn't a stitch of nothin'. Dey didn't have no floor but de ground, and back 'hind dat partition was dug out a little deeper dan in de rest of de house. Dey filled dat place wid leaves and dat's whar all de chilluns slept. Evvy day Miss Sallie made 'em take out de leaves what dey had slep' on de night before and fill de dugout wid fresh leaves. On de other side of de partition, Miss Sallie and her old man slept 'long wid deir hog, and hoss, and cow, and dat was whar dey cooked and et too. I ain't never gwine to forgit dem white folks.

"My grandma Patsy, Pappy's Ma, knocked 'round lookin' atter de sheep and hogs, close to de house, 'cause she was too old for field wuk. Ma's Mammy was my grandma Rose. Her job was drivin' de oxcart to haul in wood from de new grounds and to take wheat and corn to mill and fetch back good old home-made flour and meal. I never did hear nothin' 'bout my grandpas. Ma done de cookin' for de white folks.

"I don't know if I was no pet, but I did stay up at de big house most of de time, and one thing I loved to do up dar was to follow Miss Betsy 'round totin' her sewin' basket. When wuk got tight and hot in crop time, I helped de other chillun tote water to de hands. De bucket would slamp 'gainst my laigs all along de way, and most of de water would be done splashed out 'fore I got to de field.

"Marse David and his fambly most allus sont deir notes and messages by me and another yearlin' boy what was 'lowed to lay 'round de big house yard so us would be handy to wait on our white folks. Dey give you de note what dey done writ, and dey say: 'Boy, if you lose dis note, you'll git a whuppin'! All de time you was carryin' dem notes you had your whuppin' in your hand and didn't know it, lessen you lost de note. I never heared of no trouble to 'mount to nothin' twixt white folks and Niggers in our settlement.

"Us et good, not much diff'unt f'um what us does now. Most times it was meat and bread wid turnip greens, lye hominy, milk, and butter. All our cookin' was done on open fireplaces. Oh! I was fond of 'possums, sprinkled wid butter and pepper, and baked down 'til de gravy was good and brown. You was lucky if you got to eat 'possum and gnaw de bones atter my Ma done cooked it.

"Dey cotch rabbits wid dogs. Now and den, a crowd of Niggers would jump a rabbit when no dogs was 'round. Dey would tho' rocks at him and run him in a hollow log. Den dey would twiss him out wid hickory wisps (withes). Sometimes dere warn't no fur left on de rabbit time dey got him twisted out, but dat was all right. Dey jus' slapped him over daid and tuk him on to de cabin to be cooked. Rabbits was most gen'ally fried.

"Grown boys didn't want us chillun goin' 'long 'possum huntin' wid 'em, so all right, dey tuk us way off crost de fields 'til dey found a good thick clump of bushes, and den dey would holler out dat dere was some moughty fine snipes 'round dar. Dey made us hold de poke (bag) open so de snipes could run in. Den dey blowed out deir light'ood knot torches, and left us chillun holdin' de poke whilst dey went on huntin' 'possums.

"Atter dinner Saddays all of us tuk our hooks, poles, and lines down to Dry Fork Crick, when it was de right time of de year to fish. Sometimes dey stewed fish for old folkses to eat, but young folkses loved 'em fried best.

"Winter time dey give chillun new cotton and wool mixed shirts what come down most to de ankles. By de time hot weather come de shirt was done wore thin and swunk up and 'sides dat, us had growed enough for 'em to be short on us, so us jus' wore dem same shirts right on thoo' de summer. On our place you went bar foots 'til you was a great big yearlin' 'fore you got no shoes. What you wore on yo' haid was a cap made out of scraps of cloth dey wove in de looms right dar on our plantation to make pants for de grown folks.

"Mr. David Bell, our Marster, was born clubfooted. His hands and foots was drawed up evvy which a way long as he lived. He was jus' lak a old tom cat, he was such a cusser. All he done was jus' set dar and cuss, and a heap of times you couldn't see nothin' for him to cuss 'bout. He tuk his crook-handled walkin' stick and cotch you and drug you up to him and den jus' helt you tight and cussed you to yo' face, but he didn't never whup nobody. Our Mist'ess, Miss Betsey, was allus moughty kind at times lak dat, and she used to give us chillun a heap of ginger cakes. Deir seben chilluns was Dr. Bynam, Marse David and little Misses Ad'line, Elizabeth, Mary and Mildred. Dey lived in a big old two-story house, but I done forgot how it looked.

"Dat overseer, he was a clever man, but I can't ricollect his name. He never paid no heed to what sort of clothes slaves wore, but he used to raise merry cain if dey didn't have good shoes to ditch in. Marse David was de cussin' boss, but de overseer called hisself de whuppin' boss. He had whuppin's all time saved up special for de 'omans. He made 'em take off deir waistes and den he whupped 'em on deir bar backs 'til he was satisfied. He done all de whuppin' atter supper by candle light. I don't 'member dat he ever whupped a man. He jus' whupped 'omans.

"Evvybody was up early so dat by sunrise dey was out

in de fields, jus' a whoopin' and hollerin'. At sundown dey stopped and come back to de cabins. In wheat harvestin' time dey wukked so hard dey jus' fell out f'um gittin' overhet. Other times dey jus' wukked 'long steady lak.

"Marse David never had no sho' 'nough car'iage so he never needed no car'iage driver. He had what dey called a ground sleigh. In de spring Marse David sont a man to de woods to pick out a lakly lookin' young white oak saplin' and bent it down a certain way. Hit stayed bent dat way 'til it growed big enough, den dey sawed it lengthways and put a mortise hole in each front piece to put de round thoo' to hold de singletrees. Holes was bored at de back to fasten de plank seat to. Dey put a quilt on de seat for a cushion and hitched a pair of oxen to de sleigh. Come winter, come summer, snow or rain, dey went right on in de old sleigh jus' de same!

"Now, Miss, dis sho' is right! Many times as I is done been over dat plantation f'um one side to de other I couldn't tell you to save my life how many acres was in it. I would be 'fraid to say, how many slaves Marse David owned, but I'm here to tell you dere was a bunch of 'em 'round dar.

"Dey didn't have no jail house or nothin' lak dat 'round dat plantation, 'cause if slaves didn't please Marster dey was jus' made to come up to de yard at de big house and take deir beatin's. I seed dem traders come thoo' f'um Virginny wid two wagon loads of slaves at one time, gwine down on Broad River to a place called Lisbon whar dey already had orders for 'em. I ain't never seed no slaves bein' sold or auctioned off on de block.

"Wunst a white man named Bill Rowsey, come and begged Marse David to let him teach his Niggers. Marse David had de grown mens go sweep up de cottonseed in de ginhouse on Sunday mornin', and for three Sundays us went to school. When us went on de fourth Sunday night riders had done made a shape lak a coffin in de sand out in front, and painted a sign on de ginhouse what read: 'No Niggers 'lowed to be taught in dis ginhouse.' Dat made Marse David so mad he jus' cussed and cussed. He 'lowed dat nobody warn't gwine tell him what to do. But us was too skeered to go back to de ginhouse to school. Next week Marse David had 'em build a brush arbor down by de crick, but when us went down dar on Sunday for school, us found de night riders had done 'stroyed de brush arbor, and dat was de end of my gwine to school.

"Dere warn't no church for slaves whar us was. Marse David give us a pass so us wouldn't be 'sturbed and let us go 'round from one plantation to another on Sundays for prayer meetin's in de cabins and under trees if de weather was warm and nice. Sometimes when dere was a jubilee comin' off, slaves was 'lowed to go to deir Marsters' church. Me? I used to ride 'hind Miss Betsey on her hoss what she called Puss, and away us went jiggin' down de road to jubilees at Millstone and Elam churches. I was a rich feelin' little Nigger den.

"De chillun had to take a back seat whilst de old folks done all de singin', so I never larned none of dem songs good 'nough to 'member what de words was, or de tunes neither. Now and den us went to a fun'ral, not often, but if dere was a baptizin' inside of 10 miles 'round f'um whar us lived, us didn't miss it. Us knowed how to walk, and went to git de pleasure.

"Atter slaves got in f'um de fields at night, de 'omans cooked supper whilst de mens chopped wood. Lessen de crops was in de grass moughty bad or somepin' else awful urgent, dere warn't no wuk done atter dinner on Saddays. De old folks ironed, cleant house, and de lak, and de young folks went out Sadday nights and danced to de music what dey made beatin' on tin pans. Sundays, youngsters went to de woods and hunted hickernuts and muscadines. De old folks stayed home and looked one anothers haids over for nits and lice. Whenever dey found anything, dey mashed it twixt dey finger and thumb and went ahead searchin'. Den de 'omans wropt each others hair de way it was to stay fixed 'til de next Sunday.

"Chris'mas us went f'um house to house lookin' for locust and persimmon beer. Chillun went to all de houses huntin' gingerbread. Ma used to roll it thin, cut it out wid a thimble, and give a dozen of dem little balls to each chile. Persimmon beer and gingerbread! What big times us did have at Chris'mas. New Year's Day, dey raked up de hoss and cow lots if de weather was good. Marster jus' made us wuk enough on New Year's Day to call it wukkin', so he could say he made us start de New Year right.

"Marse David had cornshuckin's what lasted two or three weeks at a time. Dey had a gen'ral to keep dem brash boys straight. De number of gen'rals 'pended on how much corn us had and how many slaves was shuckin' corn. Atter it was all shucked, dere was a big celebration in store for de slaves. Dey cooked up washpots full of lamb, kid, pork, and beef, and had collard greens dat was wu'th lookin' at. Dey had water buckets full of whiskey. When dem Niggers danced atter all dat eatin' and drinkin', it warn't rightly dancin'; it was wrastlin'.

"Dem moonlight cotton pickin's was big old times. Dey give prizes to de ones pickin' de most cotton. De prizes was apt to be a quart of whiskey for de man what picked de most and a dress for de 'oman what was ahead. Dem Niggers wouldn't take no time to empty cotton in baskets—jus' dumped it out quick on baggin' in de field.

"Day went f'um one plantation to another to quiltin's. Atter de 'omans got thoo' quiltin' and et a big dinner, den dey axed de mens to come in and dance wid 'em.

"Whenever any of our white folks' gals got married dere was two or three weeks of celebratin'. What a time us did have if it was one of our own little misses gittin' married! When de day 'rived, it was somepin' else. De white folks was dressed up to beat de band and all de slaves was up on deir toes to do evvything jus' right and to see all dey could. Atter de preacher done finished his words to de young couple, den dey had de sho' 'nough weddin' feast. Dere was all sorts of meat to choose f'um at weddin' dinners—turkeys, geese, chickens, peafowls, and guineas, not to mention good old ham and other meats.

"Pitchin' hoss shoes and playin' marbles was heaps and lots of fun when I was growin' up. Atter while, de old folks 'cided dem games was gamblin' and wouldn't let us play no more. I don't know nothin' t'all 'bout no ghosties. Us had 'nough to be skeered of widout takin' up no time wid dat sort of thing.

"When Marse David changed me f'um calf shepherd to cowboy, he sont three or four of us boys to drive de cows to a good place to graze 'cause de male beast was so mean and bad 'bout gittin' atter chillun, he thought if he sont enough of us dere wouldn't be no trouble.

Dem days, dere warn't no fence law, and calves was jus' turned loose in de pastur to graze. Da fust time I went by myself to drive de cows off to graze and come back wid 'em, Aunt Vinnie 'ported a bunch of de cows was missin', 'bout 20 of em, when she done de milkin' dat night, and I had to go back huntin' dem cows. De moon come out, bright and clear, but I couldn't see dem cows nowhar—didn't even hear de bell cow. Atter while I was standin' in de mayberry field a-lookin' crost Dry Fork Crick and dere was dem cows. De bell was pulled so clost on de bell cow's neck whar she was caught in de bushes, dat it couldn't ring. I looked at dem cows—den I looked at de crick whar I could see snakes as thick as de fingers on your hand, but I knowed I had to git dem cows back home, so I jus' lit out and loped 'cross dat crick so fast dem snakes never had no chanct to bite me. Dat was de wust racket I ever got in.

"Marse David and Miss Betsey tuk moughty good keer of deir Niggers, 'specially when dey was sick. Dr. Bynam Bell, deir oldest son, was a doctor but Miss Betsey was a powerful good hand at doctoring herself. She looked atter all da slave 'omans. For medicines dey give us asafiddy (asafetida), calomel, and castor oil more dan anything else for our diff'unt ailments.

"Marse David's nephew, Mr. Henry Bell, visited at de big house durin' de war, and he was cut down jus' a few days atter he left us and went back to de battlefield.

"Us had been hearin' fust one thing and another 'bout freedom might come, when one mornin' Mr. Will Bell, a patteroller, come ridin' on his hoss at top speed thoo' de rye field whar us was at wuk. Us made sho' he was atter some pore slave, 'til he yelled out: 'What you Niggers wukkin' for? Don't you know you is free as jay birds?' 'Bout dat time de trumpet blowed for dinner and us fell in line a-marchin' up to de big house. Marse David said: 'You all might jus' as well be free as anybody else.' Den he promised to give us somepin' to eat and wear if us would stay on wid him, and dere us did stay for 'bout three years atter de war. I was burnt up den, 'cause I didn't have de privilege of ridin' 'hind Miss Betsey on old Puss no more when she went to meetin'.

"Whar us lived, Ku Kluxers was called 'night thiefs.' Dey stole money and weepons (weapons) f'um Niggers atter de war. Dey tuk $50 in gold f'um me and $50 in Jeff Davis' shimplasters f'um my brother. Pa and Ma had left dat money for us to use when us got big enough. A few Niggers managed somehow to buy a little land. I couldn't rightly say when de school was set up.

"Me and Carrie Rucker, us ain't been married long. I thinks big weddin's is a foolish waste of time and money. Yessum, I'm moughty proud of all of Carrie's grandchillun and I'm fond of evvyone of dem 24 great-grandchillun of hers.

"Well, it was a God-sent method Mr. Lincoln used to give us our freedom. Mr. Davis didn't want no war, and he 'posed it all he knowed how, but if he hadn't a gone ahead and fit, dere never would have been nothin' done for us. Far as I knows, Booker Washin'ton done some good things in his day and time, but I don't know much 'bout him.

"In a way, I'm satisfied wid what confronts me. A pusson in jail or on de chaingang would ruther be outside and free dan in captivity. Dat's how I feels.

"When dey read dis passage of de Bible to me, I 'cided to jine up wid de church. 'Come ye out f'um amongst dem, and ye shall be my people.' I think evvybody ought to read dat verse, jine de church, and den live 'ligious lifes. I done been changed f'um darkness to light. 'Oh, for a closer walk wid God.'

"Yes Ma'am, Miss, I done been here a long time I done seed many come and go. Lots of changes has tuk place. I done told you 'bout f'um de cradle to de grave, and I enjoyed doin' it. All dat ricollectin' sho' tuk me back over many a rocky road, but dem was de days what ain't never gwine to be no more."

ANNIE HUFF, EX-SLAVE,
of near Macon, Georgia
Jul 28 1937

ANNIE HUFF

A large windmill beside the highway, on the Houston Road near Seven Bridges, draws the attention of a traveler to a two-story house, recently remodeled, which was the colonial home of Mr. Travis Huff, now occupied by Mrs. Rosa Melton, his grand-daughter. During the days of slavery the master and an indulgent mistress with their twelve slaves lived on this property. Mr. Huff's family was a large one, all of whom were well educated and very religious. Several of his daughters became teachers after the close of the Civil War.

Among the "quarter" families were Annie Huff and her daughters, Mary being the elder. The mother cooked and the small children learned to sweep the yard and to do minor jobs in the field at a very early age. At the age of twelve, the girls were taught to card and spin as well as to knit and were required to do a certain task each day until they were large enough to assist with the heavier work. The adult females did this type of work after sunset, when their labor in the field was over. On rainy days they shucked and shelled corn or did some other kind of indoor labor.

Generally, this group was humanely treated, but occasionally one was unmercifully beaten. In spite of the fact that there was only one male among his slaves, Mr.

Huff's outbursts of temper caused him to be so cruel that his daughters would frequently beg him to end his punishment.

Frolics were mostly given at corn shuckings, cane grindings, hog killings, or quiltings. At hog killing time, huge containers of water were heated in the yard. When it reached the desired temperature, the hogs were driven to a certain spot where they were struck a hard blow on the head. When they fell, they were stuck with a very sharp knife, then scalded in the boiling water. The hair and dirt were then scrubbed off and they were a pretty light color as they hung from a rack to be dressed. When the work was completed, the guests cooked chitterlings and made barbecue to be served with the usual gingercake and persimmon beer. They then dressed in their colorful "Sunday" garments, dyed with maple and dogwood bark, to engage in promenades, cotillions, etc., to the time of a quill instrument.

On Sunday, church services were held at Old Liberty Church where seats in the rear were provided for all adult slaves. The small children were not allowed to attend these services, but they frequently sneaked away from home and attended in spite of the restriction. It was expedient that they also leave before the close of the service, but often lingered on the roadside and waited for Mr. Huff to pass. He'd stop and ask them where they's been, and as they danced up and down they replied in chorus: "We've been to church, Master; we've been to church."

The presence of slave visitors was not encouraged, for Mr. Huff usually purchased women with children and there were no married couples living on his place. However, young Negro men would often sneak in the cabins at night—usually coming through the windows—and visit with their sweethearts.

Gifts of handkerchiefs and earrings were smuggled in strictly against the rules of the Master.

Children tattlers kept Mr. Huff informed regarding the happenings in the quarters, but their silence could be bought with a few shin plasters. This "hush" money and that made from running errands were enough to keep the children supplied with spending change. Often, when their childish prattle had caused some adult to be punished, Mrs. Huff would keep them in the house for a night to escape the wrath of the offender.

All food was raised on the plantation and cooked in the family kitchen. Every one had the same kind of food and the game caught or killed by the elder sons was a delicacy relished by all. When the family meal was served, a mischievous collection of black children would sometimes crawl under the table and meddle with each person seated there. Instead of being scolded, they would receive luscious morsels from the hands of the diners. Mrs. Huff often laughingly stated that she knew not which was more annoying—"the children or the chickens, as neither were disciplined."

Probably because of the absence of male slaves, no shoe-maker was maintained. Footwear for the entire group was purchased at Strong's Shoe Store in Macon.

Superstition was usually a part of the life of a slave. Those seeking to escape from a cruel Master used to rub turpentine on the soles of their feet to prevent capture. Others collected quantities of soil from a graveyard and sprinkled it in their tracks for a certain distance. Both of these precautions were used to throw the dogs off scent. Refugee slaves often found shelter on Mr. Huff' estate, where they were assisted in further flight by the Huff Negroes. Those who remained in the woods were fed regularly.

Mr. Huff was not in favor of emancipating the slaves. One of his sons, Ramsey Huff, fought in the Confederate Army.

The slaves rejoiced at every bit of news which they heard regarding the probability of their being freed by the Yankees. During the latter part of the war, people from Macon journeyed to the outlying swampy sections to hide their valuables, many of which were never recovered.

Mr. Huff owned a place in Houston County where he hid most of his provisions, but these were stolen before the close of the war. A few Yankees who visited his home did little damage beyond the destruction of a turnip patch.

When the war ended, Mr. Huff would not tell his slaves they were free, for, it was said, that he hated the thought of a Negro being able to wear a starched shirt. Slaves from neighboring plantations spread the news. A few days later Mrs. Huff returned from a trip to Macon and called all the children together to tell them that, even though they were free, they would have to remain with her until they were twenty-one. Little Mary exclaimed loudly—"I'm free! I won't stay here at all!"

When the Emancipation Proclamation was made

public, the Yankee soldiers gave a dinner in Macon for all Negroes and poor Whites who cared to come. A line was formed on the outside of the building in which the dinner was served and no one was allowed to enter unless he was in poor circumstances. Food of every description was served in abundance and all admitted were allowed to eat as much as they desired.

Annie Huff moved to Macon when she was freed and her daughter, Mary, now eighty-seven years old, was reared here. She attributed her long life to the excellent care she has always taken of herself.

Huff, Mary, 561 Cotton Avenue, Macon, Georgia

United States. Work Projects Administration

Adella S. Dixon
District 7
May 8 1937

Bryant Huff
Old Slave Story

BRYANT HUFF

Bryant Huff was the son of Janie and Daniel Huff who were born on neighboring plantations between Camack and Augusta. They were married while they still belonged to separate owners, but when "Marse" Jesse Rigerson, to whom Janie belonged, decided to move, he bought Daniel in order that he might live with his wife and family. They moved to Warren County and it was here that Bryant was born. He was one of twelve children.

Bryant's early life was not one to inspire pleasant memories for his master, a highly educated man; ardent church worker, had a cruel nature and a temper that knew no bounds. Owning 800 acres of land in a fairly level section, he ruled his small kingdom with an iron hand. Bryant's father, Daniel, was the only man who did not fear "Marse" Rigerson.

The quarters consisted of poorly constructed cabins with worse interiors. There were no beds, only bunks made of two poles balancing sides nailed to the walls. Rags and old clothing served as a mattress and the other furniture was equally bad. Food was cooked on an open fireplace and the frying pan was the most important utensil; vegetables were boiled in a swinging kettle. The griddle stood several inches from the floor, on three small pegs. Through the middle a "pin" was placed so that the griddle might revolve as the bread etc., cooked on the side near the hottest part of the fire. Matches, a luxury, were then sold in small boxes the size of the average snuff box at ten cents per box.

All the slaves worked from sunrise to sunset; the majority did field work. Women, as well as men, shared farm work. Small boys not old enough to be sent to the field, minded horses, drove cows to and from the pasture, and did chores around the "big house". A few women prepared meals and supervised a group of younger girls who did general work in the big house.

Sunday was the only day of rest and usually all the adults attended church. On this plantation a church with a colored Minister was provided and services, while conducted on the same order as those of the white churches, were much longer. Generally children were not allowed to attend church, but occasionally this privilege was granted to one. Huff recalls vividly his first visit to Sunday services. Being very small and eager to attend he sat quietly by his mother's side and gazed with wonder at the minister and congregation. An emotional outburst was part of the services and so many of the "sisters" got "happy" that the child, not having witnessed such a scene before, was frightened; as the number of shouters increased, he ran from the building screaming in terror.

Of the 12 children in his family, 2 were sold. The eldest child, Harriet, owned by a Judge who lived on a neighboring plantation, returned to the family after Emancipation. The father left home in a fit of anger because one of his children had been whipped. The master, knowing how devoted he was to his wife, placed her and her infant child in jail. Shortly afterward, the father returned and was allowed to visit his wife and to go unmolested. A few weeks later he came back to the jail, and was allowed to enter, as before, but when ready to leave, was told that he was there for safe keeping. The next day, he and his son, Johnie, were sold to some speculators who promised to carry them so far away that they could not return. As Daniel left, he told his wife to wait for him to return, whether it be months or years. She grieved over his departure and refused, although urged, to marry again. A few months before the close of the Civil War, her husband appeared and remained on the plantation until emancipation. Johnie was accidently killed shortly after his departure.

While most of the punishment was given by the "patty-roller" and the Master, in some instances overseers were allowed to administer it. Some of these overseers were Negroes and occasionally there was trouble when they attempted to punish another slave. Huff recalls having seen one of these "bosses" approach his mother as she toiled in the field and questioned her regarding her whereabouts on the previous evening. She refused to answer and as he approached her in a threatening manner, she threw piles of twigs upon him. (She was loading a wagon with small limbs cut from trees on "new ground"). He fled in terror. That night, as the mother and her children were seated in their cabin, the same man accompanied by their Master entered, tied her hands and led her from the home. She was carried quite a distance down the road and severely beaten.

Food was provided by the Master who gave it out in regular weekly allotments. Collard greens, peas, smoked meat and corn bread were the chief items on all menus. On Sundays a small amount of flour for biscuits and some coffee was given; buttermilk was always plentiful. Holidays were usually synonymous with barbecue when large hogs and beeves were killed and an ample supply of fresh meat was given each person. As all food was raised on the plantation, everyone had plenty.

Cloth spun from cotton produced at home was woven into the material under the watchful eye of the mistress, afterwards being cut into dresses for the women, shirts and trousers for men. Winter garments were made of wool from home raised sheep. Some of this home-spun material was colored with dye made from powdered red rocks. With a shoe hammer, last, pegs (instead of nails) and a standard pattern slave cobblers fashioned shoes from the hides of their master's cattle. They were no models of beauty, but strong, durable shoes designed for hard wear.

Bryant was not superstitious, although he did sometimes wonder when "signs" proved true. Superstition, however, had a strong grip on slave life. A fellow slave named Andy was a seasoned runaway and the overseer usually set the hounds after him. (Going to a fortune teller Andy secured a "hound" which caused all dogs to be friendly with him. There after when the hounds were set upon him, he played with them, turned their ears inside out, and sent them back to their owner.)

The attitude of the slaves toward freedom varied and as they were not allowed to discuss it, their hope was veiled in such expressions as the "LORD will provide".

Some were even afraid to settle any statement and silently prayed that their release would come soon. Some feared that something might prevent their emancipation so they ran away and joined the Yankee Army, hoping to be able to destroy their former master.

During this time masters suffered as well as their slaves, for many of their sons went gaily forth to battle and were never heard of again. Simpson Rigerson, son of "Marse" Jesse Rigerson, was lost to his parents. A younger son, who lost his right hand while "helping" feed cane to a grinder, is the only member of the family now living.

Sorrow did not break this slaves group and they soon learned to sing away their troubles. One song which gives some light on their attitude toward the government went as follows:

- I.

> Jeff Davis rode the gray horse
> Ole Lincoln rode the mule
> Jeff Davis is the gentleman
> Ole Lincoln is the fool
>
> Chorus:
>
> I'll lay ten dollars down
> I'll count it one by one.
> I'll give ten dollars to know the man
> Who struck Peter Butler's son.

II.

> I lay down in my bed
> I lay down in no dread
> Conscript come and took me
> And dragged me from my bed.

III.

> I went down a new cut road
> She went down the lane
> I turned my back upon her
> And 'long come Liza Jane.

After freedom was declared, Bryant Huff's family moved several miles from the Rigerson plantation to one owned by an elderly woman. They ran from a mean master but their flight was a "leap from the frying pan into the fire", for this woman proved even worse than their former master. At the close of the war the K.K.K. was very active and their fearful exploits made them the terror of the slaves. A band of the latter was organized to attempt to curb the K.K.K. activities. Neither gang knew who was a member of the other, but their clashes were frequent. One night the K.K.K. appeared at the Huff cabin and when admitted took the father, an uncle, and a man named Mansfield from the house. After forcing the father to break a gun which he had borrowed from Mr. Rigerson, they beat him so brutally that his arm was broken. The uncle, a minister who preached a type of doctrine that they liked, was unharmed. Mansfield, accused of being a member of the anti-K.K.K. gang, was beaten unmercifully. While this was being done, two members of the gang returned to the house where they searched the back room (men slept in the front room, the women and children in the rear) to see if any adults were secreted there. The small boys under the bed said "Don't harm us, we're only children". After this outrage, done at the request of the mistress, the Huff family moved back to the Rigerson plantation.

Mr. Rigerson's harsh disposition was broken after the Civil War ended and he repented of his severe treatment of his former slaves. Daniel Huff whom he had despised and feared, became his best friend who nursed him until death. Huff's wife received three acres of ground and two houses from her former master who also gave her an apology for his past meanness and stated that he wished to provide her with a home for life.

During this period martial law prevailed in the South. The Yankee troops, placed in every town, were the only police present and all cases from the county were presented to them for settlement.

A few years after emancipation, Bryant then a young man, ran away from home and apprenticed himself to a physician who became interested in his thirst for knowledge and gave him an opportunity to attend school. After several years of hard study, he went before the board of examiners in order to teach. After 2 examinations he was immediately appointed to teach at the school where he had once been a pupil.

Huff, now on aged man, is dependent upon local relief for his sustenance. He is able to do light work like sweeping yards and is a very good umbrella mender and shoe repairer, but is not able to go in search of work. He has smoked since he was a young man and has never taken especial care of his health, so his long life may be attributed to a strong constitution.

[TR: Date Stamped May 13 1938]

PLANTATION LIFE as related by Ex-Slave:

EASTER HUFF
125 Rockspring St.,
Athens, Georgia.

Written by: Sadie B. Hornsby
Athens, Georgia

Edited by: Sarah H. Hall
Athens —
Florence Blease
John N. Booth
Augusta, Georgia.

EASTER HUFF
Ex-Slave—Age 80

EASTER HUFF

Easter eagerly complied with the request for the story of her life, "I done forgot a heap I knowed, but I allus loves to talk 'bout de old times." She declared solemnly. "Dis young race lives so fas' dey needs to know what a hard time us had."

"I was borned in Oglethorpe County on Marse Jabe Smith's plantation. I don't 'zactly know how old I is, but I was jus' a chap when de war ended. Easter is my right name, but white folkses calls me Esther. Mammy was Louisa Smith, but I don't know nothin' 'bout my gram'ma, 'cause she died 'fore I was born, and she done de cookin' in de white folkses house. I can't tell you nothin' 'bout neither one of my gram'pas.

"Us slep' on corded beds what had high postes and ruffled curtains 'round de foot. De beds what had curtains all 'round de top of dem high postes was called teester beds. When all dem curtains was fresh washed and starched, de beds sho' did look grand. Chilluns slep' on pallets on de flo'.

"Mammy was a plow hand, but us chillun didn't do nothin' much 'cept eat and play and sleep in de grass 'til she got in from de fiel' evvy night. De big old cook house had a partition 'crost it, and on one side Aunt Peggy done all de cookin' for Old Marster's household and for de slaves too. On de udder side of de partition was de loom room whar Aunt Peggy weaved all de cloth and Mrs. Lacy Hines, what lived on another plantation not far f'um us, made all our clothes.

"Chilluns didn't know nothin' 'bout gittin' no money of dey own 'til atter de war. Mammy, she made her little money knittin' socks, and patchin' clothes at night, and she had done saved up nigh $40.00 in Confederate money. Dey called it Confederate shucks atter de war 'cause it warn't no good no more den, and she let us chillun play wid it. De shin plasters was Confederate money for as low as 25 cents.

"Victuals dem days warn't fancy lak day is now, but Marstar allus seed dat us had plenty of milk and butter, all kinds of greens for bilein', 'tatoes and peas and sich lak. Chilluns et cornbread soaked in de pot liquor what de greens or peas done been biled in. Slaves never got much meat. Dey mixed butter wid home-made syrup and sopped it up wid cornbread. Dare warn't much wheat bread for slaves.

"Dere was a good 'possum hound on de plantation what was a fine rabbit dog too, and Marster let us use him to ketch us lots of 'possums and rabbits. De mens went seinin' at night in Buffalo Crick what run thoo' Marse Jabe's place. Dey used to put back all de little fishes and de turkles and tarrepins. 'Possums was baked wid sweet 'tatoes and rabbits was parbiled in a big old open fireplace in big pots and skillets. Marster had one big gyarden whar enough was growed for evvybody on de whole plantation, but some of de slaves was 'lowed to have deir own little gyardens and cotton patches what dey wukked on moonlight nights.

"De gal chillun in dem days wore little slips, and de boys had shirts split up de sides. Dey jus' wore one piece in summer, no drawers or nothin'. In de winter us had good warm clothes, made out of coarse ausenburg (osnaburg) cloth. Us wore de same clothes Sundays as evvyday, only us was s'posed to put 'em on clean on Sunday mornin'. A colored man named Clark Dogget made our shoes out of rough red leather what never had been dyed or colored up none. Sometimes Manuel would have to help him wid de shoemakin'.

"On Sundays Mammy would comb my hair and put a clean dress on me, and den take me to de white folkses' church at Salem, whar dere was two rows of benches in de back for slaves. Rev. Brantley Calloway was de pastor, and Rev. Patrick Butler preached too.

"I never seed no baptizin's or fun'als in slavery days, but atter anybody was buried Mammy tuk us to de graveyard and let us look at de grave. Dey allus put a fence made wid pine poles 'round de grave. Some few of de slaves might have read de Bible a little, but dar warn't none what could write.

"I jined church 'cause I was converted and had done changed my way of livin'. I think folkses ought to be 'ligious so dey can help others to live lak de Bible says.

"Marse Jabe Smith was a good white man. He was a grand fiddler and he used to call us to de big house at night to dance for him. I couldn't do nothin' 'cept jump up and down and I sho' did git tired. Marse Jabe warn't married. He raised his brother's chillun, but dey was all grown when de war come on.

"I done clean forgot de name of Marster's overseer and I don't ricollec' how many acres was in dat plantation, but it sho' was a big one. Dere was 'bout 25 grown slaves, and a lot of Nigger chillun rompin' round. De overseer got 'em up 'bout three 'clock and dey stayed in de field 'til sundown 'fore dey started for de house.

"When dey got f'um de fields at night, de 'omans spun, mended, and knit, and de mens wukked in deir gyardens and cotton patches. Winter nights dey plaited baskets and made hoss collars. All de slaves knocked off at twelve o'clock Sadday. Dere was allus somepin' to do on Sadday night—frolics, dances, and sich lak. Dey picked de banjo and knocked on tin pans for music to dance by. Sunday was a rest day. Slaves visited each other or went to church if dey wanted to, but dey had to git a pass.

"I seed dem patterollers on hosses jus' goin' it down de big road. I seed 'em axin' Niggers dey met if dey had passes. Attar dey looked at de passes, dey would let 'em go on. But if a slave was cotched widout no pass dey would beat him mos' nigh to death. If us had patterollers to keep Niggers f'um gallivantin' 'round so much now days, dar wouldn't be so much devilment done.

"Some of de slaves jus' had to be whupped 'cause dey wouldn't behave. On our plantation, de overseer done de whuppin'; Marse Jabe never totched 'em. Mammy told us 'bout seein' slaves put on de block in Virginny and sold off in droves lak hosses.

"Didn't none of Marse Jabe's Niggers run off to de North dat I knowed 'bout. One Nigger named Barlow what was too lazy to wuk in de field slipped off to de woods and made hisself a den to live in. He made baskets, footmats, and brooms, and used to come out at night and sell 'em. Dey said he would steal de white folkses' hogs, chickens, and jus' anythin' he could put his hands on. If dey ever cotched him, I don't know nothin' 'bout it. Mammy used to skeer us pretty nigh to death at night when she wanted us to go on to bed. She said if us didn't go to sleep Barlow sho' would git us.

"Oh! us did have a time at Chris'mas. Dey would have plenty to eat; eggnog and all sorts of good things, and sometimes mens and 'omans got drunk and cut up. Marse Jabe allus give us a little cheese to eat Christmas time. On New Year's Day all de slaves went to de big house for a council. Marse Jabe would talk to 'em and counsel 'em for de New Year and tell 'em how to live.

"Cornshuckin's! Yassum, I ricollects cornshuckin's. De folkses comed f'um all de plantations close 'round. Atter dey was thoo' wid shuckin' de corn, dey gathered 'round a long table in de yard. Marse Jabe had de prettiest level yard you ever seed; it was swept so nice and clean. De victuals was piled on dat table, and dey give us great kegs of apple and peach brandy.

"Mammy used to tell us 'bout Raw-head an' Bloody-bones if us didn't go to bed when she wanted to go out. Us sho' would pile in in a hurry den, and duck under dat kivver and most nigh die 'cause us was skeered to look out lessen he mought be dar atter us.

"Marse Jabe was mighty good to his slaves when dey got sick. I seed Mammy sick once. Dr. Lumpkin Landon was sont atter. De slaves would git fever weeds and sweetgum bark, bile 'em together, and take de tea for colds, coughs, and fever. Dey wore little sacks of assfidity (assafoetida) 'round dey necks to keep off disease, and strung hollow treadsass (treadsalve) roots on strings lak necklaces and hung 'em 'round de babies' necks to make 'em teethe easy.

"Soon atter de surrender, Marse Jabe told his Niggers dey was free as he was, but dat he didn't want nary one to leave him. He wanted 'em to stay wid him he said, and he offered to pay 'em wages. Dere warn't nary one what left. Mammy wukked and plowed right on lak she done before. Atter I was big enough, I went to Lexin'ton to wuk for Mrs. McWhorter.

"When I married Bob Willin'ham, I sho' had a nice weddin'. I was married in a blue merino dress. My under-skirt was white as snow wid trimmin's on it. I wore long drawers what was trimmed fancy at de bottom. Our white folkses give us lots of cake, turkey, ham, and sich lak for de weddin' feast. Our only child was named Minnie, and dere was five of our grandchillun, but dey's all dead now but two. One lives in Cincinnati, Ohio, and I lives wid de udder one what wuks at de chapter house here. Atter Bob died, I married Lumpkin Huff, but us didn't have no weddin' dat time. De preacher jus' come to my house and married us. I went to Elberton wid 'im, but he was so mean I didn't live wid 'im but eight months before I come back to Athens.

"Dey used to have a song 'bout Mr. Lincoln when I was a little chap, but I done forgot it. No Ma'am, I don't know nothin' 'bout Mr. Davis and Booker Washin'ton. Dem days I never heard much 'bout folkses away off f'um here.

"I b'lieve I'se done told you all I knows 'bout back days. I don't know nothin' 'bout dese fas' present-day ways o' livin'. When I was a chap and got a whuppin' and Mammy heerd 'bout it I got another one. Now dey takes you to de law. Yes Ma'am, for myself I'd rather have de old days wid good Old Marster to take keer of me."

United States. Work Projects Administration

PLANTATION LIFE, AS VIEWED BY AN EX-SLAVE

Written By: Miss Grace McCune
Athens —

Edited By: Mrs. Sarah H. Hall
Athens —

and

John N. Booth
District Supervisor
Federal Writers' Project
Residences No. 6 & 7
Augusta, Georgia
Sept. 21, 1938.

Lina Hunter
Ex-Slave, Age about 90
270 Bailey Street
Athens, Georgia

LINA HUNTER

Lina Hunter's weather-beaten house nestles at the foot of a long hill, and several large chinaberry trees furnish shade for her well-kept yard. As the visitor hesitated before the rickety front steps someone called from inside the house, "Chile, do be keerful on dem old steps 'cause dey might fall wid you; dey done went through wid some of dese chillun here."

The tall mulatto woman who came to the door had tiny plaits of white hair that covered her head in no apparent design. Her faded print dress was clean, and she wore badly scuffed brogan shoes several sizes too large on her stockingless feet. In answer to an inquiry she replied: "Dis is Lina's house, and I is Lina. Have a cheer out here on de porch, please, mam, 'cause de gals is ironin' in de house and dem fire buckets sho make it hot in dar."

Lina readily agreed to tell of her life in the ante-bellum period. "I 'members all 'bout slavery time," she laughed, "cause I was right dar. Course I warn't grown-up, but I was big enough to holp Great-granny Rose look atter all dem other slave chillun whilst deir mammies and daddies was in de field at wuk.

"Anne and Peter Billups was my mammy and daddy, and my granddaddy and grandmammy was Washin'ton and Tiller Billups; all of 'em belonged to Old Marster Jack Billups. Marse Jack stayed in Athens, but his plantation, whar I was borned and whar all my folks was borned and raised, was 'way down in Oglethorpe County. I don't rightly know how old I is, 'cause all Marster's old records is done got lost or 'stroyed, evvy blessed one of 'em, but I'se been here a mighty long time.

"Honey, dat old plantation was sho one big place. Back of de big house, whar de overseer lived, was just rows and rows of slave cabins. Dey stacked 'em up out of big logs jus' lak dey made hog-pen fences. All de cracks 'twixt de logs was chinked up tight wid red mud and, let me tell you, Honey, dey was keerful to lay on so much red mud over dem sticks dat chimblies on our place never did ketch fire lak dey did on some of de places whar dey done things sort of shiftless lak. Dem cabins had two rooms and a shed room 'crost de back whar day done de cookin'. Two famblies lived in evvy cabin.

"Dey allus had plenty to cook, 'cause dere was plenty

of victuals raised on Marse Jack's place. Chillun was all fed up at de big house whar Marse Garner, de overseer, lived. Deir mammies was 'lowed to come in from de fields in time to cook dinner for de menfolks, but dey didn't git deir chillun back home 'til atter supper. Granny Rose had 'em all day, and she had to see dat dey had de right sort of victuals to make chillun grow fast and strong. Chillun et out of wooden trays, and, Honey, dey sho was some sight; dey looked jus' lak pig troughs. Dey poured peas, cabbage, or whatever de chillun was to eat right in dat trough on top of a passel of cornbread. For supper chillun jus' had milk and bread, but dere was allus plenty of it. Marse Jack had lots of cows, and old Aunt Mary didn't have no other job but to churn enough so dere would allus be plenty of milk and butter, 'cause Marse Jack had done said milk was good for chillun and dat us was to have it to drink any time us wanted it.

"Evvybody cooked on fireplaces den. I jus' wish you could see dat big old fireplace in de big house kitchen; you could stand up in it. It had long racks clear acrost de inside for de pots what dey biled in to hang on. Bakin' was done in thick iron skillets dat had heavy lids. You sot 'em on coals and piled more coals all over 'em. Us had somepin dat most folks didn't have; dat was long handled muffin pans. Dey had a lid dat fitted down tight, and you jus' turned 'em over in de fire 'til de muffins was cooked on both sides. I had dem old muffin irons here, but de lid got broke off and dese here boys done lost 'em diggin' in de ground wid 'em. Dem victuals cooked on open fireplaces was mighty fine, and I wishes you could have a chance to see jus' how nice dey was.

"Evvy kind of vegetable us knowed anything 'bout

was raised right dar on de place and dey had big old fields of corn, oats, rye, and wheat. Us had lots of fruit trees on de plantation too. Dere warn't no runnin' off to de store evvy time dere was a special meal to be got up. Coffee, sugar, salt, and black pepper was de most Marse Jack had to buy in de way of victuals. Course dey was hard to git in war times. Parched corn and okra seed was ground together for coffee, and us had to git up dirt under old smokehouses and bile it down for salt. Dere was allus a little sugar 'round de sides of de syrup barr'ls, and us had to make out wid dat hot red pepper 'til atter de war was done over a good long time, 'fore dere was any more black pepper shipped in. Spite of all dat, Honey, dem was good old days.

"Marster raised enough cows, sheep, hogs, chickens, and turkeys for us to have all de meat us needed. He had lots of mules and oxen too. Dey used de mules for 'most of de plowin' and for goin' to mill, and don't forgit it took plenty of goin' to mill to feed as many Niggers as our Marster had. Lordy, Lady! I never knowed how many slaves he owned. Oxen pulled dem two-wheeled carts dey hauled in de craps wid, and I has rid to town in a ox-cart many a time. Dem old oxen was enough to make a preacher lose his best 'ligion. Dey had a heap of mean ways, but de wust thing dey done was to run spang down in de water evvy time dey come to a crick. It never mattered how deep it was, and you might holler all day, but dey warn't coming out of dat water 'till dey was good and ready. Dat happened evvy time dey saw a crick, but dere warn't nothin' us could do 'bout it, for Marse Jack sho never 'lowed nobody to lay deir paws on his stock.

"Folks wove all deir cloth at home dem days. Dey

made up plenty of cotton cloth for hot weather, and for de cold wintertime, dere warn't nothin' warmer dat us knowed about dan de cloth dey made out of home-raised wool and cotton. Marster kept a slave dat didn't have nothin' else to do but make shoes for evvybody on de place. Yes, mam, Honey, dey tanned de hide evvy time dey kilt a cow. Leather was tanned wid whiteoak bark. Chillun's shoes was finished off wid brass knobs on de toes, and us was sho mighty dressed up Niggers when us got on dem shoes wid deir shiny knobs. Little gals' dresses was made wid long skirts gathered on to plain waisties. Dere warn't no showin' de legs lak dey does now. Little boys had red and black jeans suits made wid waisties and britches sewed together in front but wid a long buttoned-up openin' in de back. Most of de other places jus' put long shirts on little boys, but dat warn't de way dey done on our place, 'cause us didn't belong to no pore folks. Our Marster had plenty and he did lak to see his Niggers fixed up nice. Course in summertime none of de chillun didn't wear nothin' but little slips, so dey could keep cool, but in winter it was diffunt. Honey, dem old balmoral petticoats was some sight, but dey was sho warm as hell. I seed a piece of one of mine not long ago whar I had done used it to patch up a old quilt. 'Omans' dresses was made jus' about lak dis one I got on now, 'ceptin' I didn't have enough cloth to make de skirt full as dem old-time clothes used to be." The old woman stood up to show just how her dress was fashioned. The skirt, sewed to a plain, close-fitting waist, was very full in the back, but plain across the front. Lina called attention to an opening on the left side of the front. "See here, Chile," she said, "here's a sho 'nough pocket. Jus' let me turn it wrong-side-out to show you how big it is. Why, I used a whole 25 pound flour sack to make it 'cause I don't lak none of dese newfangled little pockets. I lak things de way I was raised. Dis pocket hangs down inside and nobody don't see it. De chilluns fusses 'bout my big pocket, but it ain't in none of deir dresses, and I'se sho gwine to wear 'em 'til dey is wore out to a gnat's heel.

"Chillun never had to wuk on our plantation 'til dey was big enough to go to de fields, and dat was when dey was around 12 to 14 years old. Dey jus' played 'round de yards and down by de wash-place dat was a little ways off from de big house on a branch dat run from de big spring. On wash days dat was a busy place, wid lots of 'omans bending over dem great big wash pots and de biggest old wooden tubs I ever seed. Dere was plenty racket 'round de battlin' block whar dey beat de dirt out of de clothes, and dey would sing long as dey was a-washin'.

"Marster was sho good to his Niggers all de time. Course he made 'em wuk 'less dey was sick. Chillun never had nothin' to do 'cept eat, sleep, and play. Evvy time Marse Jack come out to his plantation he brung candy for all de pickaninnies, and, Honey, it warn't in no little sacks neither; dere was allus plenty for 'em all, and it was a mighty big crowd of us. Marster loved to come out on Sundays to see us chillun git our heads combed. Honey, dere sho was hollerin' on dat place when dey started wukin' on us wid dem jim crow combs what was made lak a curry comb 'ceppin' dey warn't quite as wide acrost. When dem jim crow combs got stuck in dat tangled, kinky wool, damn if dem chillun didn't yell, and Marster would laugh and tell Granny Rose to comb it good.

"Granny Rose larnt me to keep clean and fix myself up nice, and, Honey, I ain't got too old to primp up now.

One thing dis old Nigger ain't never done is to put hair straightener on her head, 'cause de Blessed Lord sont me here wid kinky hair, and I'se gwine 'way from here wid dat same old kinky hair. It's white now, but dat ain't no fault of mine. Honey, I sho do trust dat Good Lord. Why, I 'member when I used to pull out my own teeth; I jus' tied a string 'round 'em, laid down on my bed, and said, 'Lord, I is in your hands,' and den I would give dat string a hard yank and out come dem damn teeth.

"Yes, mam, I'se seed slaves sold. Dey jus' put dem Niggers up on de block and bid 'em off. A smart worker brought a big price, and a good breedin' 'oman sho did fetch de money, 'cause all de white folks did lak to have plenty chillun 'round. Dem breedin' 'omans never done no wuk a t'all; dey made other slaves wait on 'em 'til atter deir babies was borned. Slave 'omans what had babies was sont back from de fields in de mornin' and atter dinner so deir babies could suck 'til atter dey was big enough to eat bread and milk; den dey was kept wid de other chillun for Granny Rose to keer for.

"Slaves didn't even git married lak folks does now. Dere warn't none of dem newfangled licenses to buy. All dey had to do was tell Marster dey wanted to marry up. If it was all right wid him he had 'em jump over a broom and dey was done married. Slaves couldn't git out and do no courtin' on other plantations widout deir marsters knowed it, 'cause dey had to have passes to leave de place whar dey lived. If dey was brash enough to go off widout no pass de paterollers would cotch 'em for sho, and dey would nigh beat 'em to death. Dat didn't stop courtin', 'specially on our place, 'cause dey jus' tuk anybody dey laked; it didn't matter whose man or 'oman dey had.

"Marster had a big old ginhouse on de plantation about 2 miles from de big house, but I never seed in it, 'cause dey didn't 'low 'omans and chillun 'round it. De menfolks said dey hitched up mules to run it, and dat dey had a cotton press inside de ginhouse. Dey said it was a heap of trouble to git rid of all dem old cotton-seeds dat piled up so fast in ginnin' time. Dere was a great big wuk-shop on de place too, whar dey fixed evvything, and dat was whar dey made coffins when anybody died. Yes, mam, evvything was made at home, even down to de coffins.

"Dere didn't many folks die out back in dem good old days, 'cause dey was made to take keer of deirselfs. Dey had to wuk hard, but dey et plenty and went to bed reg'lar evvy night in wuk time. When one of 'em did die out, deir measure was tuk and a coffin was made up and blackened 'til it looked right nice. Whenever dere was a corpse on de place Marster didn't make nobody do no wuk, 'cept jus' look atter de stock, 'til atter de buryin'. Dey fixed up de corpses nice. Yes, mam, sho as you is borned, dey did; dey made new clothes for 'em and buried 'em decent in de graveyard on de place. Marse Jack seed to dat. Dey put de coffin on a wagon, and de folks walked to de graveyard. Dere was crowds of 'em; dey come from jus' evvywhar. A preacher, or some member of deir marster's fambly, said a prayer, de folks sung a hymn, and it was all over. 'Bout de biggest buryin' us ever had on our place was for a 'oman dat drapped down in de path and died when she was comin' in from de field to nuss her baby. Yes, mam, she was right on de way to Granny Rose's cabin in de big house yard.

"No, mam, I ain't forgot when de Yankees come to

our place. Dat was right atter de end of de war, not long atter us had been told 'bout freedom. When us heared dey was on deir way us tuk and hid all de stuff us could, but dey sho tore up dat place. Dey tuk all de meat out of de smokehouse and give it to de Niggers, but deir bellies was already full and dey didn't need it, so dey give it back to Marse Jack soon as dem sojers was gone. 'Fore dey left dem Yankee sojers tuk Marse Jack's mules and horses slap out of de plows and rid 'em off, and left deir old wore-out stock right dar.

"Freedom didn't make so many changes on our place right at fust, 'cause most of de slaves stayed right on dar, and things went on jus' lak dey had 'fore dere was any war. Marse Jack had done told 'em dey was free, but dat dem what wanted to stay would be tuk keer of same as 'fore de war. Dere warn't many what left neither, 'cause Marse Jack had been so good to evvy one of 'em dey didn't want to go 'way.

"Honey, back in dem good old days us went to church wid our white folks. Slaves sot in de gallery or in de back of de church. I'se been to dat old Cherokee Corners Church more times dan I knows how to count, but de fust baptizin' I ever seed was at de old St. Jean church; dere was jus' three or four baptized dat day, but Lordy, I never did hear such prayin', shoutin', and singin', in all my born days. One old 'oman come up out of dat crick a-shoutin' 'bout she was walkin' through de pearly gates and wearin' golden slippers, but I looked down at her foots and what she had on looked more lak brogans to me. I kin still hear our old songs, but it's jus' now and den dat dey come back to my mind."

For a moment Lina was quiet, then she said, "Honey,

I wants to smoke my old pipe so bad I kin most taste it, but how in hell kin I smoke when I ain't had no 'baccy in two days? Chile, ain't you got no 'baccy wid you, jus' a little 'baccy? You done passed de nighest store 'bout 2 miles back toward town," she said, "but if you will pay for some 'baccy for Lina, some of dese good-for-nothin' chillun kin sho go git it quick and, whilst dey's dar, dey might as well git me a little coffee too, if you kin spare de change." The cash was supplied by the visitor, and Lina soon started the children off running. "If you stops airy a minute," she told them, "I'se gwine take de hide offen your backs, sho' as you is borned." As soon as they were out of sight, she returned to her chair and started talking again.

"Yes, mam, Honey, things went on 'bout de same old way atter de war." Suddenly the old woman leaped to her feet and began shouting, "Bless God A'mighty! Praise de Lord! I knows de key to prayers. I'se done prayed jus' dis mornin' for de Lord to send me some 'baccy and coffee, and God is done sont Missy wid de money to answer my prayer. Praise de Lord! I'se glad I'se here, 'cause I coulda been gone and missed my 'baccy and coffee. Praise God! I'se gwine to smoke dat damned old pipe one more time." She seized the visitor by the shoulder as she shouted, "I sho laks your looks, but you may be de devil for all I knows, and you may be fixin' to put me in de chaingang wid all dis here writin', but" here she gave the startled visitor a shake that almost pulled her out of the chair, "Damn, if I don't lak you anyhow."

Her granddaughter, Callie, came out on the porch to see what was wrong with Lina. "Granny," she said, "I wouldn't talk lak dat. Missy will think you is dat way all de time."

"Git back to your ironin', gal," said Lina. "I knows I talks right smart ugly. Didn't my Miss Fannie, tell me one time she was gwine to put potash in my mouth to clean it out? Now, Nigger, I said git, 'fore I hits you." Her grandmother started toward her, and Callie lost no time going inside the house. Lina went back to her chair, and as she sat down started singing. With each note her tones grew louder. The words were something like this:

> "God A'mighty, when my heart begins to burn
> And dat old wheel begins to turn,
> Den, Oh, Lord! Don't leave me here."

It seemed from the length of her chant that the wheels would turn indefinitely, but no sooner had she finished that song, than she started another.

> "When my old mammy died a-shoutin',
> All de friend I had done died and gone.
> She died a-prayin', she died a-prayin'.
>
> "In dat day dat you died, dat you died,
> Gwine to be a star risin' in dat mornin'.
> Didn't you hear 'em say, 'gwine to be a
> Star risin' in de mornin'.
>
> "De Christians all will know in dat day,
> Dat my old mammy died a-shoutin', died a-shoutin',
> 'Cause dat star sho gwine to be dar.

"Oh, Lord! Don't leave me now, Oh, Lord!
But guide me all 'long de way, 'long de way.
'Cause I'se in trouble, dat I am.
Lord! Oh, Lord! don't leave me now."

"Honey, I jus' feels lak prayin' and cussin' too, at de same time, but it's 'cause I'se so happy. Here I is, I'se nigh 'bout crazy. If Old Marster could jus' come back I'd sho have plenty of evvy thing I needs.

"I 'members dem old frolics us had, when harvest times was over, and all dat corn was piled up ready for de big cornshuckin'. Honey, us sho had big old times. Us would cook for three or four days gittin' ready for de feast dat was to follow de cornshuckin'. De fust thing dey done was 'lect a general to lead off de singin' and keep it goin' so de faster dey sung, de faster dey shucked de corn. Evvy now and den dey passed de corn liquor 'round, and dat holped 'em to wuk faster, and evvy Nigger dat found a red ear got a extra swig of liquor. Atter de sun went down dey wuked right on by de light of pine torches and bonfires. Dem old pine knots would burn for a long time and throw a fine bright light. Honey, it was one grand sight out dar at night wid dat old harvest moon a-shinin', fires a-burnin', and dem old torches lit up. I kin jus' see it all now, and hear dem songs us sung. Dem was such happy times. When all de corn was shucked and dey had done et all dat big supper, dey danced for de rest of de night.

"Dey had logrollin's when dere was new ground to be cleared up. De menfolks done most of dat wuk, but de 'omans jus' come along to fix de big supper and have a good time laughin' and talkin' whilst de menfolks was doin' de wuk. Atter de logs was all rolled, dey et, and drunk, and danced 'til dey fell out. I'll bet you ain't never seed nothin' lak dem old break-downs and dragouts us had dem nights atter logrollin's. Dey sho drug heaps of dem Niggers out.

"When de harvest moon was 'most as bright as daylight us had cotton pickin's. Dem big crowds of slaves would clean out a field in jus' no time, and you could hear 'em singin' a long ways off whilst dey was a-pickin' dat cotton. Dey 'most allus had barbecue wid all de fixin's to enjoy when dey finished pickin' out de cotton, and den lots of drinkin' and dancin'. 'Bout dat dancin', Honey, I could sho cut dem corners. Dancin' is one thing I more'n did lak to do, and I wish I could hear dat old dance song again. Miss Liza Jane, it was, and some of de words went lak dis, 'Steal 'round dem corners, Miss Liza Jane. Don't slight none, Miss Liza Jane. Swing your partner, Miss Liza Jane.' Dere was heaps and lots more of it, but it jus' won't come to me now.

"One night not long atter day sot us free, dere was a big old Nigger breakdown on our plantation, and such a lot of Niggers as you never seed was at dat dance. Whilst us was havin' de bestest time, takin' a drink 'twixt dances, us heared a 'oman screamin' lak murder. Evvybody run, but us jus' heared a horse runnin' and dat 'oman still hollerin'. De menfolks got on horses and rid all night but dey never did find 'em. One of our gals was gone; a real young one named Rose Billups. Some damn, no 'count Nigger had done stole 'er. Us didn't larn nothin' 'bout her for nigh onto a year, den she writ to Marse Jack to come atter her. He went. It was a fur way off, and I don't 'member now whar it was. Dat mean man had done most kilt

Rose, and had left her wid a baby. No, mam, dey didn't never cotch 'im.

"Norman Green had two wives and dey didn't live fur from our plantation. I knows 'bout dat, 'cause in years to come I lived on de same farm whar dey was. It was dis way: his fust wife, Tildy, was sold off from him in slavery time. He got married again, and atter freedom come Tildy come right back to him. He kept both his wives right dar in de same one-room cabin. Deir beds sot right 'side each other. One wife's chilluns was all boys and de other didn't have nothin' but gals.

"Yes, Chile, us wuked hard. I'se seed my mammy plowin' in de fields many a time, wid her skirt pinned up to keep it out of de dirt. Yes, mam, us did wuk, but us had a good place to stay, plenty somepin t'eat, and plenty clothes to wear; dere warn't nothin' else us needed.

"Missy did you ever hear dat old sayin' 'bout folks gittin' speckledy when dey gits old? Well, 'cordin' to dat old sayin', I'se sho been here a mighty long time. Jus' look at my legs." She raised her skirts to her knees to display the white specks that stood out in clear contrast on her dark skin. "Dat's a sho sign of bein' old folks," insisted Lina.

She stood up and peered down the road, impatient for the return of the children, who were to bring her tobacco and coffee. Finally she saw them come over the hill and could hardly restrain herself until they arrived in the yard. Snatching the parcels, as the children came up the steps, Lina called out, "Callie, come here, gal, fix my pipe quick, and put dat coffeepot on de fire bucket, 'cause Glory to God! I'se gwine to smoke my old pipe and drink me one more good cup of coffee."

When Callie finally succeeded in filling and lighting Lina's pipe to suit her, and the old woman had inhaled with an exaggerated air of satisfaction for several moments, she indulged in a few more shouts of "Praise de Lord!" then she said, "Honey, I'se ready to talk some more now. Damned if I ain't gwine to git right on talkin' for you, 'fore I starts off singin' again.

"Oh, it's 'bout my marriage you wants to know now, is it? Well, me and Jeff Hunter got married up whilst I was still stayin' on Marster Jack's place. Jeff went to de courthouse and got us a license lak de white folks, and us had a nice weddin'. My dress was mighty pretty; it was white lawn, made long waisted lak dey wore dresses den. Mrs. Lizzie Johnson made it, and it had long sleeves, and a long full skirt wid lots of ruffles. De two petticoats she gimme to wear wid my weddin' dress was ruffled to beat de band and had trimmin' on evvy ruffle. My weddin' drawers even had ruffles on 'em; I was really dressed up. Us had a big fine supper and two dances. Sho, mam, dat ain't no mistake. Us did have two dances, one was at home, and den us went over to my brother's house whar he give us another one and served cake and wine to de weddin' party. Atter us drunk dat wine, it warn't no trouble to dance for de rest of de night.

"Me and Jeff moved on de Johnson place, and Jeff wuked some for Mrs. Johnson's daughter, Mrs. Fannie Dean, but for de most part he wuked in de wagon shop wid Mr. Tom Anthony.

"I'se still got one of my old weddin' petticoats; I wore out four bodies on it." Lina excused herself and went inside the house for a moment. She returned to the porch with an old-fashioned suitcase or "grip," as she called it.

"Dis here's older dan old Lina is," she said. "It belonged to Miss Lizzie's daddy, but I sewed it back together atter dey throwed it away, and I'se gwine to keep it long as I lives." She opened it and took out a petticoat that was yellow with age. It was several yards wide and was encircled by numerous embroidered ruffles. The skirt was sewed on to a tight, straight body-waist that was much newer than the skirt and this waist was topped by a rose-colored crocheted yoke. "Mrs. Fannie Dean made dat for me," declared Lina. "Look at dis old black shawl. See how big it is? Dat's what I used to wear for a wrop on church days 'fore I ever had a coat.

"I'se still sleepin' on one of Miss Lizzie's beds. Come inside, I wants you to see it." A part of the tall headboard had been removed so the bed could be used in a low-ceiled room. The footboard was low, and Lina insisted on showing the small double locks that joined the side pieces to the head and foot boards. These are rarely seen now. She was using the original old wooden-framed wire fabric springs, and a straw mattress. As she displayed the latter, she said, "Yes, Chile, I still sleeps on my straw tick, 'cause dat's what I was raised on and dere ain't nothin' sleeps as good as dat old tick when it's full of good fresh wheat straw."

Lina's coffeepot on the charcoal bucket was steaming and the visitor prepared to depart so that the old woman could enjoy her drink while it was fresh and hot. Lina followed her to the veranda and said with much enthusiasm, "God bless you, Lady. You sho is done made me happy, and I'se gwine to pray for you evvy day and ask de Lord to take keer of you all de time. I'se gwine to do dat, 'cause I wants you to come back and let me sing some more of our good old songs for you sometime." After the house was no longer in sight, Lina's high pitched voice could be heard singing My Old Mammy Died a-Shoutin'.

United States. Work Projects Administration

[TR: Date stamp: MAY 8 1937]

SUBJECT:	EMMA HURLEY OF WASHINGTON-WILKES
RESEARCH WORKER:	MINNIE BRANHAM STONESTREET
EDITOR:	JOHN N. BOOTH
SUPERVISOR:	MISS VELMA BELL
DISTRICT:	W.P.A. NO. I
DATE:	MARCH 22, 1937

EMMA HURLEY OF WASHINGTON-WILKES

EMMA HURLEY

With snow white hair peeping from underneath a spotless "head rag" and wearing a big white apron, Emma Hurley reminds one of the plantation days of the long ago. She is eighty-odd years old, but does not know her exact age. From all she remembers she is sure she was at least 7 or 8 at the beginning of the war for she clearly recalls the talk of war and all the excitement of those anxious days.

Unfortunately, Aunt Emma was born of parents belonging to a family that bought and sold slaves as they did cattle and thought of them only in terms of dollars and cents. The story she tells of her childhood would make a Simon Legree turn pale with envy. She is not resentful, but is honest in telling of those early years of her life, years of suffering and great hardship.

Although she has never been to school, she uses very little dialect: "No mam, honey, the folks I belonged to said it wouldn't do fer niggers to learn out'n books; that schools warn't fer them. They said learnin' would git us so they couldn't do nothin' wid us. After freedom I wuz nussin' here in Washin'ton. The mother of the chillun was a good lady an' she let me look on the books when she read to them an' larned me the lessons 'long with her chillun. She said it wuz a pity I couldn't ov went to school, cause I wuz a apt pupil. I larned easy, yassum, that's what she said."

"My Ma wuz name Margaret an' she had thirteen chillun, six of 'em twins. I wuz the oldest one, but I ain't a twin. I wuz born on a plantation in Wilkes County right on the line of Oglethorpe. In the white family I belonged to there wuz a mother, four boys, an' two girls, all grown. They come to Wilkes County from Maryland. All four of the men went to the war an' three of 'em died of sickness caught in the war."

Aunt Emma told of how the slaves had to live on the plantation and an unpleasant story it was. There were no neat cabins all in a row making up the "quarters" where the slaves lived. Instead they were made to live around in any old hut they could find shelter in. Her mother and three other women stayed in one room of the house the white family lived in.

The little slaves were fed pig-fashion in the kitchen, but they were given just so much food and no more. They were alloted two garments at the time, summer and winter: "Why, honey, I never had no shoes 'til after freedom come. I've walked on snow many a time barefooted with my feet so cold my toes wuz stickin' straight up with no feelin' in 'em. The white folks had a trained shoe-maker slave an' he made shoes fer them, but us little niggers didn't have none. The first shoes I ever remembers had wooden bottoms an' sich a sound as they made when the folks walked 'round with 'em on."

The slaves did plenty of hard work done on the plantation. The women labored all day in the fields and then spun at night. Each one was given the task of spinning six broaches a week. On Saturday "a white lady" reeled off the spinning and if one of the women had failed in her task she was severely beaten. The men worked all day and until ten o'clock at night shucking corn or doing other chores by lamp light.

Every Wednesday night the slaves had to go to the spring and wash their clothes by torch light. They did have all day Sunday as a resting period, but they were not allowed to go to church and no religious services were held for them. There was one day holiday at Christmas, "but I never heard of a Santa Claus when I wuz a child," said Emma.

When a slave died on the place he was wrapped in a sheet, put into a pine box, and taken to a "burying ground" where he was put in the ground without any services, and with only the immediate family attending. All other slaves on the place had to keep on working just as though nothing had happened.

There were no marriages. The slaves being told to "step over the broom stick." Many families were separated by sale. "I recollects good when Mr. Seaborn Callaway come over to the place an' bought my Grandma an' some other slaves an' took 'em away. We jest cried an' cried an' Grandma did too. Them white folks bought an' sold slaves that way all the time."

"Honey, there wuz one time when them white folks wuz good to us slaves," said Aunt Emma, "an' that wuz when we wuz sick. They would give us homemade remedies like tansy tea, comfort root tea, life everlasting tea, boneset tea, garlic water an' sich, 'cordin' ter what ailed us. Then if we didn't git better they sont fer the doctor. If we had a misery anywhere they would make poultices of tansy leaves scalded, or beat up garlic an' put on us. Them folks wuz sho' 'cerned 'bout us when we wuz sick, 'cause they didn't want us ter die."

When asked about the war and what she remembered of those terrible times, Aunt Emma slowly shook her head and said: "I never wants to live through sich sad times no more. Them wuz the hardest an' the saddest days I ever knowed. Everybody went 'round like this: (here she took up her apron and buried her face in it)— they kivered their face with what-somever they had in their hands that would ketch the tears. Sorrow an' sadness wuz on every side. The men all went off to fight an' left the women an' chillun an' niggers behind to do the best they could."

"Times wuz so hard, why, honey, in them times folks couldn't git so much as some plain salt to use on their victuals. The white folks had the dirt dug up from out'n their smokehouses an' hauled it up to Mr. Sisson's an' he run it an' got what salt he could out'n it. I 'members one day I went over there fer sumpthin' an' the dirt what he had run wuz piled way up high like sawdust these days. There warn't no soda neither, so the white folks took watermelon rinds, fixed 'em keerful like we does fer perserves, burned 'em an' took the ashes an' sifted 'em an' used 'em fer soda. Coffee giv' out an none could be bought so they took okra seeds an' parched 'em good an' brown an' ground 'em an' made coffee out'n 'em. Some folks made coffee out'n parched ground wheat too. Everybody had to do the best they could in them times."

"Durin' the war," continued Aunt Emma, "the mother died an' all her property wuz divided 'mongst the chillun. My Ma an' all her chillun fell to Miss Mary what had married an' wuz livin' in Lexington, over in Oglethorpe County. She moved us all up there an' we wuz there 'til freedom, then we moved down to Washington where we have lived ever since. Miss Mary's husband's Ma had over two hundred slaves an' she sho' did take on when they wuz all freed. I 'members how she couldn't stay in the house, she jest walked up an' down out in the yard a-carrin'-on, talkin' an' a-ravin'.

"Word come one day that the Yankee soldiers wuz comin' an' all us niggers went down to the road to watch 'em go by. It wuz a sight. They all marched by singin'. 'Fore they come, though, the white folks had all the niggers busy hidin' everything they could. Stock wuz tied out way down in thick woods, an' silver, money, an' good clothes wuz buried deep in the ground an' leaves put all over the earth so they couldn't see where it had been dug. When the Yankees did come they called all the slaves up an' went into smokehouses an' throwed out the meat to the niggers an' said: 'Here, take all this, we knows it's yours anyhow, you worked fer it.' But most of the niggers give it all back to the white folks it belonged to. The Yankees poured out all the syrup an' 'stroyed everything they could. I tell you, honey, them wuz bad times an' us all wuz skeered 'most to death."

Aunt Emma had only one sign: "No mam, I ain't 'tall

superstitious, I never thinks of things like that. But I does know when it's goin' to rain hard, an' that's when my haid itches an' itches up under my haid rag."

When asked about the amusements of her day Aunt Emma said: "I ain't never danced a step nor sung a reel in my life. My Ma allus said we shouldn't do them things an' we didn't. She said if we went to the devil it wouldn't be 'cause she give us her 'mission!"

"How come I done lived so long? I dunno, only I allus been truthful an' honest an' tried hard to treat people good as I want them to treat me. Once I wuz so sick they all thought I wuz goin' to die. I thought so too. But I lay there sufferin' an' the Spirit seemed to come 'round an' reasoned that I would be spared days longer in this low ground of sorrow. That's been long ago an' here I is livin' yet."

Not even the faintest smile crossed Aunt Emma's wrinkled face while she was talking. Although she lived to marry and have a home of her own with good children, she is sad when she thinks of her childhood with all its injustice and suffering. "I'se glad my race don't have to suffer now what we did on that plantation. Some of my old friends tells me they had good homes an' wuz took keer of an' all that, but from my own 'sperience, I'se glad my chillun never knowed slavery."

CONSULTANT:
Emma Hurley
Washington, Georgia

[TR: date stamp: MAY 13 1938]

PLANTATION LIFE as viewed by ex-slave

ALICE HUTCHESON
165 Rockspring Street
Athens, Georgia

Written by: Grace McCune
Athens —

Edited by: Sarah H. Hall
Athens

and

John N. Booth
District Supervisor
Federal Writers' Project
Augusta, Georgia.

ALICE HUTCHESON Ex-Slave—Age 76

ALICE HUTCHESON

As the interviewer approached the house she could hear Alice singing, "Good mornin' to you! Howdy you do?" and through the open window the old woman could be seen busily engaged in household duties. Her broom, moving in rhythm with the song, did not miss a stroke when the tune changed to, "Lord I'se a comin' Home."

At the first sound of rapping, the singing ceased and Alice promptly opened the door. "Good mornin' Missy," she said. "How is you?" Asked for the story of her early life as a slave, she smiled and urged the visitor to "have a seat in dis here rockin' cheer out here on de porch in de sunshine."

"My Ma and Pa was named Har'iet Bell and William Hanson, and dey b'longed to Marse Cal Robinson down in Monroe County. Ma was married two times, and de fus' man was named Bell. He was de Pa of my half brother. Only one of my three sisters is livin' now. I was born in June 1862 durin' de war. Ma's two brothers, Taylor and Bob Smith, b'longed to de Robinson's in Morgan County. Dem Robinsons was kin to our white folkses, and us was still all Robinson Niggers. Ma's four sisters is all done died out long years ago.

"I jus' kin 'member one time de Yankees come to our plantation. Dey ramsacked de place, tuk all de victuals f'um de white folkses and give 'em to de slaves. Us chillun sho' hid out whilst dey was dar, 'cause dem was skeery times, and dem sojers sung old songs I heared lots of times atter I got bigger. De captain would start de song. 'Member 1866, boys, de rebels in hell of fixes, but we'll drink and eat deir bones yit.' Atter de Yankees lef' de Niggers brung back de white folkses victuals 'cause dey was our own white folkses and dey had allus done give us plenty of evvything.

"Us chillun didn't have to do no hard wuk, jus' played 'round de yards wid de white chillun mos' of de time. One of our little jobs was to git in plenty of wood for de fires. Chestnut and hick'ry wood made de bes' fires and dere was allus plenty of good kindlin' to git 'em started. Oak and pine bark was good to make de pot bile in a hurry. Dem ovens would bake lak evvything wid heaps of hot coals piled 'round 'em.

"Dere warn't no Nigger schools den, but Miss Jane larnt us 'long wid de white chillun, and us sho' had to mind dem lessons or she'd tear us up.

"De slave quarters was jus' log cabins, and dey cooked on fireplaces jus' lak at de big house. Marster didn't have many Niggers, but us had plenty somepin' t'eat. He had a big gyarden whar he raised mos' evvything: corn, 'taters, cabbages, peas, onions, collard greens, and lots of pun'kins. When de mens plowed up de 'taters us chillun had to go 'long and put 'em in baskets. De bestes' times was hog killin' times. Us chillun wukked den. Dey hung up de hogs all night and nex' day us cut 'em, put 'em down in salt, and cooked up de lard. Us chillun got some of dem good old skin cracklin's when dey got brown.

"Atter Marster tuk de meat out of de salt, he put brown sugar and 'lasses on de hams and shoulders, sacked 'em up, and hanged 'em in de smokehouse. Den he say for us to git de fire ready. Us made a fire wid cottonseed to smoke de meat. Dat kep' it good, and it didn't git old tastin'. It was sho' good eatin' when you got some of dat meat.

"When de time come 'round to gather in de corn us wukked mighty peart lak, 'cause us couldn't hardly wait for de cornshuckin's dat Marster was gwine to let us have atter dat corn was hauled in f'um de fields. Marster 'vited all de other white folkses and dey brung deir Niggers 'long. Shucks would jus' fly off of dat corn while dem Niggers was a-singin' 'Old Liza Jane' and 'Susan Jane'. When de cornshuckin' was all done, us had a big supper— chicken pies, barbecue, and plenty of evvything good wid lots of liquor too. Atter supper dey started up playin' dem fiddles and banjoes, and de dancin' begun. White folkses danced da twistification up at de big house, but us had reg'lar old breakdowns in a house what Marstar let us have to dance in. Wid all dat toddy helpin' 'em 'long, sometimes dey danced all night, and some of 'em fell out and had to be dragged off de dance flo'.

"Marse had log rollin's and 'vited evvybody. Dey all come and brung deir Niggers. Marster had big dinners for 'em, and atter dey done rolled dem logs all day dem Niggers evermore did eat. When dey was wukkin' dey sung somethin' lak dis:

> 'I'se wukkin' on de buildin'
> And hits a sho' foundation,
> And when I git done
> I'se goin' home to Heb'en.'

"All de neighbors comed to de quiltin's, and when de quilts was finished, dey throwed it over de head of de house. Dat brung good luck.

"Us had to cyard, spin and reel cotton. Missy give us chillun six cuts of thread for a days wuk and if us wukked hard and fas' us got done in time to go chestnut and chinquapin huntin'. Us th'owed rocks 'ginst de limbs to shake de nuts down, and us had jus' de bestes' time a-gittin' 'em out of de burrs and eatin' 'em. Us used to string chinquapins and hang 'em 'round our necks.

"Marster had dese big car'iages wid de high front seats whar de driver sot. Us had buggies den too, but attar de War us jus' had two-wheeled carts and dey was pulled," the old Negress modestly explained, "by male cows."

"Niggers all laked thrashin' time. Marstar, he growed

lots of wheat and de thrashin' machine tuk turn about gwine f'um one plantation to another. Dey had big dinners on thrashin' days and plenty of toddy for de thrashin' hands atter dey done de wuk. Dey blowed de bugle to let 'em know when dey done finished up at one place and got ready to go on to de nex' one.

"Missy lef' us to look atter de house when she went off to Morgan County to see de other Robinsons, and she mos' allus fetched us a new dress apiece when she come home. One time dey was Dolly Vardens, and dey was so pretty us kep' 'em for our Sunday bes' dresses. Dem Dolly Vardens was made wid overskirts what was cotched up in puffs. Evvyday dresses was jus' plain skirts and waistes sowed together. Gal chilluns wore jus' plain chemises made long, and boys didn't wear nothin' 'cep' long shirts widout no britches 'til dey was 'bout twelve or fo'teen. Dem was summertime clothes. Cold weather us had flannel petticoats and drawers. Our bonnets had staves in de brim to make 'em stand out and had ruffles 'round de front.

"Ma done de cookin' and house wuk at de big house for Mist'ess Jane Robinson. White folkses had lots of comp'ny, and dey had de cook fix de mostes' good things for 'em. Dey kilt heaps of chickens and cooked whole hams and lots of 'tater puddin's and sich lak. When Ma steamed pun'kin 'til it was done and den fried it, hit sho' would make your mouf water. Missy's folkses was crazy 'bout de 'tater puddin's what Ma made, and when she went off to visit 'em she allus had Ma bake one for her to take 'long to 'em.

"White folkses and Niggers all went to de same church and listened to de same white preacher. Church day was second Sunday of evvy mont'. White folkses went in de mornin' and Niggers atter dinner. Dem Niggers had better behave and listen to de preacher, 'cause if dey didn't Marster would give 'em a rakin' over sho'. Us went to Mount Zion Church in Monroe County, and de Baptists and Meferdists both used de same church house.

"When anybody died, dey laid 'em out on de coolin' board 'til dey got de coffin made up. A white man lived nigh us what made all de coffins. He charged 50 cents to make one for a chile and a dollar for grown folkses. Dey had de same kind of coffins for evvybody, white and black, buried 'em all in de same graveyard, and built a fence 'round it. White mens preached all de fun'rals. When dey buried a Nigger dey mos'ly had prayer, a little talkin' and some songs. Parts of de songs went lak dis:

> "Death has been here and
> Tore away a sister from our side,
> Jus' in de mornin' of 'er day
> As young as us, she had to die.
>
> "Not long ago she filled 'er place
> And sot wid us to larn,
> But she done run 'er mortal race
> And nevermore can she return.
>
> "Us can't tell who nex' may fall
> Underneath de chasen' rod,
> One maybe fus', but let us all
> Prepare to meet our God.
>
> "And needful help is thine to give
> For Grace our souls to Thee apply,

To larn us how to serve and live,
And make us fit at las' to die."

"Part of another one was:

"Oh, come angel band
Come and 'round me stand,
And bear me away
On your snowy wings,
To my immortal home."

"Seems lak I can mos' hear de preacher read de Scripture for his tex', 'Buy de truf and sell it not.'

"Sometimes our white folkses tuk us all to old Smyrna Church, and den Ma allus cooked a fine dinner to take 'long, 'cause dey had church all day and dinner on de grounds. I ain't never gwine forgit a sermon I heared at Smyrna, onct. De tex' was, 'Be thou faithful unto death, and I will give you a crown of life.'

"One day Marster called all his Niggers together and said us was all free, and dat us could go whar us pleased anytime us got ready, but he said too, dat us could stay on wid him if us wanted to. Charlie Martin was de onlies' Nigger what didn't stay. Charlie said he wanted to go somewhars else and Marster give him a good hoss and saddle and some money when he lef', but I don't know how much dat money was.

"'Twarn't long 'fore dere was plenty of Ku Kluxers 'round 'bout. Dey had on doughfaces and long white robes what come down over de hosses dey was a-ridin'. Ma allus tole us dat if one of dem Kluxers tetched a Nigger, dat Nigger was gwine to die, and us was so skeered us stayed out of deir way so day didn't ketch none of us, but dey sho' did wuk on de hides of some of dem other Niggers what dey did git a holt of.

"I wukked for Miss Sally Yervin a while and den us moved here to Athens. My gran'pa come atter us, and Mr. Mote Robinson moved us in one of dem big, high up waggons." An ice truck passed the cabin door and Alice said: "Now jus' look, Honey, us didn't have nothin' lak dat den. Our milk and butter and sich lak was kep' in de spring house. Folkses what had wells used to put milk in buckets and let 'em down in de well wid ropes, and dat milk would keep good and cool down dar.

"I got married atter us come to Athens. Us didn't have no big weddin', jus' went to de preacher man's house to git married. De onlies' child us had is done been daid for years, and my old man died 'way over 16 years ago."

The old Negress [HW:] was reluctant to end the interview. "Goodbye Missy, I hopes you come back sometime, 'cause old Alice has had a mighty good time a-talkin' to you. Atter us gits too old to do any wuk dere ain't many folkses takes up no time a-listenin' to old Niggers."

[HW: Ex-Slave Interview: Mrs. Amanda Jackson]

MRS. AMANDA JACKSON

Mrs. Amanda Jackson was born a slave. She is unable to give her age but she can tell of some of the conditions, etc. on the plantation where she lived. Following are the things that she remembers most vividly:

"I wuz born in Glasscock county 'bout twelve miles fum Davisboro, Ga. My marster's name wuz Lowry Calhoun—he did'nt have no chillun—jes' him an' his wife an' her mother. He wus a rich man an' he had a big plantation an' 'bout fifty slaves or more—I 'members de big quarters in de back o' his house, where me an' de res' o' de slaves lived, an how we uster git up an' do 'roun."

"Besides me I had two sisters an' one brother—I wuz de younges' child."

"All of de slaves on de plantation worked in de fiel'— even de cook—dat is 'till time fer her to cook de meals. On dis plantation dey raised practically everything— corn, cotton, wheat, an' rye, an' a heap o' live stock. Dey wuz runnin' 'bout twenty-five or thirty plows all de time. Dere wuz one overseer."

"Every mornin' de slaves had to git up an' by de time it wuz light enuff to see dey had to be in de fiel' workin'". When asked how they were awakened Mrs. Jackson replied: "Dey knowed how to git you up alright—de overseer had a horn dat he blowed an' dem dat did'nt wake up when de horn wuz blowed wuz called by some of de others in de quarters". Continuing, she said: "Dey wuz in de fiel' fore de sun rose an' dere 'till after it went down—fum sun to sun". "De fiel' han's had one hour fer dinner—dem dat had families done dere own cookin' an' dere wuz a special cook fer de single ones. De women whut had families would git up soon in de mornin's 'fore time to go to de fiel' an' put de meat on to boil an' den dey would come in at dinner to come in at dinner time an' put de vegetables in de pot to cook an' when dey come home in de evenin' dey would cook some corn bread in de ashes at de fireplace".

"All dat I could do den wuz sweep de yards, water de cows an' de chickens an' den go to de pasture to git de cows an' de calves—we had two pastures—one fer de calves an' one fer de cows, I had to git de cows so de womens could milk 'em."

"All of de hard work on de plantation wuz done in de summertime. In rainy weather an' other bad weather all dat dey had to do wuz to shell corn an' to help make cloth. As a rule ol' marster wuz pretty good to his slaves but sometimes some of 'em got whupped kinda bad fer not workin' an' stuff like dat—I seen 'im cut womens on dey shoulders wid a long whip 'till it looked like he wuz gonna cut de skin off'n 'im."

"You had to do yo' own work on Saturdays an' Sundays—I members seeing my po' mother wash her clothes on Sundays many times. We did'nt have no holidays except Sundays an' den we did'nt have nowhere to go except to church in de woods under a bush-arbor".

"De white folks clothes an' all o' de slaves clothes

wuz all made on de plantation. De marster's wife could sew an' she an' her mother an' some of de slaves done all o' de spinning an' weaving on de place. I've worked many a day in de house where dey made de cloth at. To color de clothes dey made dyes out o' all kinds o' barks. If dey wanted yellowstripes dey used dye made out o' hickory bark. Dere wuz always plenty o' clothes fer everybody 'cause dey give two complete outfits two times a year—one in de summer an' one in de winter. Fer blankets we used homespun spreads."

"Even de shoes wuz made on de plantation—dere wuz a man on de place dat made all o' de shoes. Dey wuz made out o' cowhide an' wuz very stiff. You had to grease 'em to wear 'em an' after you done dat you could do pretty well. De clothes dat dey wore on Sunday wuz'nt no different fum de ones dat dey wore in de week—dey didn't have nowhere to go on Sundays unless dey had services somewhere in de woods."

"Dere wuz a always plenty to eat 'cause dey raised everything dat you c'n think of. Dere wuz all kinds o' vegetables an' big fiel's of hogs an' 'bout fifteen or twenty head'a cattle dat had to be milked everyday. Dem dat had families got a issue o' food everyday an' de others whut wuz single wuz fed at de cookhouse. De only time we ever got biscuits wuz on Sundays—de res' o' de time we et cornbread. Marster had two smokehouses—one fer de lard an' one fer de meat. Besides des he 'lowed de slaves to raise dere own vegetables in dey wanted to but dey could'nt raise no chickens on stuff like dat".

"De place where de slaves lived wuz in de back o' de white folks house. Dey called it de "quarters". Dere wuz lotsa log cabins kinda 'ranged 'roun in a sorta circle an' all of 'em had big dirt chimneys on de outside. De holes in de walls wuz stopped up wid dried mud to keep de weather out. Fer furniture dey jes' nailed up anything—dere wuz a bench or two an' a few boards nailed together fer a bed. De mattress wuz a big tickin' stuffed wid straw or dried grass. Some of de houses had big iron pots so dat dey could cook if dey wanted to. De fireplaces wuz big ones an' dey had racks in de inside of 'em so dat de pots could hang dere when dey wuz cookin'. De only light dat dey had wuz de firelight—don't care how hot it wuz—if you wanted to see you had to make a fire in de fireplace. De floors in all de cabins wuz made wid wood.

"Hardly anybody ever got sick on de plantation. When dey wuz sick de white lady would come out once in a while to see how you wuz gittin' 'long. If anybody wuz very sick de doctor would come on his horse an' bring his medicine wid 'im when he come. When you wuz sick like dis somebody from de fiel' would stay in an' do de nursin'. All de medicine I 'members is big blue mass pills an' salts—dey would give you des fer anything. When you wuz too sick to go to de fiel' an' not sick enuff to be in bed you had to report to de white lady at de house—she could tell pretty much if you wuz sick an' she would work on you—if you did'nt git better den she would send fer de doctor."

"On des plantation dey did'nt have no regular church fer de slaves an' so when de weather wuz good de slaves went to de woods an' had church in a bush-arbor. Dey made a bush-arbor by takin' some posts an' puttin' dem in de groun' an' de coverin' de top wid bushes. Later on dey had a shelter covered wid boards. De prechin' wuz done by a ol' man dey called Caesar—he wuz too old to do anything else an' so prechin' wuz de biggis' thing he done."

"My marster never did sell any o' his slaves—'course if dey wanted to go to somebody yelse he'd let 'um go p'vided de one dey wanted to go to paid fer 'em. He let one or two go like dat once. Other folks uster put 'em on de block an' sell 'em like dey would a chicken or sumpin' like dat."

"Dere wuz'nt much whuppin on our plantation—not by de marster. Dey usually got whupped fer not workin'. Others got whupped by de Paddie-Rollers when dey wuz cot off'n de plantation widout a pass. Dey would come to de plantation an' whup you if dey knowed you had been off wid out a pass. Der man whose plantation we wuz on did pretty well by us—he did'nt like fer de Paddie-Rollers to come on his place to do no whuppin'."

In reply to a query regarding the possibility of a slave buying his freedom Mrs. Jackson replied: "De only ones I knowed to go free wuz some whose marsters willed 'em enuff money to buy deyself out an' dey wuz mighty few".

Continuing Mrs. Jackson said: "When de Yankee soldiers come through we had to fit busy an' hide all de meat an' de other food dat wuz in de smokehouse so dat de soldiers would'nt take it."

"My mother an' father stayed on de plantation a long time after freedom wuz declared".

"MEMORIES OF HER CHILDHOOD", BY AN EX-SLAVE, CAMILLA JACKSON

Submitted by—
Minnie B. Ross
(Colored)

CAMILLA JACKSON

Mrs. Camilla Jackson doesn't know how old she is, but is so very old that she almost never leaves her chair. She wears a white rag around her head and is always spotlessly clean. She speaks distinctly; but her memory is a little slow, due to her old age. The events related were given only after she had thought them over carefully, for, as she stated, she did not wish to tell anything but the truth. She lives in a back room of a large house and is cared for by other people in the house.

She was born in Decatur, Georgia, the daughter of Charlotte and Joe Hoyle, and the tenth child of 18 children. Her family included her mother and father, a grandmother and 17 sisters and brothers. As far as she can remember, her family always belonged to Mr. Peter Hoyle, who was a doctor.

Dr. Hoyle's family included his wife, three boys, and three girls. He owned a very large plantation, and a large number of a slaves, probably 75 or more. All of them were required to work in the fields and tend the crops, which consisted mostly of sugar cane and cotton. Syrup was made from the sugar cane. Mrs. Jackson remembers quite well that everyone was required to work in the fields, but not until Dr. Hoyle, who was a kind master, was sure that they were old enough. She was about 12 years old when she was given a job in the house, operating the fly-brush. The fly-brush was constructed so that a piece of cloth, fastened on a wooden frame with hinges, could be pulled back and forth with a cord. This constant fanning kept the room clear of flies. As she related this, she smiled to herself as if her job was particularly amusing.

Dr. Hoyle did not find it necessary to hire out any of his slaves as he had enough work to keep them all busy. She frequently said that her master was a kind man and never punished unnecessarily. It was very seldom that he used the whip. His slaves respected him for his kindness and tried to please him. As a result of his good treatment Dr. Hoyle never found it necessary to sell any one of his slaves. Once she hesitated and seemed to go into a deep study over something. A few minutes later she related the incident of the selling of a woman slave. This woman gave birth to a baby out of wedlock and, since Dr. Hoyle was a firm believer in marriage, he immediately sold her, to prevent further trouble. Mrs. Hoyle was not as kind as her husband, and at times was cruel to the slaves.

Mrs. Jackson clearly related the method of courtship and marriage on her master's plantation. Dr. Hoyle never selected the mates for his slaves but left it to each person to chose whomever he wished. However, the selection would have to be made from among the slaves on some of his friends plantations. They were not allowed to chose anyone on their own plantation. The person chosen was allowed to call on Sundays after getting a "pass" from his master. She told how courtship was carried on in those days. A young man courted the girl in the presence of the parents. Every now and then he would be seen looking at the clock. When he left, the mother would go to the door with him. When the master was properly notified of the intended marriage, he would prepare a feast and call in his own preacher to perform the ceremony. After the ceremony everybody was allowed to take part in the feast. When Mrs. Jackson's oldest sister married the master roasted a pig and stuck a red apple in its mouth. She smiled over this incident.

A slave's home life was very simple. After work hours they were allowed to visit other plantations; however, they could not visit any plantation unless their master was friendly with the owner of this particular plantation. One of the most enjoyable affairs in those days was the quilting party. Every night they would assemble at some particular house and help that person to finish her quilts. The next night, a visit would be made to some one else's home and so on, until everyone had a sufficient amount of bed-clothing made for the winter. Besides, this was an excellent chance to get together for a pleasant time and discuss the latest gossip. Most friendly calls were made on Sunday, after securing a "pass". This "pass" was very necessary to go from one plantation to another.

Slaves did not have to prepare their food during the week. Their food was brought to them in pails from the "big house". (The master's house was called the "big house".) On Sundays they were given groceries to prepare their own meals. Mrs. Jackson remembers the bread that was made from "shorts". "Shorts" was the name given to a second grade of flour, similar to whole wheat. The first grade was always used in the master's house. As a whole, Dr. Hoyle gave his slaves enough food; however, on several occasions she remembers that a friend of her mother's, who lived on the adjoining plantation, handed pans of food over the fence to them.

Slaves were never given spending money but her grandmother was very thrifty and managed to earn a little money. This was done by collecting all the rags she could find and then carrying them to town in an oxcart to sell them. Old women used oxcarts because oxen would not run away.

She smiled when asked if she had ever worn a hoop skirt. "Yes, child", she replied, "I have worn hoop skirts. They were the fad in those days." She related how her sister made hoop skirts by cutting slits in the hem of the skirt, and running a hoop through it. "I can remember the cloth that was made on the spinning wheel", she said. She told how she had turned the reel many a day and spun the thread. She could not clearly relate the construction of a spinning wheel.

Everyone, particularly the older people, was required to attend church. For Christmas everyone was given a special Sunday suit to wear to church. The slaves did not have a separate church of their own but were allowed to attend the white church and occupy the balcony. Mrs. Jackson began to laugh outright over the memory of a funny yet serious incident that occurred in church one Sunday. She had a little white girl friend with whom she played every day. One Sunday she looked over the balcony and saw her in the audience below. They both began a little game of looking and snatching back their heads. Finally she leaned over too far and fell over the balcony into the white audience below. She hurt herself pretty badly and cried so much that the service was broken up for that day. Dr. Hoyle carried her home and administered the proper treatment. After this incident she didn't look over balconies anymore.

Before she could learn anything definite the Civil War had begun and she began to see soldiers going here and there dressed in their uniforms. One event stands out clearly in her memory and that was the time the master took all of his slaves and as many of his possession as he could and went to Camp Ground, Georgia, to dodge the Yankee soldiers. After the attack on Decatur, they returned to find all of the slave quarters torn down. The master's house, which had 13 rooms, was still standing. Most of the slaves had to stay in the "big house" until their homes could be rebuilt. Many were still living in the master's house when the papers were read telling them they were free. Dr. Hoyle asked his slaves to remain and he would pay them for their services. Her family remained with Dr. Hoyle's family one year after freedom. Afterwards they moved to Atlanta, where she has lived practically all of her life. She married immediately after freedom and proudly spoke of being the first person to wed in the old "Big Bethel Church". She is now alone without sister, brother, or child; but even at her old age she is unusually optimistic and continues to enjoy life. She believes in serving God and living a clean honest life. She has just one desire, and that is to enter the Kingdom of Heaven someday.

United States. Work Projects Administration

[TR: date stamp MAY 8 1937]

Life Story as Told by Aunt Easter Jackson
Ex-Slave

EASTER JACKSON

It was during the height of slavery days that Frances Wilkerson and one child came to make their home in Troup County, having been bought by Mr. Tom Dix from a Mr. Snow, of Virginia. Frances, being an unusually intelligent slave, able to weave, spin, and do all kinds of sewing, cost Mr. Dix $1500.00. She received excellent care, never once being allowed to do any field work, and was kept at the "Big House" to do the sewing for the household.

Frances' husband, Silas Wilkerson, was bought by the Wilkerson Family, who were neighbors.

It was here on the Dix plantation, located about one mile from what is now the Court Square, that another child, Easter, was born, a few years before the Civil War. It is with a smile of tenderness that she described her life on the old plantation.

"Yes, chile, I can see Mistus now a-ridin' up on her grey horse, "Pat", wid er basket on her arm plum full of biscuit! Yes, chile, white biscuits! and ain't no short cake ever been made what could hold a light to dem biscuits. Mistus would say, 'Where's dem chillun, Mammy?'

"Lawdy, you never seed so many little niggers pop

up in all yo' life—just 'peared lak de come right out o' de groun'. Sometimes dere 'ud be so many chillun, she'd have to break de biscuits to make 'em go 'roun' and sometimes when she's have an extry big basket, she'd say, 'Bring on de milk, and less feed dese chullun.' A big bucket o' milk would be brung and po'd in little troughs and de'd lay down on dey little stommacks, and eat jest lak pigs! But de wuz jest as slick and fat as yer please— lots fatter an us is now! And clean too. Old Mustus would say, 'Mammy, you scrub dese chillun and use dat "Jim-Crow."' Lawd, chile! I done fergot you doan know what a "Jim-Crow" wus—dat's a little fine com' what'll jest natchully take the skin plum off yo' haid 'long wid de dirt.

"Dem was good old days, plenty ter eat and a cabin o' sticks and dirt to call yo' own. Had good times too, 'specially on de 4th of July and Christmas, when old Marster Tom allus let de niggers have pigs to kill for de feas'; why chile, you should er seen de pot we cooked dem pigs in, it wus so big an' heavy, it took two to put the i'on led on. And sech music! Music played on harps, saws, and blowin' quills. Ever'body had a good time; even de "white folks" turned out for de dance which went 'way into de night.

"Den dere wus de prayer meetin's, once a week, first on one of the plantations den a nother; when all de niggers would meet and worshup, singin' praises unto the Lord; I can hear 'em now, dere voices soundin' fur away. Yes sir! Folks had religun in dem days, the "Old Time Religun." Our white folks belonged to the First Baptis' Church in LaGrange, and all de slaves went to de same church. Our services wus in de basement.

"But t'wasn' long 'fore de war broke out, and den

things wuz turrible; de niggers would huddle 'roun' de "Big House" scared ter death o' de orful tales that wus told er bout de war! It wusn't but er bout a year til young Marster Tom, John, and Bee wus called to de war. Albert and Scott Dix, two young slaves, went with Marster Tom and John and stayed by them 's close as de could, cookin' and gettin' good for de camp. But t'wus a sad day when de word come dat Marster Tom wus dyin'. Old Mistus left right straight, all us slaves goin' down to de train wid her, an' when she got on, she wave her han' an' said, 'I want all o' you, white and black, to take keer o' my baby.'

"When she got dere 'twuz a two-story house where they had Marster Tom—the blood had run down de stairs.

"Ole Mistus had stood so much she couldn't stan' no mo',—the next mornin' she wus dead in de bed! One o' de slaves, Albert, and her son, John, carried her on dere shoulders for five miles, but the war bein' so bad dey couldn't carry her no further, so dey buried her by de road and after de war wus over, de took her to de fam'ly graveyard.

"Den de word spread lak wild fire: "The Niggers wuz free". That night all the slaves went up to the "Big House", wurried an' askin' 'Young Marster Tom, where is we goin'? What is we goin' to do?' Young Marster Tom said, "Go on back to your cabins and go to bed, dey are your homes and you can stay on here as long as you want to.""

According to Aunt Easter's statement, life for the slaves on the Dix plantation changed very little after the war. She later was married to John Henry Jackson, whose mother also came from Virginia. Aunt Easter had fourteen children, six of them are now living in Troup County and have good jobs. She has made her home with her children and has the respect of all the "white folks", and she often boasts that "her white folks" will care for her till she dies. She now lives on West Haralson Street, LaGrange, Troup County, Georgia.

[TR: date stamp MAY 8 1937]

SLAVERY DAYS AS RELATED BY:

SNOVEY JACKSON

Ruth A. Chitty—Research Worker

SNOVEY JACKSON

Aunt Snovey Jackson, crippled and bent with rheumatism, lives in a cabin set in the heart of a respectable white neighborhood. Surrounded by white neighbors, she goes her serene, independent way. The years have bequeathed her a kindly manner and a sincere interest in the fairness and justice of things. Wisdom and judgment are tempered with a sense of humor.

"My name is Snovey Jackson—S-n-o-v-e-y, dat's the way I spells it. D' ain't nary 'nother Snovey Jackson in de South. I was bawned in Clarksville, Va., and owned by one Captain Williams of Virginia. I don' know jes' 'zackly how old I is, but I must be 'bout 80.

"I was jes' a small chap 'bout three or fo' years old when my folks 'cided to come to Georgia to raise cotton. You see we didn't raise no cotton in Virginia—nutten' 'cept wool and flax. De people in Virginia heerd 'bout how cotton was growed down here and how dey was plenty o' labor and dey come by the hund'eds to Georgia. Back in dem days dey warn't no trains, and travel was slow, so dey come in gangs down here. Jes' like dey had de boom down in Florida few years back, dat's de way people rushed off to Georgia to git rich quick on cotton.

"When they got here it warn't nutten' like dey thought it was go'n be. Dey thought dey could make cotton 'dout no trouble, and dey'd rake in de money. My folks lef' me in Virginia 'cause I was too li'l' to be any help, and dey thought dey could get plenty o' cheap labor here. (I'se talkin' 'bout fo' de war broke out.) Of course Virginia was a slave breedin' state, and niggers was sold off jes' like stock. Families was all broke up and never seed one 'nother no mo'.

"I don't even know who my mother and father was. I never knowed what 'come of 'em. Me and my two little brothers was lef' in Virginia when Captain Williams come to Georgia. De specalators got hol' o' us, and dey refugeed us to Georgia endurin' o' de war. Niggers down here used to be all time axin' me where my folks was, and who dey was—I jes' tell 'em de buzzards laid me and de sun hatch me.

"After we was brought to Georgia Mr. James Jackson bought me. I never knowed what 'come of my brothers. The specalators had tried to keep us together, but we got all separated. I ain't got no kin in the world today dat I knows 'bout.

"De Jacksons owned a plantation in Baldwin County, but dey sold it and moved to LaGrange, Georgia. We lived dere 'til after de war was on, den dey move back to Baldwin County. Old Miss lost her son-in-law, and later her husband died, den her daughter died. She had a little grandchild, a boy, her daughter's child, to raise. She used to say she had two pets, one pet black child and one pet white child. She was good to me. I never got no punishin's.

"Old Miss had a lot of kin folks here—high class folks. Dey was stomp down Virginians, too. Dey use to call me dey kin. Miss Kizzie Weiderman was a niece o' old Miss Jackson's, and she used to come down the street and say, 'Look here, ain't dat some o' my kin?—Come shake hands wid me.' Miss Kizzie was a sight. She alluz say when she die she want all her nigger kin to come and look on her dead body.

"Finally old Miss got dissatisfied and she 'cided de best thing for her to do was to sell her home and farm here and go to Chicago to live wid her son. Dat lef' me to seek 'nother home, 'cause I didn't want to go off up dere. So we parted.

"I come to town den (it was in 1877) and found work wid de Agent o' the Central o' Georgia Railroad here in Milledgeville. My Mistis den was Mrs. Ann Bivins. She was good to me, and when they went away, she say, 'Snovey, ef'n I had the money, nuttin' but death could separate me and you.' Den the Nesbits was made de Agent, and I work fifty years at dat Central depot. I used to get up eve'y mawnin' and cook breakfas' for all de section hands, den I'd go to de house and cook for de family. Child, I jes' worked myself to death. All my folks gone away now. De Nesbits live in Florida. I sends 'em a bag o' nuts eve'y Christmas, and dey sends me a box o' oranges. Sometime dey comes here to see me.

"I mus' tell you how de Yankees done when dey come th'ough here. I was wid old Miss Jackson at dat time. We live over de river. I was a small chap not big enough to do nothing much 'cept nuss old Miss. We heard de Yankees was comin', and did dey ruin eve'thing! Why Milledgeville was jes' tore up; twon't nuttin mo'n a cow pasture when de Yankees got th'ough wid it. Dey tuck all de stock and cattle what folks had, and burned and 'stroyed eve'ything. After de war was breakin' up, we heerd de soldiers was comin' through here and was go'n pass Town Creek on de way to Sparta, and on from Sparta to Warrenton, and from Warrenton to Augusta. I lost record after dat. Some said it was go'n be 15,000 soldiers passing th'ough. We all wanted to see them. I axed old Miss to lemme go to Sand Town to see 'em. She lemme go. Hit was a crowd of us went in a big wagon. We did see 'bout 5,000 soldiers. I was 'bout 8 or 9 years old. I 'members jes' as well how dey looked—some of 'em had canteens. Dey was tryin' to git back home. Dey seemed all bewildered like. I had alluz been skeered o' soldiers, but after I seen dem I warn't skeered no mo'.

"I had alluz wanted to own a little piece of land, and have me a one room hut like other niggers had. After I started to cookin' for de white folks at de Central depot, I 'cided I'd buy me a home. So I got my eyes on a piece of property I wanted and I started to 'vestigatin' it. It seemed like a heap o' money and me making sech a li'l' bit. I found out Mrs. Ann duBignon owned de square I wanted, so I went to see her son, de lawyer. He say, 'Snovey, you can't buy dat lot. You ain't got a chance in de world to pay for it.'

"I warn't satisfied wid dat, so I walked out to where old Miss Ann lived at Scottsboro, and I talked to her. She say she was anxious to git a buyer, but she didn't want to worry wid small payments on it, and if I could finance it, she'd sell. Well, I studied and studied, and I figgered and figgered, and my little wages for a whole year, even if I didn't spend a penny for nuttin', was mighty little. So I went down to see Mr. Samuel Walker. He owned jes' 'bout all de land in Baldwin County what he had got by loans to people dat give de land as security and never could pay off. So we talked things over, and he let me have de money to pay Miss for de square. Mind you dis here was all jes' a field and woods den. Look at it now!" She proudly pointed out the modern homes and streets.

"At de end of dat fus' year, here come Mr. Walker. 'Well, Snovey, how you gittin' 'long?' he say.

"'I'se gittin' 'long fine Mr. Walker.'

"'Well, what you go'n' do 'bout dis land?'

"I was ready for him. He thought he was go'n' come down and take de land, 'cause he knowed I didn't have de money to pay off. But I was waitin' fer him.

"'I'se ready, Mr. Walker, to settle up.' Was he surprised! He sho' was disappointed. Lot o' folks has wanted my property. Finally Judge Allen persuaded me to sell him enough to build his home. Den Mr. Bone come 'long, and he wanted to build here. So you see I done sold off several lots, and I still owns part o' my square. Dis here old nigger been de foundation of dem homes you see dere.

"I could be a grand counselor now. If I could live my days over I'd show 'em all sumpin'. Like a rollin' stone, up and down, so de world go'n' move on. I been a heap o' help to folks in my day. I done made a way out o' no way.

"I ain't never married, never had no chillun, and de

niggers says I alluz been a house-bird. I suffers a heap wid rheumatism now. Dat's de reason you see me all bent over disaway. I can't hardly raise up from my waist. I looks mighty feeble but I done out-lived a lot o' 'em. Some years ago when dey was buildin' dat fine home up dere on de lot they bought from me, de contractor boarded right across dere from me wid Mrs. Sims, and he used to say, 'Aunt Snovey, how 'bout sellin' me dis corner lot to build me a marble house on? You might not be here much longer, and I sho' love to have dis corner lot.'

"I used to laugh and tell him I might eat de goose dat ate de grass dat growed on his grave. Sho' 'nough, he died here some years ago."

"Aunt Snovey, what are you going to do with all your property—you have no family and no relatives?"

"Well, dis property was here when I come here."

"Haven't you made a will?"

"Me? No mam. Some fellow'll git it. I can't say who'll git it. I better not say."

"Aunt Snovey, I would like so much to have these old chairs you have here—how about selling them to me?"

"Child, I can't tell you de folks is wanted dem chairs. I has to have sumpin' to use. Folks done traded me out o' fust one thing then another. You see dat table? Mrs. Bone up here swapped me one she had for one I had she wanted. I ain't worrying about what's go'n' become o' things when I'se gone. It was all here when I come here, and it'll be here when I die.

"I'se a old-fashioned Missionary Baptis'. I used to go

to de white folks' church. Dat's where I got my dip. We fared a heap better back in dem times dan we does now."

"Aunt Snovey do you have any pet superstitions?"

"Go on way from here, child, I ain't got nuttin' to do wid superstitions. My old Miss never 'lowed me to believe in no signs and sech like. I could dig up a lot of sorrow in my life, but dat wouldn't do no good.

"I never did believe in bumpin' 'bout, so dat's why I settled down here and made up my mind to have me a home. You see dis ain't no fine home, but it's mine and it's paid for. Some day when I can afford it, I'se go'n' try to finish de inside o' dis house. I got one room ceiled, and maybe some day I can finish it. I don't believe in taking on no bigger load dan I can git up de hill wid. I'se seed folks go th'ough de machinery o' extravagance, and it'll eat you up sho'. I'se skeerd o' debts as I is o' a rattlesnake, but debts in de right sense makes you industrious. And I'se learned dis much—that a line fence and a dog creates more fuss dan anything in de world."

United States. Work Projects Administration

[HW: DIST. 4 Ex. Slave.]

Louise McKinney 100142

[HW: "Uncle Jake"]

"A Vessel Ob De Lawd".

UNCLE JAKE

Uncle Jake was a character up in the hills of north Georgia. I can look back and see him now as he trudged through the snow in the early morning from his little log cabin down in the field. His new home-made shoes were being worn for the first time and with every swing of the milk pail, he limped.

"Whose on de Lawd's side? I's on de Lawd's side!" His thin, cracked voice rang out clearly, and every other word received special emphasis as he tried to step lightly with his left foot.

My nose was flattened against the cold, frosty window pane as I watched the old darky go about his morning chores. Just the afternoon before I had slipped away to his and Aunt Callie's cabin to talk for a little while and found him melting tallow in an old bucket over a sputtering log fire. As he rubbed the smelly drippings over the heavy shoes he kept glancing toward the sky at the soft gray clouds, then he would say, "Look at dat smoke up at de big house. It am meeting and mingling and habin' communion wid dem clouds oberhead. We's goin' hab wedder in de mornin', and here you is Cissie Ann wid dat 'plexion o' yo's as soft as a fresh born lam'. Dis wind aint for sweet chile's like you for it soun's like de pipe what de dibbil play as it whistles roun' dis chimney corner".

With all of my six years' wide experience, I always learned something new from Uncle Jake and somehow I enjoyed the musty smell of the dark cabin, the strings of red pepper draped in festoons, twists of "chawing baccer" and bunches of onions which hung from the rafters and the soft goose feather bed which Uncle Jake said warded off dampness and kept him from having "the misery in his stiff ol' jints". In spite of his protests as to me remaining longer, I settled myself on a three-legged stool and with the aid of his fumbling fingers took off my bonnet. My mother insisted that a bonnet was for protection from wind and sun, so I always wore mine, but I had to have assistance in removing it because mother braided my hair near the top of my head and pulled the plait through a hole in the bonnet left for that purpose, then the top was buttoned around it so my fingers could not remove it. Uncle Jake always laughed when he helped me take it off because we had to be rather secretive and not let mother find out.

Mammy Callie was in the kitchen churning, so I continued to ply Uncle Jake with questions while I waited for a glass of fresh buttermilk. I knew that my father was away at war and that Uncle Jake and Mammy Callie were looking after my grandparents, my mother and me, but they would not tell what war was like or why I could not go and play with other children—they always watched me when I played and everything was kept locked and hidden. It was all so strange and different from what it had been, but Uncle Jake was just the same and all he would say was, "Dis ol' worl' am just a vessel ob de Lawd and sometimes de contents of dat vessel jest don' agree, dey gets bilin' hot like when water am poured on burning embers, a powerful smoke do rise. So it is now, chile, dis ol' worl' jest got too hot wid sin and God am trying to cool it off wid refreshin' showers ob his love, but de dibbil am makin' sech a smoke it am smartin' God's eyes", and Uncle Jake would pat me on the head and I would smile and nod as if his explanation had been perfectly clear.

These thoughts of the afternoon before ran through my mind as I watched Uncle Jake as he limped through the snow with a big brown shawl wrapped around his stooped shoulders, a piece of home spun jeans pinned around his head and a pair of patched jeans trousers supported by heavy bands of the same material for suspenders. As he returned from milking, I wondered if he had my gray kitten in his pocket, but suddenly I realized he was hobbling hurriedly, the milk pail was thrown aside and he seemed badly frightened. I ran to find out what had occurred to upset Uncle Jake's usual carefree manner.

"De lock am gone! Dat mule am gone! Dem bushwhackers done tuk it off and I's done gone atter 'em, right now". His eyes flashed as he shouted without stopping and he hobbled down to his cabin. Grandfather went down and tried to convince him that the weather was too cold to attempt to follow the thief and to wait until later, but the old negro began quoting scripture as he put on another coat and heavy knit gloves. "De Lawd say, 'Dey shall not steal', and de white folks is sho' to think I tuk 'at mule off. Fuddermore, in de 'pistle ob de 'postle, Isaiah, he say, 'Be a clean vessel ob de Lawd God', and I gonna find out de truf and prove my position 'fore dese people. Dat low-down scallawag what come here wid no 'nouncement ob his 'pearance is gwine suffer for dis here axident. He nebber reckoned wid me". And with that Uncle Jake waded into the deep snow and was last seen following the creek down through the meadow as it meandered underneath an icy crust.

Several days passed and anxiety began to show on the faces of those at home, but one morning Mammy Callie came to get breakfast with her face aglow. After praying most of the night, she said "The good Lord has given me a sho sign, for He done showed me a vision of a man up 'fore a Jedge and den I see Jake wid a bucket of oats and dat mule was toggin' behin' him".

His spirit was contagious and we lived in an atmosphere of expectancy during the day and were not surprised when we heard shouts of joy and praises to "de good Lawd" from Jake as he rode up on the old mule.

He had been unable to locate any tracks, but he had walked miles in the cold and sneaked around the barns and in the chimney corners to eavesdrop at the homes of those whom he suspected of being disloyal to the Confederate cause. While hiding under a haystack late one afternoon, he heard voices and he recognised his master's mule as it was sold by a stranger with a decided northern brogue to the owner of the place on which he was hiding. Uncle Jake almost shouted for joy, but he realised he was on "alien" territory so he remained out of sight. When the mule was fed and stabled, he skipped in under cover of darkness and led the mule away. In the excitement of getting away he forgot that he had crossed the county line, so no excuse was taken when the sheriff of that county took him into custody. Uncle Jake was hailed into court the next morning with the "owner" as witness against him.

"How old are you?" asked the judge in a stern manner.

"I's ol' enuf to know dat am de mule what belongs to Marster. I knows him by his bray", answered the negro, as he looked over the crowd and saw and felt no sympathy from any of them.

"You were caught with stolen goods out of your county and from all appearances you were hurt in the attempt to escape for I see you are limping. What do you say to that?"

Uncle Jake was trembling as he looked down at his smelly shoes. "No, sir, Jedge. You is sho' wrong. I jest receibed a commandment from my heabenly Father to walk in de Truth and I was serbing my white folks by getting back what is ders. Dis mule was stole by some po' sinner what don' know de scriptures".

At this point the sheriff from Jake's county, who was a good friend of our Marlow family, walked into the courtroom to see if he could help Jake in his difficulties. When the frightened negro saw him, he forgot the dignity of the court and shouted, "Praise de Lawd. I's been a vessel ob His for nigh onto sixty years and He's done fill me full ob Grace and Glory dis very hour".

And without further ado, he left the sheriff to make all explanations. As he ran to the hitching post the mule began to bray and as Uncle Jake mounted he shouted, "We're shaking de dust ob dis place from off our feet and goin' back to our (Fannin) county where we can con-tinue bein' vessels ob de Lawd and servin' our white folks".

As long as he lived, Uncle Jake was a faithful servant to his white folks. Every time I slipped away to spend a little time at the log-cabin, I always asked him to repeat the story of how he returned the mule and with each repeating he praised the Lord more for being a direct instrument in helping him prove to the countryside that he was "a clean vessel ob de Lawd", but he blamed the new shoes and his skinned heel for not getting across the county line before he was caught.

- **BIBLIOGRAPHY.**

An old negro by the name of Jake identified a mule of his master's in court at Morganton. The little girls in the Morris family in Fannin County were made to wear bonnets with their hair pulled through so they could not be removed.

These two facts told me by Mr. J. R. Kincaid of Blue Ridge.

Slave Narratives

PLANTATION LIFE as viewed by Ex-Slave

MAHALA JEWEL
177 Berry Street
Athens, Georgia.

Written by: Grace McCune
Athens —

Edited by: Sarah H. Hall
Athens —

John N. Booth
District Supervisor
Federal Writers' Project
Residencies 6 & 7.

MAHALA JEWEL Ex-Slave—Age 76.

MAHALA JEWEL

Mahala Jewel, known in the community as "Aunt Hailie," was sitting on her tiny porch when the interviewer arrived. "I'se a-tryin' to git my foots warm," she declared. "Dey was cold all last night, and didn't warm up none even when I had done walked all de way up to de courthouse to git dem cabbage what de welfare ladies had for me today. Yes Ma'am, hit sho' is hard times wid old Hailie now. I was raised whar folks had plenty. Our white folks warn't no pore white trash, and if my old Marster and Mist'ess was a-livin' today dey sho' would do somepin' for old Hailie in a hurry, 'cause dey allus give us plenty of evvything dey had."

Aunt Hailie's rickety chair was kept in vigorous motion as she talked and the visitor was fearful it would collapse at any moment. One rocker was broken and on top of the cushions in the low seat of the chair she was sitting on an old cheese box. Suddenly she arose to go in the house to "see if dem cabbages is a-burnin'," and when she returned she carefully adjusted the box before resuming her precarious perch in the old rocking chair. When she was sure that her feet were in a sunny spot, she began her narrative.

"Gracie Wright was my Ma's name 'fore she tuk off and married my Pa. He was named Tuggle, and both of 'em belonged to Marse Hamp McWhorter on his plantation down in Oglethorpe County. Marse Hamp was sho' a rich man and on his big old plantation dey raised evvything dey needed lak, peas, 'tatoes, ingons, collards, cabbages, and turnip sallet, beans, punkins, and plenty of corn, wheat and rye. Marse Hamp had lots of cows, hogs, sheep, and goats too. Miss Liza was our Mist'ess, and she raised more chickens dan dey ever could use. I just tells you, my white folks warn't no pore folks.

"I was born and raised up right dar. Ma wukked in de fields, and Mist'ess brung me up in de big house 'cause she said I was gwine to have to wait on her when she got old. Dare was sho' a moughty big lot of slave chillun a-comin' on all de time and Marster and Mist'ess was good as dey could be to all of 'em. Marster and Mist'ess had seben chillun. Deir boys was William, Joe, James, and Mack. Miss Tildy and Miss Mary was two of deir gals, but I just can't ricollect de name of deir oldest daughter.

"Whilst us was little, slave chillun didn't have much wuk to do. De littlest ones just picked up trash when de yards was bein' cleant up and done easy jobs lak dat.

"Marse Hamp never fooled wid dem little one track stores at Maxeys, de town nighest our plantation. When he needed somepin', he just cotch a train and lit out for 'Gusty (Augusta), Georgie. Mist'ess knowed when he was comin' back, and she allus sont de car'iage to meet him. When us chillun seed 'em gittin' out de car'iage and hosses, us didn't wait, us just lit out and when dat train got to de crossin' all of us was right dar a-waitin' to see our Marster step off. Den us followed dat car'iage down de big road plum back to de plantation, 'cause us knowed Marster never forgot none of us. Dere was new dresses for de gals and clothes for de boys too, and us felt moughty proud when us dressed up in dem store bought clothes f'um 'Gusty. Chilluns' evvy day clothes was just slips cut all in one piece, sleeves and all. Boys wore long shirts 'til dey was big and strong enough for field wuk. Clothes for de grown folks was made out of cloth wove in de loom house right dar on de plantation, but dere was some beaded cloth too.

"Us sho' did have a pretty place. De big house was painted white, and dere was big old yards wid lots of flowers. De slave quarters was white too. Dey was one room cabins built in long rows, way off f'um de big house. Home-made beds was nailed to de wall and had just two laigs, and de big ticks stuffed wid straw made dem beds moughty good places to sleep.

"Most of de slaves et at de two long tables close by de kitchen up nigh de big house. De kitchen warn't built on to de big house, but hit sot out in de yard a little piece. Dat's de way evvybody had deir kitchens built dem days. Marster kept a big strong man to do de cookin' for his slaves. Pa was de boss for Marse Hamp. I don't 'member much 'bout him. My brother stayed in de cabin wid Pa and Ma, but I was all time up at de big house wid Mist'ess. She was good to me as she could be. She told me to allus do right and never do no wrong to nobody. I had a little highup cheer what I sot in to keep de flies off of Mist'ess.

"All de slaves went to church wid deir white folks, and sot in de back part of de meetin' house. Us went to old Beard (Baird) Church, off out in de country, and sometimes I had to take de littlest white chilluns out and stay in de car'iage wid 'em, if dey got too restless inside de meetin' house. Out dar in de car'iage us could listen to de singin' and it sho' did sound sweet. Meetin' days was big days. Dey fetched deir dinners and stayed all day. De McWhorter family allus carried great big baskets, and one of deir biggest baskets was kept special just to carry chickens in, and de barbecue, it was fixed right dar on de church grounds. Slave gals sot de long tables what was built out under de trees, and dem same gals cleant up atter evvybody had done got thoo' eatin'. Niggers et atter de white folks, but dere was allus a plenty for all. Little Niggers kept de flies off de tables by wavin' long branches kivvered wid green leafs for fly brushes. Some few of 'em brung home-made paper fly brushes f'um home. Most of dem all day meetin's was in July and August. Some folks called dem months de 'vival season, 'cause dere was more 'vival meetin's den dan in all de rest of de year. De day 'fore one of dem big baptizin's dey dammed up de crick a little, and when dey gathered 'round de pool next day dere was some tall shoutin' and singin'. White preachers done all de preachin' and baptizin'.

"Somehow I don't 'member much 'bout de celebratin' when dey got in de wheat and done de thrashin'. Dey was so busy wid de cotton 'bout dat time on our place dat dere warn't much frolickin', but de sho' nuff big celebratin' was in de fall atter all de corn was gathered and dey had cornshuckin's. Marse Hamp 'vited all de white folks and deir Niggers. De white folks visited and de Niggers done de wuk. De fust thing dey done at cornshuckin's was to 'lect a gen'ral. All he done was to lead de singin' and try to git evvybody to jine in his song 'bout de corn, and as dey sung faster, de shucks dey flew faster too. Atter de corn was all shucked, dey et de big feast what us had done been cookin' for days and days. Hit tuk a passel of victuals, 'cause dem shuckers could sho' hide 'way dem good eats. Den de fiddlers started up deir music wid Turkey in de Straw. De old breakdown dancin' was on, and hit was apt to go on all night.

"Syrup makin' time at Marse Hamp's was a frolic too. Us raised plenty of sugar-cane to make dat good old 'lasses what tasties so good wid hoecake and homemade butter.

"Atter de War, Ma and Pa stayed on wid Marse Hamp a long time. Mist'ess died when I was just a little chile, but she had done willed me to Miss Mary and told her to allus take keer of Hailie. Miss Mary stayed right on dar wid Marse Hamp. My Ma and Pa had done left, and I ain't never heared nothin' more f'um 'em since dey went away f'um Marse Hamp's place.

"Den Marster he done went and got kilt. He had rid off on a middle size pony what must a runned away wid him, 'cause dey found him plumb daid in a ditch. It was all so sudden lak us never could find out if he died happy. Us knowed Mist'ess died happy 'cause she told de folks 'round de bed dat de Lord was a-takin' her home out of dis old world of trouble.

"Atter Marse Hamp died, Miss Mary married Marse Pleaze Winter, and us all moved to Flatwoods, what warn't so fur f'um Marse Jim Smith's place. I 'members when dat Smith man died. Dey buried him in de graveyard on his own plantation at fust, but den dey said nobody didn't want to live dar atter he was buried dar, so dey tuk him up and buried him somewhar else.

"I didn't lak to live at Flatwoods, but I stayed on wid my Miss Mary and nussed her chillun 'til me and Joe Jewel got married. Joe was named atter his old Marster, Captain Joseph Jewel, and dey lived on de Jewel place in Oglethorpe County. I never did keer much for fine clothes and Miss Mary said what clothes I had was all right, but she just would give me a nice white weddin' dress. She had us git married at her house, and she 'vited lots of mine and Joe's folks and our friends to a big supper she had fixed for us. Miss Mary sho' did give me a grand send off. Atter dat, I visited my Miss Mary whenever I wanted to, and still helped her wid her babies when she needed me.

"Miss Mary is done daid now, but if she was a livin' old Hailie would have what she needs. I'm a gittin' moughty old now and my old man is done gone on to glory, but Hailie will soon be wid him dar. Whilst I did go and git married to a Jewel, I ain't forgittin' I was borned and bred a McWhorter, and I'm here to tell you dat I'm still just de same—a McWhorter."

BENJAMIN JOHNSON EX-SLAVE

BENJAMIN JOHNSON

Following is Benjamin Johnson's own account of some of his experiences as a slave and of conditions on his plantation.

"On our plantation de white folks been feedin' de slaves off fat meat, jowls, an' heads an' jaws. Dey kept all de meat out in de smoke house in de back yard. In dis house dey kept de hams all hangin' up high an' above dem dey kept de sausages and den above dem dey kept de finest hams all trimmed an' everything. De slaves eat dat fat meat an' thought dat dey wus eatin' pound cake. Come down to chicken—if you got it you stole it when de white folks wus sleep at night an' den you had to be careful an' bury all de feathers in de groun' 'cause if you burned 'em de white folks would smell 'em. We boys in de fiel' used to be so hungry 'till we didn't know what to do. De overseer would be settin' down under a tree an' he would holler 'keep goin.' De sweat would be jes' running' off you and sometimes you could smell one another.

"Dere wus a spring nearby an' when we would git to it we would fall down an' drink fum de branch. De women would be plowin' an' hoein' grain an' de spanish needles an' cockle burrs would be stickin' to dere dresses fum dere knees to dere feet. Further down dere would be a man diggin' a ditch. Every now an' den white folks would walk over to de ditch an' see if it wus de same width all de way."

"You go off to see somebody at night—jes' like you an' me want to laff an' talk—an' if dey ketch an' you ain't got no pass den dey gwine to whup you. You be glad to git away too 'cause when dey hit you, you wus hit. I wus down to ol' John Brady's place one night talkin' to a lady an' ol' man Brady slipped up behin' me an' caught me in de collar an' he say: "Whut you doin' over here?—I'm goin' to give you twenty-five lashes" an' den he say to me: "come here". He wus jes' bout as tall as I am an' when I got to 'im he say turn 'roun' and' I say to 'im dat I ain't doin' nuthin' an' den he say: "dats whut I'm goin to whup you fer 'cause you ought to be home doin' sumpin'. 'Bout dat time when I stooped over to take off my coat I caught 'im in his pants an' throwed 'im in a puddle o' water an' den I lit out fer home. If you git home den dey couldn't do nuthin' to you. He tried to chase me but he did'nt know de way through de woods like I did an he fell in a gulley an' hurt his arm. De next mornin' when I wus hitchin' up de boss man's horse I seed 'im comin' an' I tol de boss dat he tried to whup me de night befo' an' den de boss man say "did he have you?" I tol' 'im dat he did but dat I got away. An' den de boss say: "He had you an' he did'nt have you—is dat right?" Den he say "don't worry 'bout dat I can git you out of dat. If he had you he shoulda whupped you an' dat woulda been his game but he let you git away an' so dat wus yo' game." 'Bout dat time ol' man Brady had done got dere an' he tol' de marster dat I wus on his place de night befo' an' dat I got away an' when he tried to whup me an' de marster say to him: "dat wus his game—if you had him you shoulda whupped 'im. Dats de law. If you had whupped 'im dat woulda been yo' game, but you let 'im git away an' so dat wus his game."

Ol' man Brady's face turned so red dat it looked like he wus gonna bus'.

"We worked in de fiel' every day an' way in de night we shucked an' shelled corn. De cook done all de cookin'. When all of de marster's 75 slaves wus in de fiel' dey had two cooks to feed 'em. At twelve o'clock de cooks would blow a horn at de stump in de yard back o' de cook house. Even de hosses an' de mules knowed dat horn an' dey would'nt go a step further. You had to take de mule out of de harness an' take 'im to de spring an' water 'im an' den take 'im to de house where a colored man up dere named Sam Johnson had all de feed ready fer de hosses. When you git dere all de hosses go to dere own stalls where dere wus ten ears o' corn an' one bundle o' fodder fer each hoss. While dem hosses is eatin' you better be out dere eatin' yo' own. Sarah an' Annie, de cooks had a big wooden tray wid de greens an' de meat all cut up on it an' you pass by wid yo' tin pan an' dey put yo' meat all cut up on it along wid de greens an' den you could eat anywhere you wanted to—on de stump or in de big road if you wanted to. Sometimes some of 'ems meat would give out or dere bread would give out an' den dey would say: "I'll give you a piece of my bread for some or yo' meat or I'll give you some of my meat for some of yo' bread". Some of 'em would have a big ol' ash cake an' some of 'em would have jes' plain corn bread. Dere wus usually a big skillet o' potatoes at de cook house an' when you eat an' drink yo' water den you is ready to go back to work. Dey wus goin' to let you lay down in de shade fer 'bout a hour but you would make de time up by workin' till dark. Some of 'em worked so 'till dey back wus gone. Dey could'nt even stand up straight.

"Sometimes ol' missus would come 'long an' she would be mad wid some of de women an' she would want to go to whuppin' on 'em."

"Sometimes de women would'nt take it an' would run away an' hide in de woods. Sometimes dey would come back after a short stay an' den again dey would have to put de hounds on dere trail to bring dem back home. As a general rule dere wus'nt much whuppin' on our plantation. 'Course if you did'nt do what dey tol' you to do dey would take you out an' put yo' hands round a pole an' tie you so yo' feet would jes' touch de groun' an' den dey would go to work on you wid a cowhide. Everytime dey hit you de blood would fly wid de whip."

"De clothes den wus'nt but ol' plain white cloth. Most of 'em wus patched fum de legs to de waist. Some wus patched so till dey looked like a quilt. Some of de women wore dese long striped cotton dresses an' when dey would go in de fiel' de Spanish needles an' de burrs would stick all over 'em. De only shoes dat you got wus red brogans. If you got anything better it wus some dat de marster give you fer brushing off his shoes at de house. You wus so proud whenever dey give you a pair o' shoes or a ol' straw hat dat dey wus through wid at de house you went back an' showed it to everybody an' you wus mighty proud too. I used to drive my marster's hoss an' buggy fer 'im an' so I used to git a lotsa stuff like dat."

"Ol' marster wus a judge an' his name wus Luke Johnson. His wife wus named Betsy an' his sons wus named Jim, Tom, Will, an' Dorn. His daughters wus Janie, Mary, Catherine, an' Lissie. He had 300 acres of land an' 75 slaves."

"All de houses on de plantation 'cept ol' marster's wus built out o' logs. Ol' marster lived in a fine house. Sometimes when one o' de slaves had a chance to go inside his house all de rest of de slaves would be waitin' outside fer you to come out. When you did come out dey would say: "You been in de marster's house—how did it look in dere—whut did you see?" Dey would tell 'em: "you ought to go in dere—it's so pretty". Whenever you got a chance to go in dere you had done pulled off yo' hat long' fore you got to de door.

"On Sunday we would take soot out of de chimney an' wet it an' den go an' borrow de marster's shoe brush an' go an' brush our shoes. We wus gittin' ready to go to church."

"At church all de white folks would sit in de front an' all de slaves would sit in de back. De preacher would preach an' say: "Obey yo' master an' yo' missus an' you will always do right. If you see eggs in de yard take 'em to yo' marster or yo' missus an' put 'em at her feet. If you don't do dis she will needle you well or break bark over yo' head an' de bad man will git you."

"Sometimes dey would give us a dollar at Christmas time an' if somebody did'nt take it fum us we would have it de nex' Christmas 'cause we didn't have nuthin' to spend it fer."

"When de war broke out ol' marster enlisted an' he took me 'long to wait on him an' to keep his clothes clean. I had plenty o' fun 'cause dere wus'nt so very much work to do. I 'members seein' 'im fightin' in Richmond an' Danville, Virginia. I had a good time jes' watchin' de soldiers fightin'. I did'nt have to fight any at all. I used to stand in de door of de tent an' watch 'em fight. It wus terrible—you could hear de guns firin' an' see de soldiers fallin' right an' left. All you could see wus men gittin' all shot up. One day I seed one soldier git his head shot off fum his body. Others got arms an' legs shot off. An' all de time all you could hear wus de guns goin'—bam, bam, bam—it wus terrible to see an' hear. One mornin' as I wus standin' in de door of de tent I had a dose of it. I wus leanin' against de side of de tent wid my hand stretched out a load o' grape shot fum de guns hit me in de hand an' de blood flew everywhere. I jes' hollered. It come pretty near scareing me to death. After de doctor got it patched up (and he held the hand up to exibit the scar) it wus as good as it every wus."

"After de war wus over ol' marster wus all shot up an' I had to take him on back home. When we got dere all de slaves crowded 'roun me an' wanted to know if dey wus gonna be freed or not an' when I tol' 'em dat de war wus over an' dat dey wus free dey wus all very glad. After de war a whole lots of 'em stayed on de plantation an' a whole lots of 'em left as soon as dey could git away."

PLANTATION LIFE as viewed by Ex-Slave

GEORGIA JOHNSON
1537 W. Broad Street
Athens, Georgia

Written by: Grace McCune
Athens —

Edited by: Sarah H. Hall
Athens —

Leila Harris
Augusta

GEORGIA JOHNSON
Ex-Slave—Age 74

GEORGIA JOHNSON

Almost without exception the old Negroes who have given their "ricollections" have had life stories centered around one plantation. Unlike these Aunt Georgia Johnson, 74 years old, of Athens, Georgia, moved about considerably during her childhood, lived in several states and had many and varied experiences. After coming back home she is of the opinion shared by all Georgians: "Dar's no place kin tetch Georgie."

"Ma's fust name was Myra. I don't 'member what her other name was. Atter her white folkses had done died out up in Maryland, her Pa, her brudder and sister was sold off up dar, and a man named Jim Grisham brung de rest of de slaves from dat plantation down to Lexin'ton, Georgie to sell 'em. Marse Duncan Allen bought my Ma and her Mammy dar at de sale in Lexin'ton and tuk 'em to his big old plantation in South Callina.

"Ma said her didn't never see no hog meat 'til she come to dis country. Her said dey et all sorts of fishes; just went to de beach and got crabs, oysters, and swimp (shrimp) wid de hulls still on 'em, but when her done et some hog meat at Marster's plantation, her said hit sho' was good. Marse Duncan Allen give my Ma to his gal, Mist'ess Laura, for her maid. My Pa, he was Charlie Allen; he b'longed to Marse Duncan Allen too. When Mist'ess Laura done went and married Marse Blackwell of E'berton, Georgie, Marse Duncan give 'em my Pa for a weddin' present and dey fetched my Ma and Pa wid 'em to live in E'berton, Georgie. Atter dey got moved and settled, my Ma and Pa dey got married. Ma, her wukked in de big house and done most of de cookin'. Pa driv' de carriage for de white folks. Marster and Mist'ess was powerful good to deir slaves. Marster, he run a big store at E'berton, and 'sides dat he had a big plantation and a heap of Niggers too.

"On de plantation dey had big gyardens whar dey raised heaps of cabbages, potatoes, colla'd greens, turnip sallet, onions, peas, rutabagas, and pun'kins and sech lak. Dey raised plenty of chickens, tukkeys, hogs, cows and sheep, and dey wove good wool cloth on de plantation looms out of de wool f'um dem dar sheep.

"Slave quarters was just one room log cabins what was built so de corners come together to big old chimneys. Yessum, I 'members dey just had one big chimney to evvy four cabins. Dey cooked on de fireplace and had pot racks for to hang de pots on, and ovens to bake in. Us sho' could do 'way wid a heap of sweet 'tatoes what had done been roasted in de ashes. Cabins was planked up on de inside and de outside was daubed wid mud in de cracks to keep out de wind and rain. Our home-made beds, nailed to de side of de cabins, had ticks filled wid wheat straw. White folks had nice corded beds. Ma said hit was lots of trouble to keep dem cords tight. Dey had hooks for to draw 'em up tight and den peg 'em down wid wooden pegs.

"Marster allus give his Niggers passes on Sundays so as dem paddyroller folks wouldn't ketch 'em and beat 'em up, if dey went off de plantation. Niggers went to de white folks church and listened to white preachers. When Ma jined de church, dey had to break de ice in Beaver Dam Crick to baptize her. Her was so happy and shouted so loud, dey had to drag her out of de crick and take her way back in de woods to keep her from 'sturbin' de rest of de folks at de baptizin'.

"I was borned in de last year of de War so I don't have no sho' 'nough ricollections 'bout dem hard times what old folks says dey had dem days. Atter de War was over, us all stayed on wid Marster for a long time. Mist'ess was moughty good to us chillun. Us played wid de white chillun, and one day Mist'ess cotch us all a-fightin', and her switched us all, but it didn't hurt. Marster used to git my sister to shout for him. I kin just see her now, a-twistin' and jumpin' and hollerin' for all de world lak grown-up Niggers done at meetin's and baptizin's, 'til she done fell out. Den Marster, he say, 'Take her to de kitchen and feed her good.'

"Pa and Marster had a fallin' out, 'cause Marster wouldn't have no settlement wid 'im. He just wouldn't give my Pa no money. Marster said us younguns still b'longed to 'im and dat us had evvything us needed, and could git anything us wanted at his store and he thought he had done 'nough for us. But my Pa said he didn't wanter take up evvything he wukked for in trade, 'cause he would lak to have some money too.

"Bout dat time Marse Pope Barrow was a gittin' up lots of Niggers to go wid him to Mis'sippi for to raise cotton out dar, whar he said dey was makin' heaps of money. Pa tuk us all and went 'long wid 'im. I just kin 'member dat place. Hit was all kivvered wid water. Marse Pope, he hired a lot of Irishmen to help dig ditches for to dreen de water off his land. Den dey planted cotton and Pa said hit sho' was fine cotton, just a-growin' to beat de band, when dem Irishmens got mad 'cause dey said Marse Pope hadn't paid 'em for deir wuk, and dey blowed up de dams and let all dat water back on de cotton. Hit was plumb ruint. Den Marse Pope, he left dar and tuk my Pa and all of us along wid him to Arkansas. Us made a big cotton crop out dar, but when all de cotton done been sold us Niggers didn't git nothin'. Ma, her had done all de cookin' for de mens what wukked for Marse Pope. His wife, Mist'ess Sallie Barrow used to come to see him and her allus brought her maid along wid her, and de maid, her stayed wid us. Ma said us chillun used to cry to go back to Georgie wid Mist'ess Sallie, 'cause her rid on one of dem boats what was run wid steam. Pa left Marse Pope 'cause he wouldn't give 'im no pay. Us sold our things and come to Memphis, Tennessee and went to farmin' for Marse Partee, and us just stayed dar long 'nough to make one crop. Whilst us was out dar, our little sister died. Just 'fore her died her said her was goin' to see God. Her told de debbil to git away f'um dar, 'cause her warn't gwine wid him. Dey put a little white dress on her and laid her out on de bed, 'til dey could make up a coffin out of plain pine wood for her. Dey just had a prayer and sung 'Hark F'um De Tomb,' and den dey buried her away in de groun'.

"Pa got his money for dat crop and den us come on back to da plantation in E'berton, Georgie, 'cause Old Marster had done been a-wantin' us back. He said he needed us, chillun and all, and us was sho' glad for to git back home. Ma done de cookin' and Pa driv' de carriage and done little jobs 'roun' de barns and hosses. Sometimes he wukked a little in de fiel's. Us chillun used to clean yards, git in de wood, feed chickens and on Sundays atter dinner when dar warn't no company at de big house us would go up to de big plunder room in de attic and us would have de bestes' times wid de white chilluns, a-dressin' up in de old clothes what Mist'ess had stored away up dar. Sometimes when Marster would ketch us up dar all dressed up, he would make us come down and preach for him. Den he made us all set down 'cep' one what was to do de preachin'. Sometimes it was his own son he called on to preach to us, and dat white boy sho' told us Niggers 'bout our sins. Den dey would make my sister, Millie, sing, 'Po' Sinner Man, Done Gone Down Yonder'. One time when Marster's son was a preachin' he told all about a fight us done had once when I hit him wid a rock. He said I sho' was goin' to de debbil for dat. I just knowed Marster was gwine git atter me 'bout dat, but he just laughed and said hit warn't de fust time a preacher had done been hit wid a rock."

"Marse Deadwyler, de mayor, up at E'berton, lived on de plantation next to ours, and he had a big old deer what sho' hated chillun. Hit would try to stomp 'em to death, and us sho' did make tracks fast sometimes when dat old deer got out. And Marster had a old mule what would fight at us chillun too. One time us didn't know he was in de parstur when us went out dar to play. De gate was wukked wid draw poles and us couldn't git 'em down, so us had to crawl under a old crib house and hit was plumb dark when Marster foun' us. Us sho' didn't go in de parstur no more lessen us knowed dat mule was fas'ened up good and tight at de barn."

"One time, in de middle of de night, long atter us chillun had done gone to bed us heared grown folks runnin' 'roun', and dey told us to git up and see Mr. Deadwyler's house a burnin' up. Dat was de bigges' fire I ever seed. Blazes and sparks went way up, and dey didn't save nothin'. Us chillun got so 'cited us didn't go back to bed no more dat night."

"Niggers didn't have no church of dey own, but dey did have prayer meetin's. Dey would kindle 'em a big fire for light and to keep 'em warm, off clost to de woods, whar deir racket wouldn't 'sturb de white folks, and dey would gather 'roun' dat fire and pray. Sometimes slaves would just go off by deirselfs in de woods to pray. One night when Ma was out in de woods a prayin' her heared a loud fuss back of her lak somebody was tearin' down de woods, and hit skeered her so her quit prayin' and run to de big house. Marster told her, hit was de debbil atter her."

"Pa got mad again at Old Marster 'cause still he wouldn't have no settlement wid 'im, so us left E'berton again and went back to South Callina to de old Allen place where Pa had come f'um. Den Pa bought me a doll what would dance when you wound it up, and I sho' did love dat little dancin' doll. Soon Miss Laura come to see her pa, Marse Duncan Allen, and her brung me a little doll too. Her said I needed somebody to play wid 'cause I couldn't go to school on account of my eyes. Dey was bad and I warn't 'lowed to read nothin', but Ma larnt me to do a little sewin'. I felt moughty big and grown up soon as I could make my own dresses and chemise. Dey warn't hard to make, but I was moughty proud 'cause I had done made 'em my own self."

"Marse Duncan Allen didn't have no little chillun of his own den, but he sho' seed atter us. For supper us had bread and milk, wid butter and 'lasses sirup. Dey says dats 'nough for chillun at night. Us was still dar on Marse Allen's place when me and Isaac McCollie got married. De white folks said I was too young 'cause I was just 15 den, but my Ma told me I could go ahead and git married if I wanted too. Isaac's two brudders was married at de same time. Whilst de boys was gone atter licenses and de preacher, us three gals was a-waitin' up at Marse Tom Young's house whar de weddin' was to take place. Dem other two gals was so skeered dat Marse Tom's house-keeper give each one of us a glass of gin to quiet our nerves, but I warn't skeered a bit, not me, when I had a chanst to be all dressed up lak dat, in a satin striped white weddin' dress wid a long train a-trailin' off de back of it. All de ten ruffles 'roun' dat dress was aidged wid pink and de big puffed sleeves had pink cuffs. Hit did seem an awful long time 'fore dem boys got back wid Preacher Lockhart. Us was married dar at Marse Tom's and den us went back to Marse Duncan Allen's place whar de bigges' surprise I ever had was ready for us. Marster and Mist'ess had done 'lowed dat if I just had to git married dey would do de best dey could for me. Out in de big house yard was long tables just loaded down wid everything good—chickens, barbecue, pies, and a great big weddin' cake, what my good old Mist'ess done baked for me her own self, and den us just had de bigges' sort of time a-dancin' and frolickin' atter us et all dat good supper. Isaac's Pa said he owed him one more year 'cause he was just 19 when us got married, and all us got for dat whole year's wuk was a little corn and one heifer.

"Old Marse Blackwell had done died and Miss Laura was a-beggin' my Pa to come back and wuk for her, but he wouldn't go nowhar 'til atter Marse Duncan Allen died, den he moved back to Georgie, down nigh de Jim Smith place. Den Pa got a farm whar de stockade is now. Us wukked moughty hard a-gittin' a start, and dat hard wuk made good crops and us raised most all us needed to eat—veg'tables, hogs, cows, chickens, tukkeys, and sech lak. In de fall atter us had done wukked so hard all thoo' crop time, Pa let us have cornshuckin's. Us cooked for two or three days 'fore dem cornshuckin's 'cause dere was allus a big crowd to be fed. When de big day come, fust thing us done was choose a gen'ral. He just walked 'roun' de big piles of corn and led de singin'. Somehow, I can't 'member how dat song went, but it was all 'bout corn. De gen'ral started de song slow and den got it to goin' faster and faster and de livelier de song went de faster de shucks would fly, and de more often dey would pass 'roun' de liquor. Soon as all de corn was shucked, us had de big feast wid plenty of good coffee and toddy to go wid dem good victuals us had done been cookin' up; dem chickens, all dat fresh killed hog meat and a big spread of lightbread and pies and cakes. Dem was de good old days, and dey don't have no sech grand times a helpin' each other, and a-celebratin' de harvest time no more.

"Atter Isaac died, I wukked for diff'unt white folks, cookin' and washin' 'til I married Alec Johnson. Dis time us just went to de preacher for to git de knot tied and didn't have no big weddin'. I did have on a nice white dress, but hit warn't nigh so pretty and fancy as my fust weddin' dress. A few friends come 'roun' dat night and us handed 'em out a little cake and ice cream, but dere warn't no big supper.

"Bofe my husbands is done been daid and gone long ago, but I'se still got two of my chillun, my gran'chillun and four great gran'chillun. Dey's all sweet and good to me, and sees dat I has all what I needs. I done lost de sight in one eye and de other one is failin' moughty fast. I prays and prays dat de good Lord will let me see a little, what time I'se got left to live.

"One of my chillun died de fust of dis year and soon I'm gwine to jine her. I hopes you laks what I ricollected, but somehow I can't call dem old times back to mind since I done got so old, lak I use to. Come back to see me again, Honey. Good-bye."

United States. Work Projects Administration

MANUEL JOHNSON of WASHINGTON-WILKES

by

Minnie Branham Stonestreet
Washington-Wilkes
Georgia

MANUEL JOHNSON

Seventy-four year old Manuel Johnson, "about de younges'" of the nine children of Milford and Patsey Johnson, is a tall ebony-black old man with the whitest hair and the roundest, merriest face. He lives in Washington, but even at his age he farms.

Although he was too young to remember much about slavery, Uncle Manuel recalls the happy old plantation days: "My Pa an' Ma cum frum ole Virgin'y five years befo' de Wah, Jedge Harris here in Wilkes County went up ter Virgin'y an' bo't dem frum de Putnams an' bro't 'em home wid him. You know, Miss, in dem days us niggers wuz bo't an' sole lak dey does mules ter-day. I wuz borned down on de Harris place de same year Miss Carrie (the youngest Harris daughter) wuz—we's de same year's chillun, dat's de onlies' way I knows how ole I is, Miss Harris tole me.

"Jedge Harris had er lot ov slaves—I specks I kin name er hunderd now, dey all lived in log cabins in de Quarters an' wuz happy an' well took keer ov as dey could be. De white folks took me in de house when I wuz leetle an' raised me kase dey wanted me fer er house boy.

I waited on de table, washed dishes, an' atter I got big 'nough, I milked de cows. I et in de kitchen out'n young Marse Jimmie's plate. I tho't so much ov him I allus et out'n de same plate he did. We sho' had er plenty ov ev'ything good too. All de y'uther niggers cooked an' et in de cabins. I wuz gittin' 'long in years 'fo' I knowed you could buy meat in a sto'. Yassum, us lived well on dat plantation—had plenty ter eat an' ter wear. Miss Cornelia—(the oldest Harris daughter)—made all my clothes. De nigger wimmens spun an' wove, but I never paid dem much mind when I wuz er comin' on. I 'member hearin' dem talk 'bout dyin' de cloth out er bark an' things dey got out'n de woods. Jes' so I had somethin' ter wear I never tho't how hard dey had ter wuk ter mak hit.

"I lived on de Harris plantation wid dem 'til I wuz nineteen years ole an' I allus felt lak I belonged ter dem—dey wuz so good ter me. When I fust could 'member, Miss Cornelia would git on ole Ruben, dat wuz her saddle horse, an' mak me git up behind her an den she'd go anywhere she wanted ter go. 'Nough times she took me ter ole Mt Zion Church wid her.

"No nigger wuz ever 'lected on de Harris place. Ef we wuz sick er needed sumthin' us got hit. Ef we wuz real sick de horseback doctor cum. In dem days de doctors rid 'roun' in de country on horseback an' took medicine wid em. Ef we warn't so sick de ole white folks cum ter see us an' 'scribed fer us. Dey use ter mak us little niggers take hoehound tea an' fat lightwood tea fer coles. Dat lightwood tea is er good medicine, I takes hit lots ov times now when I has er cole. Us had ter take Garlic water—no'm, not Garlic and whiskey, but jes' plain Garlic water, an' hit wuz a bad dose too. Dey give us candy made out'n Jerusalem oak an' sugar, dat warn't so bad."

Uncle Manuel said when he first could remember the negroes had services in their cabins at night. "Chair-back" preachers went around from one plantation to another holding services and much good was done. "On Sunday evenings, our Mistess called all us little folks up to de house an' read de Bible to us an' tole us Bible stories an' talked ter us 'bout livin' right. I 'members dat jes' as good."

When asked about the funerals and marriages when he first remembered, Uncle Manuel said: "Dey keeps dead folks out too long now. When I wuz comin' on, ef somebody died lak terday, dey wuz buried ter-mor-rer'. Dere wuz a settin' up an' prayer service dat night, de body wuz put in er plain home-made coffin blacked wid blackin' an' speerits turpentine, an' when de wag-gin cum ter take de body ter de buryin' groun' ev'ybody went out behin' de corpse singin' some good ole song lak 'Amazin' Grace' an' 'Hark Frum de Tomb'. Den dey went on ter de grave an' had a little service tellin' 'bout how de departed 'un had gone ter peace an' rest—dere warn't no long 'ictionary lak dey has now—none ov dese great long sermons an' gwines on—ev'ybody had jes' er common funeral an' hit wuz so much better.

"My Marster wuz a Jedge so he married all his niggers whut got married. He married lots ov y'uther couples too. I 'members dat dey use ter cum fer him ter marry dem."

Uncle Manuel said he tried superstitions and signs, but they didn't "prosper me none", so he gave up all he knew except the weather signs, and he plants his crops by the moon. "I watches de fust twelve days ov de New Year an' den I kin tell jes' whut weather ev'y mont' ov de year gwine ter bring. Dat's de way mens mak almanacs. 'Course I ain't got no edercation—nuver been ter school in my life—but dat's my fault kase I could have went, but long 'bout den I wuz so mannish I wouldn't go an' ev'y day I wishes I had er went so I could read now, but I didn't have sense 'nough den ter want ter learn."

About planting crops, Uncle Manuel advises: "Plant ev'ything dat makes under de groun' lak 'taters, goobers, tunips an' sich, on de dark ov de noon; plant ev'ything dat makes on top de groun' on light nights. Plant yo' crap on de waste ov de moon an' dat crap sho' gwine ter waste er way, an' dat's de truf, I ain't nuver seed hit fail yit. Plant corn on de full ov de moon an' you'll have full good-made years, plant on de growin' ov de moon an' you'll have a full growed stalk, powerful stalks, but de years won't be fulled out. I pays 'tention to dem signs, but as fer all dese y'uthers, dey ain't nothin' ter dem, 'cept meetin' er cat, I jes' has ter turn clean er 'roun' when I meets er cat an' dat turns de bad luck dat hit means, er way."

Uncle Manuel grew sad as he recalled the good old days long gone. He made an unusual statement for one of his race when he said: "Mistess, ef somebody had er thousan' dollars in one han' an' in de y'uther a pass fer me ter go back to dem ole days an' axed me which 'un I'de tak', I'de go back to dem ole days an' live de rest ov my life. Dere aint' nothin' to dese times now—nothin' 'cept trubble, peoples is livin' so fast, dey don't tak' no time ter stop an' 'sider, dey jes' resh right into trubble. I use ter drive oxen—four ov 'em—an' dey took me 'long all right. I'se plowed oxen too, now yu nuver see 'un kase dey's too slow; hit's autymobiles an' gas-run things, no'm, folks don't 'sider on de ways ov life lak dey use ter.

"Why is I livin' so long? Dat's easy—I'se 'onest, ain't nuver stole, nuver been in no trubble ov any kin', been nigh ter death two times, but I'se been spared kase I jes' ain't lived out my days yit. I'se on borrowed time, I knows dat, but dat ain't worryin' me none. An' I tell yu somthin' else; I ain't botherin' none over dis ole age pensun business fer I'se gwine ter wok on pensun er no pensun. No mam, I ain't gwine ter set back an' 'speck no govermint ter feed me long as I kin' scratch er 'roun'. I got wuk ter do—I got mo' wuk ter do an' gwine ter do hit long as I'se able."

It was easy to see from Uncle Manuel's manner he meant every word he said about "wuk". An independent old soul, and a good example to the younger ones of his race.

United States. Work Projects Administration

[HW: Ex-Slave]

Mary A. Crawford
Re-search Worker

Susie Johnson—Ex-slave

SUSIE JOHNSON

Susie was only four years old when The War Between the States began, but recalls a great deal about the old days, and remembers a great deal that her mother told her. Susie's parents were Jim and Dinah Freeman who belonged to Mr. and Mrs. Henry Freeman.

The Freemans lived on a large plantation near The Rock, Georgia, and had so many slaves "they could not be counted".

The old Freeman home is still standing, but is occupied now by negroes and is in a bad state of repair.

Susie is around seventy-five or seventy-seven years old, as nearly as she can "figger it out". A good many years ago when she first came over here from Upson County, she found "Mr. Frank Freeman, her young marster, away back yonder", and he told her lots and lots about her mother and father and gave her her correct age—July 4th.

Susie says that Mr. and Mrs. Freeman were "sho" good to their slaves but they surely did control them. For instance, if any of them had the stomach ache "Ole Miss" would make them take some "Jerusalem Oak tea" and if they had a bad cold it was "hoar hound tea". If you did not take the medicine "Ole Miss" would reach up and get the leather "strop" and (Susie chuckled) "then you'd take it".

When asked if Mr. Freeman whipped the slaves very much, Susie said he did not and that if he had been a mean master that "all the niggers wouldn't a wanted to stay on with him after freedom".

When asked about the negro marriage customs of slavery days, Susie stated that her mother said that "she and Jim (Susie's daddy) when they got in love and wanted to marry, jest held each others hands and jumped over the broom and they was married".

"Yes, I believe in lots o' signs", Susie replied on being asked about that. For instance, the "scritch' owl is a sho' sign o' death. And the reason I knows that is cause my papa's death was fo' told by an owl. Papa was took sick like this morning at nine o'clock and about eleven o'clock a little scritch' owl come and set right on the corner of the roof right above the head o' papa's bed and scritched and scritched—and by two o'clock that day papa was a corpse!"

Susie remembers one day when she and her mother were picking cotton when all of a sudden her mother began to sing "Glory to the Dying Land" and sang so much that "atter a while she got so happy she couldn't be still and she danced all over Masta's cotton patch and tromped down so much cotton I jest knowed Masta was gwina whup her. Den I laffed at her so hard 'Ole Miss whupped me wid dat strop! Law! Law!"

Susie Johnson—232 East Tinsley Street, Griffin, Georgia
September 4, 1936

United States. Work Projects Administration

EX-SLAVE INTERVIEW

ESTELLA JONES
1434 Wrightsboro Road
Augusta, Georgia

Written by: Louisa Oliphant
Federal Writers' Project
Augusta, Georgia.

Edited by: John N. Booth
District Supervisor
Federal Writers' Project
Residencies 6 & 7
Augusta, Georgia.

ESTELLA JONES

At least one old Augusta Negress has vivid recollections of childhood days on plantations in the pre-Civil War days. Outstanding in their memories are the methods of rearing slave children and the amusements indulged in by their mothers and fathers.

"I was born and raised in Powers Pond Place," said decrepit Estella Jones, "and, though I warn't but nine years old, I 'member dey had a nuss house whar dey put all de young chillun 'til dey wuz old enough to work. De chillun wuz put at dis nuss house so dey Ma and Pa could work. Dey had one old 'oman to look atter us and our some'pin [HW:] t' eat wuz brought to dis house. Our milk wuz put on de floor in a big wooden tray and dey give us oyster shells to eat wid. All de chillun would gather 'round dis tray and eat. Dey always let us eat 'til us got enough. I kept some of de oyster shells dey give us for spoons 'til my own chillun wuz grown.

"De nuss house wuz close to de marster's house. It wuz a wooden house wid two great big rooms. De sleepin' room wuz furnished wid little bunk beds three or four feet apart. The other room wuz used for a playroom and dinin' room. De floor wuz bare and de seats and benches wuz built from undressed lumber.

"Slaves on our place had a hard time. Dey had to work night and day. Marster had stobs (staves) all over de field to put lights on so dey could see how to work atter dark. De mens, more so dan de womens, had to work every night 'til twelve o'clock. But dey would feed 'em good. Dey had dey supper sont out in de field to 'em 'bout nine o'clock by a cripple boy who didn't do nothin' but tote water and do things lak dat.

"Dey wuz always glad when de time come for 'em to shell corn. Dey enjoyed dat better dan dey did Christmas, or at least jist as much. Dey always had to work durin' de day time and shell corn at night. De overseer wuz real good to 'em and it looked lak he enjoyed corn shellin's as much as dey did. Most times slaves from other plantations would come over and help 'em. Dey used to put on dey good clothes 'cause dey wanted to look dey best.

"It always tuk 'bout two weeks to shell corn 'cause de real old mens and womens never did help. Dey always had somethin' good to eat at dese times. Dey would pick out de best six cooks and dey wouldn't help shell corn, dey jist looked atter de cookin'. Dey would have chicken, sometimes fish or anythin' dey could get. Now and den dey had jist chitt'lin's and sweet 'tatoes.

"De men have even stole hogs from other people and barbecued 'em, den dey would cook hash and rice and serve barbecue. The overseer knowed all 'bout it but he et as much as anybody else and kept his mouth shut. He wuz real good to all de slaves. He never run you and yelled at you lak you warn't human. Everybody loved him, and would mind him better dan dey would anybody else. He always let de slaves shell corn 'til 'bout ten o'clock, den everybody would stop and have supper. Atter dat he would let 'em dance and play games 'til twelve. Our marster didn't say nothin' 'bout what de slaves done so long as de overseer wuz wid 'em.

"When corn-shellin' time come, everything would be tuk out of a big room, and one half of de room would be filled wid corn. Every pusson had a bucket dat held de same amount. Every time a bucket wuz filled it wuz tuk to de scorekeeper to be credited to his name. Whenever de huskin' wuz over, de number of buckets you had filled wuz counted and de one who filled de most always got a prize.

"Whenever anybody wuz late gittin' his cotton picked out, he always give a moonlight cotton pickin' party. Dese parties wuz always give on moonshiny nights and wuz liked by everybody. Atter while dey give everybody somethin' good to eat, and at de end of de party, de pusson who had picked de most cotton got a prize. Sometimes dey had pea shellin's 'stead of corn huskin's, but de parties and frolics wuz all pretty much alike.

"At quiltin' bees, four folks wuz put at every quilt, one at every corner. Dese quilts had been pieced up by old slaves who warn't able to work in de field. Quiltin's always tuk place durin' de winter when dere warn't much to do. A prize wuz always give to de four which finished dere quilt fust. 'Freshments went 'long wid dis too.

"Sometimes de grown folks all went huntin' for fun. At dem times, de womens had on pants and tied dey heads up wid colored cloths.

"Cake walkin' wuz a lot of fun durin' slavery time. Dey swept de yards real clean and set benches 'round for de party. Banjos wuz used for music makin'. De womens wore long, ruffled dresses wid hoops in 'em and de mens had on high hats, long split-tailed coats, and some of 'em used walkin' sticks. De couple dat danced best got a prize. Sometimes de slave owners come to dese parties 'cause dey enjoyed watchin' de dance, and dey 'cided who danced de best. Most parties durin' slavery time, wuz give on Saturday night durin' work seasons, but durin' winter dey wuz give on most any night.

"I still 'members some of de songs dey used to sing at frolics and at church too":

The Wind Blows East

>The wind blows east and the wind blows west,
>It blows like the Judgment Day.
>And all them sinners who never have cried,
>Will surely cry that day.

>Let me tell you, sure to cry that day, sure to cry that day,
>All them sinners who never have cried,
>Will surely cry that day.

You'd Better Be Praying

You'd better be praying while you're young,
You'd better be praying while you're young,
You'd better be praying without waiting any longer,
You'd better be praying while you're young.

You'd better seek religion while you're young,
You'd better seek religion while you're young,
You'd better seek religion without waiting any longer,
You'd better seek religion while you're young.

Come Change My Name

Bright angel, bright angel, come change my name,
O angel come change my name.
Come change my name from Nature to Grace,
O angel come change my name.

Sweet Jesus, sweet Jesus come change my name,
O Jesus come change my name,
Come change my name from Nature to Grace,
O Jesus come change my name.

I'm On My Way

If a seeker gets to Heaven before I do,
Look out for me, I'm on my way too.
Shout, shout the Heaven-bound King!
Shout, shout I'm on my way!

United States. Work Projects Administration

If a brother gets to Heaven before I do,
Look out for me, I'm on my way too.
Shout, shout the Heaven-bound King!
Shout, shout I'm on my way!

EX-SLAVE INTERVIEW

FANNIE JONES
37—12th Street
Augusta, Georgia

Written By:
Emily Powell
Augusta, Georgia

Edited By:
John N. Booth
WPA Residencies No. 6 & 7
Sept. 1, 1938.

Fannie Jones Ex-Slave, Age 85 37—12th St. Augusta, Georgia

FANNIE JONES

Fannie Jones lives in a ramshackle, two-story, rooming house near the banks of the Savannah River. She is an old Negress with iron gray hair and a gingercake complexion. Her ill-fitting old dress was none too clean, and her bare feet exposed toe nails almost a half-inch long. Fannie apparently hadn't a tooth in her head, but she was munching some bread.

The old Negress thought the purpose of the visit was to see about an old age pension for her, and she was very much disappointed when she learned the real reason; however, she invited her visitor into a bedroom. This place was much too dark, and the interview finally took place on the back porch where an old cat was made to get out of the only chair. Fannie settled herself on the doorsteps, while the visitor fanned flies and gnats with one hand and took notes with the other.

"I was born on Marse Jim Dubose's plantation 'bout de year 1853," she began. "My Marster and Mistiss was de overseer and his wife. You see, honey, I was born in de overseer's house. When my Ma was 12 year old she was give to de overseer's wife, Miss Becky Ann, when she married. My Marster was named Jesse Durden. I never did see Marse Jim Dubose's house nor none of de slave quarters, and I don't know nothin' 'bout dem or none of his Niggers. I jus' stayed in de house and waited on Marster and Mistiss. I cleaned up de house, made de beds, churned for Mistiss, and made fires for Marster. My Ma, she cooked for Marster and Mistiss, cleaned up de house, and waited on Mistiss 'cause she was a invalid.

"Marse Jim Dubose's plantation covered thousands of acres, and he owned hundreds of slaves. You see, my Marster was de man what handled all of dese here Niggers. Evvy mornin' Marster Jesse would git up and go out and blow his horn, dat was de way he called de Niggers to de fields.

"De overseer's house was a one-story buildin' and it was furnished in de old time stuff. De beds was teestered and had slats to hold de mattresses. When Marster would come in from de fields he would be so tired he never did go nowhar. Sometimes I would say to him, 'I'se cold,' and he would say, 'Nig, you jus' crawl up on de foot of my bed and git warm.' He would say 'Nig, what you want for supper?' and I would say, 'I wants some bread and milk and a little syrup.' He give me anything dat I wanted to eat, and us had good things to eat. Us had chickens, hogs, and good milk cows. I kin see de big bowls of milk now dat us used to have. Us made a heap of butter and sont it to Augusta onct a month and sold it for 25¢ a pound.

"Atter freedom come, Marster said to me and Ma, 'you all is free now to go wharever you wants to.' Ma, she wanted to go, but I jus' cried and cried 'cause I didn't want to leave Marster and Mistiss; dey was too good to me. So Ma tuk me and us went to her grandma's down at Barnett. Us stayed dar awhile, den us lef' and went to Thomson. Us stayed at dat place a long time, and I was married dar to a man by de name of Claiborne Jones. Us had 'leven chillun, but dey is all daid now 'cept two. I lives here wid one of my daughters.

"My husband b'longed to Marse John Wilson. Durin' de war Marse John wuz a captain, and he tuk my husband 'long to cook and to wait on him. He said one night de Yankees was atter 'em and him and Marse John jumped in a big ditch. Later in de night it rained and dey couldn't git out of de ditch, so de rest of Marse John's company lef' 'em alone. De next mornin' when dey got out of de ditch, dey didn't know which way dey had went, but Marse John got a hoss and dey got on and rid 'til dey caught up wid de company.

"At Christmas dey give us anything dat us wanted. Dey give me dolls, candy, fruit and evvything. Mistiss used to git a book and say, 'Nig, come here and let me larn you how to read.' I didn't pay no 'tention to her den, but now I sho' does wish I had. My Mistiss didn't have but one chile, Miss Cornelia."

At this moment Fannie, tired of sitting on the doorsteps, abandoned the back porch for her room. The place was very untidy, but she explained this by saying that she was not able to clean it up. On one side of the room hung a picture of the Sacred Heart and on another a reproduction of the Lord's Supper. An enlarged family portrait decorated the front wall. The symbolic pictures aroused curiosity as to whether Fannie was a church member. She answered questions on the subject by saying "Yes honey, I joined de Mount Pleasant Baptist Church 58 years ago and wuz baptized by Brother Mike Wilson." When she was asked to sing, the cracked voice broke into this song:

> "I am a Baptist born,
> And my shoes cried,
> And my eyes batted,
> And when I'm gone
> Dere is a Baptist gone."

Fannie was now completely tired out, but when her visitor arose to leave, she sang out cordially: "Honey, God bless you; goodbye."

Alberta Minor

[HW: over 100 years old]

Rastus Jones, Ex-slave

Place of Birth:
Chapel Hill, North Carolina

Date of Birth:
Apparently, between 1825 and 1830

Present residence:
Near Vaugn, Georgia On Farm of Mr. W.M. Parker

Interviewed: August 18, 1936

RASTUS JONES

Rastus Jones, born the slave property of Mr. Sidney Jones, a North Carolina planter, is a very old man, probably between 107 and 110 years of age. His earliest memory is that of the "Falling Stars," the most brilliant display, perhaps, of the Leonids ever recorded, that of November 12-13, 1833, which establishes his age as being in excess of 103 years.

"Uncle" Rastus states that the Joneses were good to their slaves—gave them clothing each spring and fall, issued them shoes as needed, fed them well, and furnished them medical attention when ill.

The Negro children and white children played together and the life of the slave was usually happy and care-free. At Christmas time, the slaves were always remembered by their masters with gifts.

The Jones family owned about twenty-five Negroes and, some years prior to the Civil war, moved to DeSoto County, Mississippi, taking their slaves with them, all making the trip in wagons. In both North Carolina and Mississippi, it was a custom of Mr. Jones to give each deserving, adult Negro slave an acre or two of land to work for himself and reap any profits derived therefrom.

While living in Mississippi, Rastus ran off with a crowd "o' Niggers" and joined the Federal forces at Memphis. During the siege of Vicksburg, he was employed as cook in General Grant's Army, and later marched east with the Yankees. Subsequently, he seems to have become attached to Sherman's forces. Near Marietta, Georgia, in July or August, 1864, he was captured by the Confederates under General Hood, who confined him in prison at—or near—Macon until the close of the war. After his release, in May, 1865, he had "a pretty hard time of it" for several years. Still later, he came to Spalding County and hired out to Mr. Jones Bridges. He remained with Mr. Bridges for seven years, then went to work for, and farming with, the Parker family, with whom he has since remained.

He is the Father of fourteen children and has a large number of grand and great-grandchildren.

For a man of his years, "Uncle" Rastus is well preserved mentally and physically. He is a widower and now lives with a daughter, the only one of his children that he knows the whereabouts of.

Transcribers note:

[TR:] = Transcriber Note
[HW:] = Handwritten Note

Every effort was made to faithfully reflect the distinctive character of this document. Some obvious typographic errors have been corrected. The above notes are placed inline, to cover all other unusual comments.

Hover over HW: with a mouse to see the changes made.

www.ingramcontent.com/pod-product-compliance
Lightning Source LLC
Chambersburg PA
CBHW071649160426
43195CB00012B/1404